EMERGENT ACTORS IN WORLD POLITICS

PRINCETON STUDIES IN COMPLEXITY

FORTHCOMING TITLES

Robert Axelrod, *The Complexity of Cooperation: Agent-Based Models of Competition and Collaboration*

Scott Camazine, Jean-Louis Deneubourg, Nigel Franks, and Thomas Seeley, *Building Biological Superstructures: Models of Self-Organization*

James P. Crutchfield and James E. Hanson, *Computational Mechanics of Cellular Processes*

Ralf W. Wittenberg, *Models of Self-Organization in Biological Development*

EMERGENT ACTORS IN
WORLD POLITICS

HOW STATES AND NATIONS

DEVELOP AND DISSOLVE

Lars-Erik Cederman

PRINCETON UNIVERSITY PRESS   PRINCETON, NEW JERSEY

Library of Congress Cataloging-in-Publication Data
Cederman, Lars-Erik, 1963–
Emergent actors in world politics : how states and nations develop
and dissolve / Lars-Erik Cederman.
p.   cm. — (Princeton studies in complexity)
Includes bibliographical references and index.
ISBN 0-691-02149-X (cl : alk. paper). — ISBN 0-691-02148-1 (pb :
alk. paper)
1. International relations.   2. National state.   3. World
politics—1989– I. Title. II. Series.
JX1391.C37   1997
327.1'01—dc21   96-45562 CIP

This book has been composed in Times Roman

Printed in the United States of America by Princeton Academic Press

2   4   6   8   10   9   7   5   3   1

2   4   6   8   10   9   7   5   3   1
(Pbk.)

IN MEMORY OF MY GRANDMOTHER

Märta Malmberg

BORN IN 1905, THE YEAR THAT THE
PEACEFUL DISSOLUTION OF THE SWEDISH-
NORWEGIAN UNION WAS AGREED UPON IN
KARLSTAD, THE CITY OF MY CHILDHOOD

Contents

Tables

Figures

Preface

THE DISAPPEARANCE and formation of states after the end of the cold war has proved puzzling to both theorists and policymakers. This lack of conceptual preparation stems from two tendencies in Western thinking. First, the dominant focus on cohesive nation-states as the only actors in world politics obscures crucial differences between the state and the nation. Second, traditional theory usually treats these units as fixed.

To circumvent these limitations, this study presents a series of models that separate the state from the nation and incorporates these as emergent rather than preconceived actors. The models draw on both formal and constructivist theories in an attempt to integrate them. This requires methodological innovations ranging from minor deviations from existing deductive models to more unconventional frameworks based on simulations of complex adaptive systems.

This work would not have been possible without the inspiration and assistance of my dissertation adviser, Robert Axelrod. He supported this project from its earliest, haziest stage through its completion, providing an invaluable—and apparently inexhaustible—supply of intellectual guidance. I am also indebted to the other members of my dissertation committee: Michael Cohen helped me develop my skills in computer modeling and simulation; John Holland introduced me to the theory of complex adaptive systems; and William Zimmerman provided badly needed area expertise for the empirical work.

Besides my committee, I would like to thank Cheryl Shanks for reading the entire manuscript and giving me essential substantive, presentational, and linguistic advice. The reviewers of Princeton University Press, Joshua Epstein and Jack Snyder, also provided thorough critiques of the whole text. I am also grateful to the following individuals for their helpful comments on parts of the manuscript: Hayward Alker, Gary Goertz, Simon Hug, Peter Katzenstein, Ellen Lust-Okar, Urs Luterbacher, Jonathan Mercer, Peder A. Olsen, George A. Reisch, David Rivera, David Sylvan, Philip Tetlock, Stephen Mitchel Tull, Patricia Weitsman, and Alexander Wendt.

Most of the work on this project was done at the Institute for Social Research at the University of Michigan, which provided an excellent research environment. I would especially like to thank the faculty and graduate students who participated in the presentations I gave there. The informal Complex Adaptive Systems Study Group at the University of Michigan with Erhard Bruderer, Helen Klein, and David Lazer added an ideal interdisciplinary forum to discuss modeling of complex systems.

In addition, the current project benefited greatly from the Summer School of the Santa Fe Institute, which I attended in June 1992. It is hard not to be infected by the enthusiasm and novel ideas at the Institute. I would also like to thank Urs Luterbacher for inviting me to teach a course in international relations at the Graduate Institute for International Studies in Geneva in the spring of 1993. The interaction with colleagues and students proved instrumental in making this work more policy relevant. Later the same year, I had the privilege of presenting an early version of chapter 4 to the *Arbeitsgruppe in Internationalen Beziehungen* in Arnoldshain, Germany. This group has been convened biannually by Christopher Daase and Bernhard Moltmann, whose invitation I greatly appreciate.

I am also grateful for the excellent support from the editorial staff at Princeton University Press, including Malcolm DeBevoise, Malcolm Litchfield, Karen Verde, and Heidi Sheehan. Tim Mennel carried out professional copyediting of the highest class.

Finally, I acknowledge the generous financial support from a two-year fellowship in Peace and Security of the Social Science Research Council and John D. and Catherine T. MacArthur Foundation, as well as the permission to use the material in chapter 4 and chapter 8, which previously appeared as "Emergent Polarity: Analyzing State-Formation and Power Policies," *International Studies Quarterly* 38 (1994): 501–33 and "Competing Identities: An Ecological Model of Nationality Formation," *Europeann Journal of International Relations* 1 (1995): 331–65.

EMERGENT ACTORS IN WORLD POLITICS

CHAPTER 1

Introduction

THE FALL of the Berlin Wall in 1989 triggered an astonishing series of epochal events that led to the dissolution of multiethnic communist states and the creation of dozens of new sovereign units. While the collapse of communism accelerated the splintering of the Soviet Union, Yugoslavia, and Czechoslovakia, other parts of Europe experienced a trend toward unprecedented levels of political integration. Germany reunited, and despite certain delays associated with the ratification of the Maastricht Treaty, Western European integration progressed toward a deeper and a wider union.

What explains this simultaneous trend toward integration and disintegration? Clearly, this puzzle differs from the typical research questions of the cold war. During that historically unique period, most analysts found it natural to engage in "problem solving theory" (Cox 1986), focusing on interstate behavior rather than on the more fundamental question of why states and nations form and disintegrate. Thus, the main debate in postwar International Relations (IR) theory revolved around the question of whether cooperation or conflict dominates the international arena. The only major exception to this tendency, integration theory, was almost completely abandoned as a result of impatience with the sluggish pace of the European integration process.

This behavioral focus made sense against the backdrop of the cold-war environment. The post-1945 era was marked by exceptional stability and simplicity that derived from the small number of major actors—only two superpowers—and their unitary character. Moreover, the ideological rift between East and West overshadowed other political and cultural conflicts. Compared to the historical record, the stability of this relatively simple structural situation reached an exceptional level. Many observers thought that "the long peace" would last virtually indefinitely.

If simplicity and stability characterized the postwar world, the opposite certainly holds for the present era. The post–cold war period exhibits remarkable complexity and change. The dominance of the two superpowers has been replaced by a more complicated power distribution involving an open-ended set of players. The United States remains the strongest actor on the world stage, but it is becoming increasingly clear that, while still impressive in absolute terms, its power falls short of unipolarity.[1] With the demise of communism and the ascendance of ethnic and national conflict dimensions, it is no longer fruitful to view the world as a duel between two ideologies. Moreover, not only has the complex web of relationships changed but the main actors themselves are also now in flux, with revolutionary changes affecting the actors' identities. In the wake of the Soviet and Yugoslav dissolutions, the geopolitical map continues to evolve.[2]

It is precisely the issue of unstable agency that poses the most serious conceptual problems to existing IR approaches. Almost without exception, these perspectives assume the actors are exogenously given before analyzing their behavior. The general bewilderment surrounding the collapse of the Soviet Union reveals the limitations of this assumption. Preoccupied with behavioral-research puzzles, scholars and policymakers alike were simply not ready to confront the possibility of a major player vanishing abruptly. Developed to cope with the strategic problems of the cold-war era, mainstream IR theory has had little to say about the structural changes that the world is currently undergoing.

Of course, it may be argued that the transition to a new power equilibrium will be brief and that it will soon be possible to reapply conventional theories. This response is not helpful, regardless of the transitional period's length. Even if these transformations come to a quick close, this does not automatically imply that the new stable period will be as uncomplicated and lasting as the cold war. We would also have to worry about being surprised next time the balance was upset. To suspend analysis until the dust settles because current tools do not let us grasp dynamic processes is a deeply unsatisfactory position, especially since the interludes of swift historical change profoundly influence the institutions, norms, and power distribution of the stable periods that follow such discontinuities. Policymakers cannot afford the luxury of a wait-and-see attitude, and neither can theorists. Conceptual innovation is needed now and not after the action has already taken place.

Indeed, the present situation forces the IR theorist to aim at a moving target. To hard-wire actors and specific strategic exchanges into the theoretical framework defeats the purpose of understanding historical novelty.

---

[1] Here I am using unipolarity to designate world dominance by a single empire or hegemon (cf. Gilpin 1981, 29) such that "its capabilities are formidable enough to preclude the formation of an overwhelming balancing coalition against it" (Layne 1993, 5). Although the United States is by far the most powerful power in today's world, the crises in Somalia and the former Yugoslavia illustrate the limitations of American military power (see Layne 1993 for further arguments along these lines).

[2] The contrast should not be exaggerated. The Third World did experience momentous structural change throughout the cold-war era, as dozens of former colonies emerged as independent states.

Instead of presupposing simplicity and stability, students of political change should make these system properties emerge spontaneously from a backdrop of disorder and chaos. It is the cold war that is the exception from the constant flux of world history, not the other way around (Gaddis 1992). The goal of this study therefore, is to develop new heuristic devices that deal directly with complexity and change in world politics. This requires a dynamic and emergent, as opposed to static and reified, approach to agency.[3] To this end, I present a series of models that represent both states and nations as inherently history-dependent actors. In addition to stressing their emergence, the proposed formal frameworks also distinguish clearly between states and nations as actor categories, a distinction that is often blurred in contemporary IR scholarship.[4]

The emergent-actor approach thus lends itself to explicit studies of state formation and nationalism, historical processes that play central roles after the end of the cold war. Turbulent periods, such as the present one, force the analyst to reconsider conventional assumptions adopted under more stable circumstances. The common tendency to treat all actors in world politics as if they were nation-states is such a postulate. Allowing for alternative forms of organization promises to fill the current theoretical vacuum between the extremes of cohesive internal order and external anarchy. This extension is of particular importance since system-transforming structural change takes place precisely in the zone between order and chaos. More specifically, it is hard to trace either completed or aborted transitions from anarchy to full-fledged nation-states without paying attention to the intermediate stepping-stones of multinational states and multistate nations. While Germany's reunification constitutes a major move toward national consolidation, both the Soviet Union and Yugoslavia are nation-building failures. Of course, these examples constitute but the tip of a historical iceberg containing a multitude of nation-building experiences, many of which are now forgotten. Thus, we speak of the French nation, and not of the Burgundian one. Indeed, "there is a very large number of potential nations on earth. Our planet also contains room for a certain number of independent or autonomous political units. On

[3] In social theory, agency stands for the way in which microlevel explanations depict actors, including their purposes, beliefs, and identities. The corresponding concept, structure, refers to macrolevel phenomena such as social institutions and norms (Bohman 1991, 146; see also Giddens 1979, 55–57, and Wendt 1987 for an application to IR). Although this study focuses on the problem of analyzing actors in world politics, it also deals with structural issues such as polarity (see chapter 4). Reification refers to the tendency to treat social entities as if they were natural objects (see chap. 2).

[4] It is important not to confuse the concepts of state and nation. The state is a formal institution that possesses the power to control a bounded territory through enforcement. The nation is a psychosocial community held together by emotional bonds. These two notions converge in the nation-state (see chap. 2).

any reasonable calculation, the former number (of potential nations) is probably much, *much* larger than that of possible viable states" (Gellner 1983, 2).

The analytical objectives of this study should be seen as steps toward the metatheoretical goal of combining various formal modeling techniques with the insights of sociologically oriented perspectives outside mainstream IR theory. Broadly speaking, critical theory of this type designates a wide range of "dissident" perspectives, including postmodernism, neo-Marxism, feminism, and social constructivism (Wendt 1995, 71). Leaving the first three literatures aside, I focus on the constructivist paradigm because of its direct relevance to emergent agency in IR. Constructivist scholars insist that social structures, including individual and collective actors and their practices, are all socially constructed rather than naturally given. Distinguishing this interpretation from neorealist practice, Wendt points out that "constructivists think that state interests are in important part constructed by systemic structures, not exogenous to them; this leads to a sociological rather than micro-economic structuralism" (72).

Social constructivism is attractive for our purposes because of its ability to capture complex historical processes. Yet these dynamic and contextual extensions come at the price of abandoning the parsimony of conventional rational-choice modeling. Ironically, constructivists' call for richer analytical frameworks amplifies the need for formal heuristic tools, a fact often overlooked by these scholars. It is hard to overestimate the difficulties of grasping complex identity shifts and of tracing involved counterfactual arguments. Viewed as a complement to qualitative theoretical and historical work, formal models are useful in assisting the scholar in disentangling thorny conceptual puzzles and in keeping track of involved spatiotemporal processes, as advocated by constructivist scholars.

Despite their unquestionable value as heuristic guides to simpler contexts, conventional rational-choice models are often unable to render these badly needed services in the richer contexts studied by sociologically inspired IR theorists. Two methodological limitations substantially block progress toward a fully dynamic and history-dependent rendering of states and nations. First, to preserve mathematical tractability, modelers almost always rely on equilibrium analysis, a methodological choice that yields elegant theories but that also assumes away historical accidents. In some cases, this simplification is warranted, but the emergent perspective on political institutions and culturally defined groups adopted here is badly served by such a contingency-free approach to historical change. Second, conventional modeling frameworks rest on methodological individualism, a principle that usually entails a purely materialistic and self-interested approach to human agency. Yet nationalism is a process that involves both deliberate strategic manipulations and unconscious redefinitions of collective identities, phenomena that remain beyond the conceptual horizon of individualist approaches, which exclude identity-formation a priori.

In order to circumvent this impasse, I propose a series of models of varying complexity that move modeling beyond the current individualist and materialist orthodoxy. These theoretical explorations belong to a class of unconventional frameworks that imply radically increased theoretical complexity as compared to traditional formal models. This type of model can be summarized under the label *complex adaptive systems*, or CAS. Methodologically, CAS models differ from traditional mathematical models in their reliance on computer simulation of a particular decentralized type. The computer methodology allows for systematic explorations of artificially created complex networks featuring large numbers of locally interacting agents. These counterfactual thought experiments make it possible to rerun history, thus opening the door for a truly path-dependent analysis of institutions and cultural forms. Thus, the flexibility of the CAS approach facilitates modeling states and nations as emergent phenomena rather than reified entities frozen into the theoretical assumptions and model specifications.

Although CAS simulations sacrifice the deductive elegance of conventional rational-choice models, treating the actors as dependent rather than independent variables introduces new research questions that cannot easily be addressed or even conceived without such an approach. From where do realists' great powers come? Why do some multiethnic states collapse while others survive? How fast can political mobilization be pushed in such states without causing disintegration? Why do national identities vary in scope? Within the behaviorist paradigm, these are puzzles that are hard not only to resolve but also to recognize.

Furthermore, the CAS approach generates surprising and counterintuitive insights about existing theories. For example, it is seldom realized that neorealism implicitly assumes the existence of a self-feeding process of conquest that sometimes leads to "hegemonic takeoffs." Neorealism cannot explain the contraction of a massively multipolar system into the traditionally presumed small number of great powers without postulating that conquest pays, but the resulting positive feedback of such an assumption threatens to undermine the power balance. A dynamic CAS model helps to elucidate the consequences and robustness of neorealist assumptions. The introduction of balancing mechanisms such as defensive technology and alliances sometimes, contrary to realist expectations, perversely *undermines* rather than strengthens the balance of power.

To take another example, journalistic accounts and traditional anthropological scholarship often regard nationalities in empires as givens. Yet such a reified view obscures the fact that the political identities of such groups vary systematically with the underlying resource balance between an imperial center and a culturally fragmented periphery. I suggest that the stronger the imperial government, the more inclusive and encompassing the peripheral identities. This insight explains the difficulties of unification encountered by nation-building elites in the postcolonial phase. With the threat gone, parochial identities regain terrain, thus undermining the efforts to create a new, independent nation.

Although this book stresses theory development, it does purport to offer insights about the real world. This goal, however, should not be confused with the identification and testing of context-free laws and regularities. Instead of relying on massive data bases of individual observations, the validation of macroprocesses such as state formation and nationalism requires a genuinely contextual and historical approach. The study of epochal change must rest ultimately on the systematic collection of patterned observations from larger regions and time frames than the social scientists' "country cases," "conflict dyads," or the like.

Before taking on such an ambitious project, however, it is necessary to identify the patterns to be validated. I have used empirical examples for illustrative purposes to bolster the plausibility of the theoretical results and to develop the reader's intuition of general patterns and processes. The historical references range from the Italian Renaissance and nationality formation within the Habsburg Empire to more topical material covering the European Union and the nationalist reactions within the Soviet Union to Mikhail Gorbachev's reform policy.

All of these examples are drawn from European history. This focus is natural since both nationalism and state formation, in their modern, territorial sense, both originated in Europe. For sure, states existed long before the Westphalian system, but their control was much more amorphous and their boundaries less well defined than the absolute states that emerged in early modern Europe. Likewise, it is not proper to talk of nationalism as a consciously propagated ideology prior to the French Revolution. As with territorial sovereignty, popular sovereignty crystallized in Europe. While it is logical for historical reasons to make Europe the starting point the processes studied apply to most of the world as colonialism spread the idea of the nation-state as the dominant organizational form across the globe.

Despite their variety, the historical illustrations have another thing in common: they highlight transitional episodes of great importance. The centrality of the balance of power among the Italian city-states for the origin of the European state system can hardly be underestimated (Padgett and Ansell 1993). Likewise, more than the future of Europe hinges upon the development of the European Union; it can even be argued that the future of the nation-state depends on European integration (see references in Mann 1993b). Furthermore, the end of the cold war depended to a large extent on the nationality question within the Soviet Union, because "besides chronic economic woes, the greatest threat to both the Soviet state and its potential for reform [was] the emergence of mass nationalist movements" (Suny 1993, 2). Finally, it is hard to understand the outbreak of World War I without reference to nationality politics in the southern slavic lands under Habsburg rule. Hall (1993, 51) puts it even more starkly: "Bluntly, no international relations theory that fails to recognize the ability of intellectuals to imagine national communities within Austria-Hungary at the end of the nineteenth century has any chance of understanding the origins of World War I."

These historical junctures fall between the more stable periods that scholars traditionally select as their cases. Social scientists tend to let history decide how to delimit their samples, rather than designing general theories that encompass both stable and turbulent eras. This procedure is sound as long as it is applied to unchanging periods, but it will not suffice for any theory claiming to offer explanations of historical change. By contrast, studying historical discontinuities facilitates the anticipation of future structural transformations of the international system.

There is a more profound reason why the empiricists' demand for tests of simple predictive laws must be qualified. Historical contingency and path dependence thwart such efforts to generalize from empirical regularities. For example, we will never know what would have happened had nuclear weapons not been created, so it is unclear whether the "single run" of history that actually occurred warrants any strong beliefs in their effectiveness. Comparing the post-1945 world to previous eras may give us some hints, but there are so many uncontrolled factors that not even the largest army of data collectors would ever be able to establish causal knowledge akin to that possible in the natural sciences. There is often no adequately sized sample from which to generalize.

Many of the problems in the social sciences are of this type, including the phenomena studied here. There are only so many nuclear periods, bipolar international systems, great social revolutions, collapses of communist empires, etc. If historical accidents do not wash out but instead switch the flow of events onto dramatically divergent tracks, there is no alternative to counterfactual exploration since, in such cases, the empiricists' imputation of uniformly operating causal laws ceases to be meaningful, dependent as it is on large statistical samples. What, then, does the counterfactual alternative to empirical generalization entail? Realizing that research problems of this difficult type leaves the analyst with no choice but to generate "possibilities" mentally, Max Weber (1949) suggested that the counterfactual approach "involves first the production of—let us say it calmly—'imaginary constructs' by the disregarding of one or more of those elements of 'reality' which are actually present, and by the mental construction of a course of events which is altered through modification in one or more 'conditions'" (173).Equipped with such abstract devices, the researcher is in a position to examine "judgments of possibility" by drawing on empirical regularities and theoretical knowledge. Thus, the counterfactual method does not replace comparative studies of real cases; rather, it offers an invaluable complement to these more conventional approaches, especially when evidence is scarce.

In fact, Weber's counterfactual procedure should sound familiar to nuclear-deterrence theorists who faute de mieux have always been forced to rely on formal models to overcome the paucity of empirical evidence in their field. Despite the abstract flavor of their models, these theorists have had a considerable impact on policy-making: "Rational deterrence is a highly influential social science theory. Not only has it dominated postwar academic thinking on strategic affairs, but it has provided the intellectual framework of Western military policy in the same period as well" (Achen and Snidal 1989, 143). Whether one applauds or deplores the particular ways in which their reasoning impacted policy, it is hard to deny the importance of model-based counterfactual explorations.

Although the CAS approach shares the counterfactual method with these deductive studies, there are important differences. With the possibility of "rerunning the tape," albeit in an artificial world, one gets a more direct feeling for the complex and unanticipated consequences of policy choices than is offered by simpler frameworks that rule out historical contingency and path dependencies by assumption. Instead of focusing on clearly defined sequences of strategic exchanges, this study addresses a completely different set of problems that cannot be reduced to prespecified bargaining protocols. In macrohistorical contexts of the type considered here, not even the identity of the actors can be taken for granted.

Hopefully, the open-ended counterfactual experiments will contribute to reducing the often exaggerated faith in deductive solutions to policy problems. The IR literature abounds with predictions and prescriptions based on ultraparsimonious frameworks. While such work clarifies complicated dilemmas, the analytically expedient simplifications suggest a higher level of certainty than is empirically warranted. The CAS approach encourages a more humble attitude toward policy advice by forcing the analyst to factor in accidental influences. The likely loss of unique equilibrium predictions may be disappointing to those who argue for theoretical elegance, but in the end it is better to be sensitized to historical contingency while theorizing than to be unpleasantly surprised after having implemented the theory, however elegant it may be.

More generally, the principles of emergent agency and separation between state and nation have important policy implications. The models advanced in this study conceptualize the main actors, whether states or nations, as historically emergent. In addition, the analytical attention extends beyond cohesive nation-states to alternate, fragmented, and fluid institutional forms. Much of the confusion among Western policy analysts with the security problems in Eastern Europe stems from lack of experience with and awareness of situations characterized by noncongruent states and nations; this lack has been reflected in the scholarship to date. The unsuccessful attempts to mediate the Yugoslav conflict, for example, reflect not only a poor knowledge of Balkan history, but also an underdeveloped theoretical understanding of how state formation and nationalism interact in culturally fragmented settings. The temptation to ignore national communities that do not conform to political boundaries, as well as the tendency to reify those that do, bedevil even the most careful applications of contemporary IR theory.

This study is organized as follows. Chapter 2 introduces the problem of modeling actors in world politics, focusing especially on the risks of confusing the state with the nation and reifying these actor types. The discussion proceeds by locating the present approach with respect to other theoretical paradigms. Having defined the metatheoretical goal as one of improved communication between conventional IR scholars and constructivist theorists, I explain why the latter should reject their current misgivings over formal tools. This proposition does not imply an unqualified endorsement of existing rational-choice theory. On the contrary, new, more flexible models are needed.

Chapter 3 explores the prospects for these methodological extensions. Endogenizing agency requires overcoming two conceptual obstacles. First, both states and nations are inherently history-dependent structures and should ideally be modeled as such. The problem, however, is that this approach forces the analyst to confront the problem of contingency and counterfactuals. Identifying causal regularities in the presence of accidents and path-dependent processes is not an easy task. Second, while often a useful analytical starting point, methodological individualism threatens to lock the modeler into a conceptual trap that obscures the use of political symbols to transcend collective-choice dilemmas. Nationalism, in particular, cannot be understood without explicit reference to "imagined communities" (Anderson 1991), categorically defined constructs that defy purely individualistic and material representation.

The discussion of these hurdles is followed by a presentation of the

CAS methodology, which promises to circumvent the two theoretical dilemmas. An inventory of the weaknesses of CAS modeling is also included. While CAS theory can serve important purposes, it should be seen as a complement to existing methodological tools rather than a replacement. Therefore, I draw on both simpler, deductive techniques and the richer CAS frameworks.

Chapter 4 addresses the problem of state formation in the pre-Napoleonic era. The theoretical goal is to put neorealist theory on an explicitly dynamic footing. This is achieved by developing a CAS model, the Emergent Polarity Model, that traces not only the persistence of great powers but also their emergence. The simulations start with a great number of small statelike units that engage in a quasi-Darwinian struggle for power. Counterfactual experiments allow for systematic evaluation of neorealist propositions pertaining to structural invariance in power politics, as well as of the impact of defensive technology and alliances.

Chapter 5 extends the Emergent Polarity Model in theoretically significant directions. The purpose of these extensions is not only to achieve greater realism but also to test the robustness of the earlier results. The changes concern the alliance mechanism, strategic adaptation, resource allocation, and two-level action. The latter modification is major, and therefore receives more attention than others.

Chapter 6 introduces the remaining models with a conceptual overview of nationalism, expanding the neorealist dichotomy between interstate anarchy and cohesive nation-states by adding two new categories: multistate/stateless nations and multinational states. This taxonomy helps to identify three types of nationalism that arose first in Western Europe, Central/Southern Europe, and Eastern Europe. The last section provides an overview of the last two modeling chapters in terms of these historical processes.

Chapter 7 also goes beyond the equilibrium methodology of traditional rational-choice models, but the model is much simpler than the Emergent Polarity Model. The Mobilization Model is based on a dynamic framework, formalized as a two-level Markov process, the lower, demographic level of which is deductive. The superimposed level, which focuses on domestic and foreign collective action, requires counterfactual simulation of the CAS type. The analysis yields insights about the tradeoff between state-induced assimilation and the mobilization of peripheral nationalism within a multinational setting.

The formal rendering can be used to distinguish between three analytically distinct processes: assimilation theory, delayed-assimilation theory, and provocation theory. The different trajectories depend on the expected effectiveness of the imperial core's nation-building efforts. As suggested by its name, assimilation theory harbors the most optimistic expectations of success. Delayed-assimilation theory shares the previous paradigm's belief in ultimate assimilation, but takes a less sanguine view of the short-term prospects. Provocation theory, finally, argues that the center's attempts to impose its culture are likely to backfire by fueling peripheral nationalist mobilization rather than imperial centralization.

The last possibility receives explicit attention in the collective-action phase of the model. In addition to nationalist secession, the multinational elite has to consider external challenges to state sovereignty. This dilemma makes mobilization a precarious process, at least under the conditions of provocation theory. An empirical section illustrates the model's logic with references to political-mobilization processes within the Habsburg Empire, the Soviet Union, and the European Union.

Chapter 8 retains the focus on nationalism in multiethnic states but concentrates on coordination and competition among nationalist movements rather than mobilization. If the periphery can no longer be assumed to be culturally uniform, political identity-formation assumes a new level of complexity; ethnic variety opens the door for strategic manipulation of political symbols. Because nationalist leaders have a choice among the cultural traits to elevate as constitutive features of their nationalist platforms, a trade-off appears between narrow and universalistic identities. In a competitive ethnopolitical and culturally fragmented environment, the power balance between the center and the subordinated nationalities governs the scope of the national identity used by the oppositional movement(s), and thus ultimately affects the prospects of collective action.

Chapter 9 discusses theoretical contributions and extensions. The research developed here could be continued along three lines, by pursuing more advanced internal models, simulations of simultaneous emergence of states and nations, and the internal-external interaction between domestic and interstate politics. Pulling the theoretical threads together, the concluding chapter also dwells on the policy consequences of the modeling exercises.

CHAPTER 2

Modeling Actors in World Politics

INTRODUCTION

Despite the centrality of agency in International Relations theory, there is no consensus on how to conceive of actors in world politics. Realists and liberals have debated the relative importance of states versus international and transnational organizations for decades. Whether the emphasis falls on either type of organization, the overwhelming complexity of world politics usually forces analysts to rely on an anthropomorphic view of actors as both unitary and rational. While this perspective makes intuitive sense in many cases, it also entails considerable risks. The surprise felt among scholars and policymakers at the collapse of the Soviet Union illustrates the dangers of treating states as monolithic entities. Focusing on the nation-state as the ideal or typical actor, Western observers paid little attention to the signs of the impending seismic shift in world politics, such as nationalist upheaval in the Soviet republics.[1]

Not everyone has regarded states as unproblematic, homogeneous units. Arnold Wolfers (1962) highlighted the conceptual difficulties of modeling agency in world politics:

> If the nation-states are seen as the sole actors, moving or moved like a set of chess figures in a highly and abstract game, one may lose sight of the human beings for whom and by whom the game is supposed to be played. If, on the other hand, one sees only the mass of individual human beings of whom mankind is composed, the power game of states tends to appear as an inhuman interference with the lives of ordinary people. (3)

To consider either the state or the individual as the fundamental actor creates insoluble paradoxes. The former, state-centered perspective, represented by realists, often boils down to viewing the masses' influence on diplomacy as distorting interference in the game of "high politics" (e.g., Morgenthau 1985). It is not without a certain nostalgia that observers with a penchant for realpolitik have longed for the days when statesmen and diplomats divided the world as a pie (cf. Kissinger 1957). Attempts to resurrect this outlook in an era of mass politics have met with little success (e.g., Howard 1994).

[1] For early exceptions, see Collins (1978), Carrère d'Encausse (1980), and self-references in Moynihan (1993).

As Metternich discovered in 1848, followed by generations of politicians after him, the world simply isn't what it used to be. Nationalism has come to stay. Instead of ignoring "the revolt of the masses," to use Ortega y Gasset's ([1930] 1957) apt term, there is no choice but try to understand and domesticate this force: "The fact remains that a sufficient number of men identify themselves with their state or nation to justify and render possible governmental action in the name of state interests" (Wolfers 1962, 6).

The national interest depends crucially on popular perceptions, and this fact inevitably undermines the applicability of the realist approach. Whereas some eras lend themselves more readily to a state-centric perspective, others are singularly ill-suited for this simplification.[2] In Wolfers' words: "In losing sight of the individuals who comprise a state, exponents of the states-as-actors theory may come up with a relatively accurate analysis of national behavior in a period when value patterns remain static, but they are more likely to be mistaken in a period of upheaval when elites and values undergo rapid and radical change" (6). Indeed, the post–cold war period is precisely such an era. History is not kind to those leaders who "forget" their civil societies; nor is it kind to theories that take public support for granted.

Unfortunately, the other, individualist extreme is equally misleading. While it is true that only individuals, not states, "are capable of desires and intentions, preferences and feelings of friendship or hatred," ignoring the collective nature of decision making seriously distorts an analysis on the state level. Rejecting such a "psychologistic" approach to the actor problem, Wolfers concludes:

> There can be no "state behavior" except as the term is used to describe the combined behavior of individual human beings organized into a state. Not only do men act differently when engaged in pursuing what they consider the goals of their "national selves," but they are able to act as they do only because of the power and influence generated by their nations organized as corporate bodies. (8–9).

If the agency on the world stage cannot be conceived of unitary and discrete states, nor as the aggregate of individual actions, what then? This is the classical dilemma of agency in International Relations (Singer 1969). Its solution requires nothing less than a theoretical merger of state-centrism and liberal individualism. Arriving at this uncompromising conclusion, Wolfers suggests that "all events occurring in the international arena must be conceived of and understood from two angles simultane-

[2] Though see Schroeder (1994) for the argument that neorealism does not even capture the pre-Napoleonic Westphalian system.

ously: one calling for concentration on the behavior of states as organized bodies of men, the other calling for concentration on human beings upon whose psychological reactions the behavior credited to states ultimately rests" (9). Despite some recent attempts to link the two levels (Putnam 1988; Moravcsik 1992; Evans et al. 1992), the bulk of today's IR literature does not even confront Wolfers's dilemma. Most theorists continue to assume that states can and should be viewed as coherent actors, moving across the international stage, not unlike the chess pieces to which Wolfers alluded.

DEFINING THE STATE AND THE NATION

Finding a way out of this impasse calls for a more drastic approach. It is unlikely that theoretical progress will be made without a clearer definition of the actors' identities. Wolfers's two perspectives can be brought together by explicit reference to states and nations as separate entities. In addition to the states-as-actor approach, people enter the analysis not as individuals but as national communities held together by subjectively constructed emotional bonds. Both these actor types have to be viewed in a historical light rather than as exogenously existing units. Accounting for their origin, development, and disappearance is a necessary ingredient of any long-term explanation of world politics.

Despite their heavy reliance on the state as the basic ontological unit, realists have remained strangely uninterested in its definition. Their lack of concern for definitional issues can be understood by reference to the history of the realist paradigm. Originally (and to some extent still) a normative school rather than a scientific theory, the realpolitik approach emerged as a set of policy guidelines helping the Prince govern his state. For Machiavelli and his followers, the state already existed, and the question was which foreign policy would maximize its interests.[3]

The normative character of realist thought became even clearer as the idea of sovereignty developed territorial and popular components in the eighteenth century (Hinsley 1986). Faithful to the ancien régime, realists from Metternich to Morgenthau have clung tenaciously to a territorial definition of sovereignty. Yet, as Alexander George and Robert Keohane (George 1980) eloquently explain, this outlook became increasingly problematic as the rulers' right to rule came under attack:

---

[3] Yet, even Machiavelli ([1513] 1981) held strong views about actor identities, as suggested by the last, often ignored chapter of *The Prince* in which he deplored the disunity of Italy.

With the "democratization" of nationalism . . . the relative simplicity of the concept "raison d'état" was eroded, and the state itself came to be seen as composed of different interests. In the era of liberal democracy, "l'état, c'est moi" was no longer an acceptable answer to the question of sovereign legitimacy. The national interest came to reflect a weighting of various diverse interests . . . as different groups within the policy competed to claim it as a legitimizing symbol for their interests and aspirations, which might by no means be shared by many of their compatriots. (219)

Ironically, the behavioral revolution in the social sciences has reinforced the normative character of realism. Since they focus on behavior, neorealist scholars do not care whether the unit can be defined as a city-state, empire, or nation-state as long as it acts according to the "national interest." Indeed, they maintain that the laws of international politics remain the same regardless of actors' identity and type. In neorealist studies of the contemporary world, the nation-state is implicitly or explicitly referred to as the dominant actor type, but actor type has little bearing on the analysis.

Using "state" and "nation" interchangeably is a major obstacle to disentangling Wolfers's actor dilemma. Despite their convergence in the modern nation-state, any theory that claims generality beyond a world populated by such units cannot treat the two concepts as identical. This point is not easily recognized, given the common habit of referring to the *national* interest, inter*national* relations, and trans*national* relations when the references really are to state interests, interstate relations, and transstate relations (Connor 1972, 1978, 1994; Claude 1986; Ferguson and Mansbach 1988, 129).

This blurring should not be attributed exclusively to realist scholarship. Indeed, liberals are as prone to restrict their theories to explanations of state behavior, albeit choosing independent variables on the domestic level. The Anglo-Saxon dominance of the entire discipline cements the common neglect of the state/nation dichotomy. For all their variety, there has never been any doubt that the foreign policies of Great Britain and the United States can be described and analyzed as that of nation-states. Unsurprisingly, scholars from these countries often write as if the entire world conformed with this pattern. Walker Connor (1978, 382) points out that if the nation-state was indeed the rule rather than an exception, the analytical costs would be insignificant: "Where nation and state essentially coincide, their verbal interutilization is inconsequential because the two are indistinguishably merged in popular perception. The state is perceived as the political extension of the nation and appeals to one trigger identical, positive psychological responses as appeal to the other."

This state of affairs, however, does not apply to many other areas. Connor (1978) cautions that "the invoking of such symbol has quite a different impact upon minorities. Thus, 'Mother Russia' evokes one type of response from a Russian and something quite different from a Ukrainian" (383). Since it is precisely the failure to realize this distinction that causes so much confusion among policymakers and scholars in the post–cold war era, the call for clear definitions cannot be brushed aside as conceptual nit-picking. For the purposes of the current analysis, I define the state in Weberian terms, as a territorial organization exercising legitimate control over its own territory, undisturbed by internal power competition or external intervention (cf. Weber 1946, 78). Likewise, I turn to Weber for a definition of the nation as "a community of sentiment which would adequately manifest itself in a state of its own" and hence "tends to produce a state of its own" (176).

Because Weber's definitions benefit from clarity and wide use, I refrain from reviewing alternative conceptualizations, although there is a wide literature on the conceptual difficulties involved (see, e.g., Poggi 1978; Gellner 1983; Ferguson and Mansbach 1988; Hall and Ikenberry 1989). Therefore, a few words about the distinction between the two organization types are in order.

Weber's state concept emphasizes the exclusivity of control. This automatically rules out organizations falling short of power monopoly, such as feudal principalities (Ruggie 1983, 1993), amorphous empires with ill-defined frontiers lacking the means to enforce internal order (Kratochwil 1986), and supranational organizations such as the European Union.[4] National cohesion differs in that the nation is held together by an emotional bond, while the state does not presuppose any particular loyalty from its subjects. In principle, if not in practice, internal order can be maintained by threat. Furthermore, not every community counts as a nation. The nation, in Weber's view, is a special type of community in that it aspires to, or already enjoys, statehood. This makes it different from other types of ethnic and regional communities. Tribal organizations, rural village units, and other *ethnies*, to use the French term (cf. Smith 1986, 1991), are usually all very cohesive, but their lack of ambition to form a state disqualifies them as nations.[5] The absence of a political consciousness expressed in territorial terms also currently marks the great cosmopolitan communities of faith, such as the Catholicism and Islam. When religion

---

[4] As would be expected, realists challenge the medieval state as different from the modern one (e.g., Fischer 1992; for a rebuttal, see Hall and Kratochwil 1993).

[5] Smith (1986, chap. 7; 1991) adds more criteria distinguishing a nation from an ethnic group, including greater size, territorial attachment, secular rather than religious identity, sharp boundaries, and so on. See also Suny (1993, 13).

has been exploited for nationalist purposes, the church must be subordinated to the state.[6]

When the state and the nation coincide territorially and demographically, the resulting unit is a nation-state. Nation-states combine the emotional cohesion of the nation with the territorial integrity of the state by conferring citizenship to their subjects and regulating the movement of people across their borders (Brubaker 1992). In the following, I will use the notion of nation-state in this restrictive sense. Since common conceptual usage often fails to distinguish between the nation and the nation-state, the nation will sometimes be referred to as a national community or a national identity whenever necessary. To further reduce the risk of confusion, I will use the term "multinational state," or "imperial state" whenever applicable, to designate states that do not live up to the ethnic homogeneity required by the nation-state category (see definitional discussions in chapters 6 and 7). Such fragmented states consist of two or more nationalities, which are nations that share political organization with other nations. For example, before the fall of Yugoslavia, we spoke of Yugoslav nationalities when referring to the Serbs and Croats (see chapter 6 for more on this issue).[7]

FROM REIFICATION TO EMERGENCE

Though indispensable for a general theory of world politics, clear definitions of the state and nation do not suffice. The concepts must also be set in motion. While static and objectified approaches to agency are justified as long as the temporal scope remains limited, they tend to conceal the inherently history-dependent and socially constructed nature of states and nations. The behavioral focus of contemporary IR theory has reinforced such a reified notion of actors.

In social theory, reification stands for "the apprehension of human phenomena as if they were things, that is, in non-human or possible supra terms" (Berger and Luckmann 1966, 106; see also Wendt 1992, 410). Anthony Giddens (1984, 180) explains that "reified discourse refers to the 'facticity' with which social phenomena confront individual actors in such a way as to ignore how they are produced and reproduced through

---

[6] Henry VIII's break with Rome is an early example of a church being nationalized (cf. Greenfeld 1992, chap. 1). The emergence of autocephalous Orthodox state churches in the Balkans also illustrates this trend (Kitromilides 1989). Theocracies constitute a possible exception, although even such states are ruled by national religious leaders rather than cosmopolitan elites.

[7] See Suny (1993, 12) and Alter (1989, 18) for alternative definitions of "nationality."

human agency." As an important corollary, reification grants concepts an unproblematic status, implying that they do not require any explanation.

Vernacular reasoning would hardly be possible without reification of both individual and collective actors (Gilbert 1989). This mental shortcut serves important heuristic purposes, which is why it is so hard to break away from. When applied to large-scale social organizations and long-term processes, however, reification often obscures more than it clarifies. In such contexts, neither the state nor the nation can be treated as given objects without assuming away much of what is essential for a complete explanation of their behavior, not to mention their structural origin and historical unfolding. The habit of reifying actors thus unduly narrows the research agenda by removing important research questions.

Neorealism offers perhaps the best example of a theory resting upon an explicitly reified notion of agency (Wendt 1987). Richard Ashley (1986) asserts that, in neorealist theory, "the state must be treated as an un-problematic unity: an entity whose existence, boundaries, identifying structures, constituencies, legitimations, interests, and capacities to make self-regarding decisions can be treated as given, independent of transna-tional class and human interest, and undisputed (except, perhaps, by other states)" (268). It would be a mistake, however, to single out this para-digm as the only one that considers actors to be unproblematic. Despite their willingness to rely on domestic-level explanations and a more inclu-sive set of actor types than realists do, most neoliberals also tacitly ad-here to a reified approach to agency. According to Wendt (1994), "they either bracket the formation of interests, treating them *as if* they were exogenous, or explain interests by reference to domestic politics, on the assumption that they are exogenous, although not necessarily constant" (384). In fact, to find exceptions from reified actors, one has to turn to integration theory (e.g., Deutsch et al. 1957) and constructivist theory (e.g., Wendt 1987) and historical sociology (e.g., Tilly 1990).

To a large extent, this theoretical lacuna depends on the strong behav-iorist bias of contemporary, especially American, social science (Hoff-mann 1977). Many theorists are unaware of the built-in limitations of the conventional IR agenda. Generations of graduate students have been so-cialized to concentrate on one predominant theme: the explanation of cooperation and conflict. The causal nexus implied by the dominant metatheoretical scheme in IR, the levels-of-analysis framework, implic-itly presupposes the existence of actors. Introduced by Kenneth Waltz (1959), and repeated with minor or major variations by several other authors (e.g., Singer 1969; Russett and Starr 1981), the levels-of-analysis model organizes causes of social behavior, such as war or economic co-operation, on different levels of aggregation. While this conceptual scheme serves a useful purpose as one of the rare common reference points in a theoretically and methodologically fragmented discipline, it has unfortunately also tended to divert attention from sociological questions pertaining to the anatomy of the actors themselves.

As we have seen, the conceptual standing of the nation is if possible even more precarious. To the extent that references to culture and nationalism enter the analysis at all, the nation almost always plays a reified role not unlike the state in mainstream IR theory. To take one recent example addressing units greater than nations, Samuel Huntington (1993) suggests that a "clash of civilizations" will replace interstate conflicts in the post–cold war period. It is clear that Huntington has a reified notion of culture in mind for, emphasizing the allegedly immutable character of cultural identities, he states: "In conflicts between civilizations, the question is 'What are you?' That is a given that cannot be changed" (27).

Journalistic coverage of ethnic conflicts in former Yugoslav and Soviet republics also contains many examples of reification of entire nations. According to one common outlook, dubbed the "Sleeping Beauty" view by Ronald Suny (1993), these conflicts are "eruptions of long-repressed primordial national consciousness" (3; see also Snyder 1993b and Hardin 1995). Like the tendency to reify the state, this habit mirrors everyday reasoning. Pointing to the dangers of reification of communities in general, Craig Calhoun (1992, 8) contends that

> we habitually refer to ethnic groups, races, tribes, and languages as though they were clearly unities, only occasionally recalling to ourselves the ambiguity of their definitions, the porousness of their boundaries, and the situational dependency of their use in practice. The point is not that such categorical identities are not real, any more than the nations are not real, it is, rather, that they are not fixed but both fluid and manipulable. Cultural and physical differences exist, but their discreteness, their identification, and their invocation are all variable.

Although culture may be close to immutable, political categories are not. This point has also been stressed by David Laitin (1986, 1988) who proposes a "two-faced" notion of culture. Instead of reducing cultural influences on politics to a matter of value consensus, Laitin emphasizes the instrumental aspects. Political leaders consciously manipulate identities by highlighting "points of concern" rather than taking entire cultural packages for granted.

This conceptualization promises to offer an escape from the polarized debate between primordial (reified) and modernist (instrumental) approaches to nationalism (see reviews in Laitin 1986; Smith 1986, 1988, 1995; and Calhoun 1993). In their reaction to naively reified notions of nationality, modernist scholars sometimes go too far in the other direction by exaggerating the ease with which nations can be invented and individuals persuaded to believe in their myths. This view takes the deep ethnic roots of nations too lightly (Smith 1986). The challenge consists of capturing the constraints placed upon the manipulative creativity of political leaders without resorting to reification: "What is necessary . . . is a sense of the mutability of group boundaries and yet their dependence on antecedent affinities that are not easily manipulated" (Horowitz 1985, 66).

To sum up, understanding long-term political change requires an inherently historical perspective on both states and nations. It is convenient to refer to this conception of agency as the *emergent-actor approach* in contrast to reified notions. For now it is sufficient to define emergence somewhat loosely as the opposite to reification, with the status of actors problematic and thus requiring explanation. In standard social-science language, this means that the actors are not treated exogenously, but endogenously as dependent variables. In the following, I will use "problematic" and "emergent" synonomously.[8]

Due to its historical character, the emergent-actor approach is of necessity process based. More specifically, states and nations emerge from two macrohistorical processes: state formation and nationalism. Although it is useful to keep the two processes analytically separate, in reality they are intertwined:

> States are created by war, colonization, conquest and peaceful settlement, through amalgamation of different parts and through their separating from each other; and all this is bound up with an alternating process of intermingling and separation of races and civilizations, tribes and languages. The European peoples have only gradually developed their nationalities; they are not a simple product of nature but are themselves a product of the creation of states. (Hintze 1975, 161)

The organization of this book reflects this analytical distinction. Of the four models to follow, the first two deal explicitly with state formation (see chapters 4 and 5). Chapter 6 provides a brief introduction to the remaining models, which both concentrate on different aspects of nationalism (see chapters 7 and 8). In broad outline, the phase of "pure" state formation corresponds to the absolutist period in early modern Europe. It was not until the Napoleonic revolution of warfare that nation building became a wider concern beyond a strictly Western European setting.

---

[8] This preliminary definition says nothing about how deep the account must be to be called emergent. Chapter 3 introduces a stricter concept of emergence requiring a subjective distance between the assumptions and the phenomenon to be explained. There is also a rich literature on emergence in sociology starting with Durkheim's (1938) notion of "emergent properties." See also Phillips 1976; Giddens 1984, 171; Alexander 1988, 275–78.

AN OVERVIEW OF THE LITERATURE

Some IR theories, as mentioned above, treat both state and nation as given; other work holds one of those categories constant and addresses the question of how the other develops in that context. Such analyses build on work in some of these categories and initiate work in others. To locate the current modeling projects relative to these traditional and non-traditional approaches, it is helpful to combine the state/nation dichotomy with the classification of actors as reified or emergent.

The latter classification can be extended to include three possibilities pertaining to the theoretical status of a particular actor type: (1) absent/implicit; (2) reified; and (3) emergent/problematic.[9] A few examples make these classes clearer:

1. Due to their microeconomic focus, neither neorealism nor neoliberalism refers to nations except implicitly as a qualification of the state concept (i.e., the nation-state). Neomarxist perspectives, by contrast, usually treat states as an implicit category or even omit them.

2. In conventional social-scientific parlance, reified status translates into exogeneity—that is, the actor in question figures either in explicit assumptions or as an independent variable. In neorealism, for example, states are explicitly assumed. While sticking to a reified concept of the state, some neoliberal theories also treat the state as an independent variable. Recent scholarship on the democratic peace belongs to this category (e.g., Russett 1993).

3. Finally, if the actor concept is made entirely endogenous in the sense alluded to in the previous section, it deserves to be called emergent. Examples include historical and sociological approaches to the state (e.g., Poggi 1978; Tilly 1990).

The contrast between states and nations generates two theoretical dimensions. Figure 2.1 presents this classification, using the three theoretical role categories to grade the axes. Without pretending to offer an extensive review of IR theory and related literatures, I will go through the cells to illustrate the flavor of corresponding theories. The way the figure is organized implies that the further one moves down and to the right, the more complex the theory becomes. Theories in the upper left corner tend to be more tractable than those in the lower right. Conversely, the constructivist perspectives usually reflect complex environments better than the traditional ones. The ultimate choice of theory cannot be made a priori but depends on the empirical circumstances at hand. Since the goal

---

[9] See also Therborn (1991) for a similar classification of theories with respect to their view of actors.

States

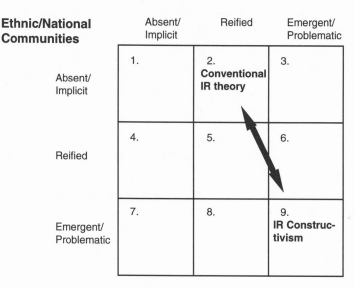

Figure 2.1. The theoretical landscape of IR theory

of this work is to promote an emergent approach to both states and nations, however, cell 9 represents an analytical goal.[10]

Cell 1 is least interesting for our purposes since it is silent about both the state and the nation. Here we find theories of domestic politics that view the state as an arena containing other actors, such as interest groups and parties (see Nettl 1968). This is also the analytical starting point of global perspectives that rely on various nonstate actors such as nongovernmental organizations and classes. More recently, however, comparative politics has seen a tendency to view the state as an actor in its own right. Attempts to "bring the state back in" shift the focus gradually from cell 1 to cell 2 (Evans, Rueschemeyer, and Skocpol 1985).

Cell 2 combines an explicit but reified treatment of the state with minimal references to nations as actors in their own right. Most conventional IR theory fits into this cell since both neorealism and neoliberalism tend

---

[10] I add cultural communities to the vertical axis since, strictly speaking, the definition of the nation would have otherwise left cells 4 and 7 empty. The nation presupposes the existence, or at least the aspiration, of statehood, something that is ruled out by default in the first column. In these cases it is proper to talk of ethnic communities. With this wider interpretation of the vertical dimension, these cells become more interesting. In the remaining cases (cells 5, 6, 8, and 9), we can legitimately refer to nations thanks to the state's explicit status.

to treat states as given and unchanging while almost completely ignoring nations as independent actors. Despite their different predictions about cooperation and conflict, their rationalistic assumptions imply a common behavioral approach to process and institutions (Wendt 1992, 391). Deriving their philosophical inspiration from Hobbes and Locke, these paradigms adopt a fundamentally voluntarist and contractarian approach to agency that downplays history. We have already seen that liberal efforts to problematize the state are often restricted to explaining behavior by references to domestic politics while holding the state itself constant. Since most (American) IR theorists count themselves as either neorealist or neoliberals, I will refer to this position alternatively as "mainstream" or "conventional."

Cell 3 represents a theoretical generalization of cell 2 by which the state, but not the nation, becomes an emergent concept. The question of national identity thus still lurks in the background. It should not come as a surprise that many theorists have found the mainstream outlook wanting. In many respects, classical (as opposed to neo-) realists have always been closer to this position (Ashley 1986). Because of their suspicion of behaviorism and rationalist orthodoxy, these traditional scholars have had a penchant for historically and sociologically inspired approaches that lend themselves more readily to an emergent-actor approach (e.g., Aron 1966). But some neorealists have also pushed their theories in this direction (e.g., Gilpin 1981). The endogenization of the state is not restricted to realists. Unlike their neoliberal colleagues, "strong liberals," to use Wendt's (1992) terminology, show a greater interest for learning and identity formation, a perspective that opens the door for emergent conceptualizations of the state. In this camp, we also find neofunctionalist theories of integration that stress social learning as a way to shift peoples' loyalties to a higher-level state structure (e.g., Haas 1958). While such theories trace institutional developments in terms of interests, they deliberately shun any explicit discussion of national identities and national communities (Taylor 1983), which is why they belong to cell 3 rather cells 6 or 9.

Once we leave the first row, the nation acquires its own role. To find explicit references to nationalism, it is usually, and ironically enough, necessary to leave political science. There are rich and long-standing literatures on the topic within history, sociology, social psychology, and anthropology. As we shall see, the nation plays very different roles in these fields, and these variations intersect with the conceptual status of the state in complicated ways.

Cell 4 introduces culture but leaves no room for the state as an actor. This class of studies corresponds to traditional approaches in anthropology, especially those concerned with primitive, prestate organizations (e.g., Geertz 1973). Huntington's (1993) study of civilizations, cited above, also falls into this box because of its conscious attempt to replace interstate relations with a reified notion of cultural communities, whether tribes or entire civilizations.

Cell 5 goes beyond the previous one by treating both the state and the nation as explicit, albeit reified, actors. This is where we find traditional studies in comparative nationalism organized as country cases. While such studies offer detailed information about the specific areas of focus, they often frame their explanations in terms of "national characters" or "national traditions." For example, David Laitin (1991) detects these tendencies in comparative work on Soviet nationalities.

Cell 6 marries the emergent-state perspective with a reified approach to the nation. Taking nations for given, these studies focus on the development and integration of states. Modernization theory and classical functionalist integration theory are cases in point to the extent that they treat nation building as a trivial process. Chapter 7 classifies these approaches under the label "assimilation theory."

Cell 7 captures the endogenization of ethnic groups in an essentially stateless environment. Fredrik Barth's (1969) work on emergent ethnic boundaries belongs in this class of theories. Reacting to reified conceptions of cultural categories in traditional anthropology, Barth suggested an ultimately subjectivist view of cultural identity formation. The Bristol school of social psychology also stresses self-categorization as opposed to objectivist notions of social groups (Tajfel 1981; see also Turner 1987). We will return to these perspectives in chapters 7 and 8.

Cell 8 builds on work from cells 5 and 7. Like studies of national character in cell 5, these studies typically proceed by holding the state constant, but here national identities evolve over time, as in cell 7. Since they limit their time scopes to the medium-long run, these analyses often explain the impact of state policies on nationality formation within fixed multiethnic states (e.g., Brass 1974, 1991; Laitin 1986). While useful for limited comparisons, this analytical position can be carried too far, especially if the goal is to provide a general theory of nationalism. The reification of the state inherent in country-based studies of nationalism frustrates such ambitious projects despite their endogenization of national identities over time (e.g., Greenfeld 1992).

Cell 9, finally, constitutes the most general of all these categories in that it endogenizes both the state and the nation. To the extent that it manages to free itself from materialist shackles without resorting to speculation about deterministic cultural trends in world history, historical sociology reaches this category. I know no better examples of such studies than Charles Tilly's (1990) and Michael Mann's (1986, 1993a) sophisticated historicosociological approaches to state and nation formation.

Within the IR literature, it is critical theory in general, and social constructivism in particular, that aspires to populate this cell, although much
scholarship in this genre belongs in other cells. As we have seen, critical
theory can be defined negatively in opposition to mainstream IR approaches. Yet it exploits its full potential in its positive function, combining a constructivist conception of structural determinants (Giddens 1979,
1984) with a nonreified approach to identity formation, which draws on
social psychology and symbolic interactionism. So far, constructivists
have stressed the need for a theory of state formation more than that of
nation formation (e.g., Ashley 1986; Ferguson and Mansbach 1988;
Wendt 1987) but more recently progress has been made in analyzing the
coevolution of national identities and state structures.[11]

We now turn to the debates that rage among the various perspectives of
states and nations. Because of the popularity of neorealism and neoliberalism, most of the controversies that fill the IR journals actually take
place within cell 2. These exchanges usually derive from the traditional
conflict between realism and idealism. The more technical language of
today's contributions cannot obscure the continued centrality of this ideological fault line, whether the arguments concern relative versus absolute
gains (Baldwin 1993) or the possibility of cooperation through iterated
games and other individualistically based devices (Axelrod and Keohane
1985).

Critical theorists challenge the orthodoxy of the mainstream research
agenda as defined by cell 2. Launching their attacks from the lower right
corner of figure 2.1, especially from cell 9, these scholars pit their own
more sociological outlook against the rationalist approaches of neorealism and neoliberalism. In a review of this division, Robert Keohane

---

[11] In his most recent writings, Alexander Wendt (1994, 1995) backs away from his earlier
commitment to an endogenized view of the actors themselves. Drawing on Mead's distinction between "I" and "me," he separates corporate identities, defined as "the intrinsic, self-
organizing qualities that constitute actor individuality," from social identities, referring to
"sets of meanings that an actors attributes to itself while taking the perspective of others,
that is, as a social object" (Wendt 1994, 385). Having labeled his position "weak or essen-
tialist constructivism," Wendt admits that, while his theory endogenizes social identities, he
leaves corporate ones unexplained: "Corporate identities have histories, but these do not
concern me here; a theory of the state's system need no more explain the existence of states
than one of society need explain that of people" (p. 385). Furthermore, Wendt adopts an
explicitly state-centric agenda, which makes it hard to study nationalism as an autonomous
process (Chakrabarti Pasic 1996). Because this book explicitly considers the emergence and
evolution of states and nations, I have to turn to "stronger" types of constructivism than that
proposed by Wendt. Christopher Daase's (1993a; 1996) "sociational" perspective belongs to
the most promising attempts along these lines. For other less restrictive constructivist
studies, see also Waever (1993), Waever and Kelstrup (1993), and Biersteker and Weber
(1996).

(1988) labeled these two positions reflectivism and rationalism respectively. Yosef Lapid (1989) refers to the same controversy as the "third debate," since it is preceded by two other great exchanges: the "idealism versus realism" schism of the interwar period and the "history versus science" controversy of the early postwar era. More recently, a debate provoked by John Mearsheimer's (1994–1995) attack on critical theory as one of several "institutionalist" perspectives raged in the pages of *International Security* (see Wendt 1995 for a rebuttal).

In contrast to other scholarly disputes in IR, the "third debate" has revolved mostly around metatheoretical issues. This reflective turn is related closely to the demise of logical positivism in philosophy of science (Lapid 1989; Bohman 1991). Drawing on these post-positivist and post-behaviorist developments, social constructivists assail mainstream scholarship for its naturalist ontology and empiricist epistemology (e.g., Wendt 1987). While some diehard defenders of the conventional camp tend to brush these attacks aside as being irrelevant and even damaging for scientific progress, there is a growing awareness within the mainstream IR community that not all the critics can be stamped as destructive "theory wreckers." Likewise, as some of dissidents have managed to secure a firmer material basis for their research, their battle cries have become less shrill and their willingness to engage in productive exchanges with the mainstream scholars greater.

To use a somewhat exotic metaphor, the vast depopulated desert area between the main IR oases at cell 2 and cell 9 has seen an influx of pioneers ready to profit from new theoretical water holes wherever possible. Although there is not yet any steady flow of caravans from one oasis to the other, and the supply of water (read: research grants) may be somewhat unreliable outside the populated areas, the latter grow at a steady pace. As the previously arid landscape starts blooming, new excursions set out into the shrinking void. In terms of this analogy, the metatheoretical goal of this book is to encourage contact between the two main oases by establishing new water holes. Clearly this strategy falls well short of a building a bidirectional highway connecting the two camps. Nevertheless, the new outposts will hopefully attract new settlers, bringing us closer to the goal of an interconnected, flourishing theoretical landscape that leaves no spot unexploited.

One has to be realistic about the risks associated with this bold campaign of frontier cultivation. The desert road is littered with theoretical carcasses and methodological bones. Speaking as an experienced inhabitant of the conventional oasis, Robert Keohane (1988) sees the issue clearly: "Eventually, we may hope for a synthesis between the rationalistic and reflective approaches—a synthesis that will help us to understand both practices and specific institutions and the relationships between them. Such a synthesis, however, will not emerge full-blown, like Athena from the head of Zeus" (393).

My own mission aims at discovering methodological water holes, here interpreted as formal models. The remainder of this chapter will be devoted to justification of this strategy. Since only qualitative theories, but no models, have hitherto tended to be available beyond cell 2, there is no choice but to start the expedition from this point. In the next section, I show why modeling is not only desirable for any point in the landscape, but also why its desirability actually increases the further away from the conventional camp one ventures. Below I clarify why conventional modeling tools are insufficient to take us beyond the mainstream position. These two points combine into a dilemma: The demand for models is inversely proportional to the supply. Paradoxically, the more complex reality becomes, the more we need formal tools, but the less current models fit.

WHY MODELS ARE NEEDED

Critical theorists typically reject formal research in mainstream IR as model driven rather than motivated by substantive concerns. Though not opposed to theoretical elegance and empirical observation as a matter of principle, the dissident scholars question the prominence of mathematical tractability and empirical falsifiability as the guiding principles in theory building. In their view, this "methodological monism" forces theoretical concepts into a formal procrustean bed that frustrates scientific progress (Lapid 1989).

Expressing similar concerns, Shapiro and Wendt (1992) suggest that contemporary mainstream scientific practice often falls into the trap of "logicism." Deriving its raison d'être from the prestige of economics, the rationalist research program all too often degenerates into "an exercise in trying to derive an ever widening class of phenomena from the theory rather than an attempt to validate the theory empirically" (202).[12] Nevertheless, Shapiro and Wendt also realize the potential of rationalist explorations: "Taking an explanation and running with it, driving an as-if causal theory to the hilt, may reveal as faulty the assumptions that hitherto had been taken for granted and may generate research problems and hypotheses for investigation that otherwise would not have been thought of" (203; see also Giddens 1979, 258). Thus their quarrel is not with

---

[12] Many theorists rightly attack the various attempts to escape the scant predictive success of rational-choice models. See Moe (1979), Miller (1987), and Green and Shapiro (1994).

modeling per se, but with the imperialistic ambitions present in some strands of political economy (e.g., Becker 1986):

> By confusing what can never be more than devices for hypothesis generation with the conduct of social science itself, they often lose sight of the phenomena that their theories purport to explain, and the disputes about the fine points of analytical models that occupy much of their attention often reside so deeply in a world of counterfactuals that they would never be tested empirically. (Shapiro and Wendt 1992, 203)

While these points represent an unusual tolerance for formal approaches, they underestimate both the need for modeling approaches in the constructivist paradigm and the potential for modeling innovations outside the rational-choice paradigm. In the next chapter, I will address the second point by exploring alternative modeling techniques. This section addresses the first point by highlighting the often overlooked value of formal modeling as a complement to constructivist approaches. Though Shapiro and Wendt (1992) correctly stress the heuristic, as opposed to directly empirical, role of formal tools, their implicit confidence in the alternative—verbal analysis—is somewhat overdrawn. Formal modeling is not a mere toy that is best left for game theorists to tinker with. Ironically enough, because of the inherent complexity and context dependence of their theories, constructivists and other dissident scholars need the heuristic power of formal tools even more urgently than neorealists and neoliberals. In their eagerness to increase empirical accuracy and accommodate real-world complexity, these theorists often lose sight of the risks associated with verbal theorizing. Without the logical straitjacket of modeling, it is hard to maintain coherence and consistency. Of course, these problems can be reduced by lowering the ambition to narration, but such a concession inevitably defeats the goal of understanding complex social systems. Like the rationalist obsession with technical details, social constructivism's lack of precision hinders formulation of precise testable hypotheses. Mainstream theorists have good reasons to be impatient with the lofty theoretical constructs imported from social theory (Skocpol 1987; Keohane 1988; Jervis 1993).

Following Anthony Giddens and other social theorists, IR dissidents are prone to call for "rich" frameworks including explicit spatial and temporal contextuality, intangible entities such as beliefs and ideas, and most importantly for our purposes, abandonment of reification. These principles are neatly presented as scientific realism (Wendt 1987), but when it comes to their practical implementation, it is less obvious how to proceed.[13] Indeed, it is hard to overestimate the difficulties of overcoming

---

[13] Scientific realism should not be confused with political realism.

reification and other conceptual hurdles. Although particularly conscious of the risks of reification, constructivist theorists cannot always escape the traps of vernacular reasoning. Creating a theory that "acknowledges the historic and dynamic character of cognitive schemes and assumptive frameworks" is easier said than done (Lapid 1989, 248).

No one was more keenly aware of these limitations than the German sociologist Norbert Elias. In many ways, Elias anticipated the ideas of modern social theory and can therefore be counted as an early social constructivist. Unlike most historically oriented scholars, he never overlooked the formidable obstacles to human understanding of complex and dynamic systems. "Even bearing in mind that social forces are forces exerted by people over themselves and over one another, it is still very difficult when thinking and speaking to guard against the social pressure of verbal and conceptual structures. These make social forces seem like forces exerted on objects in nature—like forces external to people, exerted over them as 'objects'" (Elias [1970] 1978, 20).

Though he devoted his life to conceptual innovation, Elias clearly saw the limitation of his own metaphorical devices. In his view, the dilemma remains that "the social apparatus for thinking and speaking places at our disposal only either models of a naïvely egocentric or magico-mythical kind, or else models from natural science" (ibid., 17). It is not hard to see the parallel to loose qualitative theorizing and sterile formal modeling. The basic problem still applies to the social sciences: "No matter how painfully aware we are of their inadequacy, more adequate means of thought and communication are in many instances simply not available at present" (ibid.).

Writing almost a half century later, James March and Johan Olsen (1984) reiterate Elias' call for more precise heuristic tools:

> There is good sense in noting that history is not necessarily efficient, but it would be of greater help if we were able to show the specific ways by which specific history-dependent processes lead to outcomes that are either non-unique or long delayed under some conditions. It is plausible to argue that politics is filled with behavior that is difficult to fit into a utilitarian model, but the plausibility would be augmented if we could describe an alternative model. And it is provocative to note the importance of symbols, ritual, ceremony, and myth in political life, but we cannot sustain the provocation without a clearer specification of how theories of politics are affected by such a vision. (742)

Thus more systematic ways of theorizing would serve an essential function as a complement to more intuitive, verbal conceptual development. The question is whether existing formal frameworks can meet the challenge of modeling emergent actors.

WHY CURRENT MODELS WILL NOT DO THE TRICK

Almost without exception, formal applications in IR rest upon rational-choice theory. Mostly of a game-theoretic type, these models have played an especially important role in elucidating the strategic intricacies of nuclear deterrence during the cold war (Schelling 1960, 1966). Moreover, collective-choice schemes such as the prisoner's dilemma type have also helped us grasp the difficulties of achieving cooperation among states (e.g., Jervis 1978; Axelrod and Keohane 1985). Yet outside the relatively well defined and stable setting of the cold war, these approaches have proven less useful. In a more complex and fluid setting, game theory's virtues turn into vices. Rational-choice models impose a strict and unchanging structure on strategic situations, assuming actors to be fixed and given, perfectly informed, and acting in ways that always produce equilibria.

Fixed and Given Actors

Because of their focus on choices and actions, game theorists treat the actors and their identities as given. Hard-wired into game forms and utility functions, the actors remain the same throughout the game. Since most models focus on short-term interactions rather than macrohistorical processes, this assumption makes sense. If the time scope extends to longer periods, however, the exogenization of agency becomes problematic: "Within the static one-shot game the persistence of the players' identity may be ignored; but with any repetition or learning this condition becomes critical" (Mirowski 1988, 85).

The problem of given actors does not concern only the constancy of the actors' preferences, but their identities as well. More recently, rational-choice theorists have started to question the adequacy of the assumption of exogenous preferences, though more attention has been paid to the direct influence of culture and norms on behavior (Elster 1989). Nevertheless, the more fundamental issue of identification and self-perception still remains conspicuously absent from the rationalist research agenda (Therborn 1991, 183; though see Hirschman 1984; Sen 1987; and Richards 1995). This lack of awareness of symbolic aspects of social life stems directly from methodological individualism to which almost all modelers adhere for ideological and/or methodological reasons.[14] Assum-

---

[14] Methodological individualism often makes more sense in economic settings, such as large markets consisting of individual consumers. Yet the value of the principle becomes

ing self-interested individual actors undoubtedly simplifies model building substantially. What these theorists often fail to notice, however, is that this assumption begs the question of how the self should be defined. Human individuals are far from being the only possible candidates in whose name action could take place. As we have seen above, individuals frequently identify with a symbolically defined group, such as a national community, and predicate their actions upon this identity. In fact, it is hard to conceive of mass politics in the modern world without referring to such symbolically mediated identifications. Methodological individualism makes it impossible to study nations and other "latent groups" as emergent actors.[15] We will return to the problems of relaxing this philosophical principle.

Common and Complete Knowledge

Virtually all game-theoretic models assume actors possess complete knowledge about all aspects of the game, including the identity, preferences, and resources of the other players. The only exceptions to this rule are incomplete information games that permit uncertainty about a very restricted set of features, usually the other players' payoffs (Kreps and Wilson 1982). For technical reasons, only minor deviations from this assumption are allowed, and in fact, common knowledge must hold at least with respect to probability distributions over actor types. Equilibrium analysis as it is commonly practiced would simply be impossible without the common-knowledge assumption (Binmore 1990).

Again, small social systems observed over limited periods pose few problems. But as the temporal and spatial scopes expand, the plausibility of common knowledge decreases dramatically. In these situations, "we are likely to encounter patterns of interdependent choices whose size and complexity are beyond the ability, of actors and researchers alike, to identify equilibrium solutions in large n-person games" (Scharpf 1991, 281). The actors' knowledge in complex social systems is by necessity local and bounded rather than global and complete.

Accustomed to assume common knowledge to such an extent that it has acquired a self-evident, almost transparent character, most game theorists fail to realize the limitations of conventional game theory in fluid

---

more dubious in other contexts, especially those relating to large-scale historical change involving the manipulation of political symbols.

[15] The typical rationalist stance toward latent groups is that they tend to fall apart, or that they remain inconsequential, unless their leaders possess means of achieving coercive control or loyalty induced by selective incentives (Olson 1965).

and involved contexts, though there are notable exceptions (e.g., Aumann 1976; Binmore 1990). We will return to this topic while looking at ways to model bounded rationality. In the end, the question is whether theories should strive to model the way human actors really think, however limited and parochial their strategies may be, rather than attempt to identify ideally rational courses of action regardless of the cognitive models actually employed by real-world actors (Schutz 1962, 43–44).

Unwilling to abandon their elegant models, most rationalists tend to answer no to this question, but affirmative responses become more common among those theorists who face the complexities of large-scale historical processes beyond the cognitive horizon of single decisionmakers. Douglass North (1990) belongs to this category:

> Social scientists have incorporated the costliness of information in their models, but have not come to grips with the subjective mental constructs by which individuals process information and arrive at conclusions that shape their choices. . . . Our preoccupation with rational choice and market hypotheses has blinded us to the implications of incomplete information and the complexity of environments and subjective perceptions of the external that individuals hold. (111)

It would seem hard to avoid North's position if the goal of liberating modeling from the reification of actors is ever to be attained. In a steadily evolving, complex social system, common knowledge loses all its attractiveness even as an approximation. Instead of devising elaborate explanations based on rational expectations, a much simpler explanatory approach based on heuristic rules appears reasonable.

Equilibrium Analysis

Like the previous two principles, the assumption that model building boils down to finding equilibria enjoys virtually unanimous support in the modeling community (for examples, see Green and Shapiro 1994, 23–30). Models that do not produce a unique equilibrium are usually confined to the modelers' wastebasket. For all its mathematical attractions, however, this obsession with unique Nash equilibria rests on shaky philosophical foundations. To support the move toward a postulated equilibrium, the theorist needs to postulate the existence of a Walrasian auctioneer. If such processes of *tatônnement*, driven either by conscious adjustments or selective mechanisms (Binmore 1990), all produce the same equilibrium outcome, history can be safely treated as efficient, that is immaterial. If these processes diverge, however, history reclaims its central role. In fact, the metaphysical conviction that equilibria are always "out there" waiting to be discovered can blind the analyst to the possibility of adjustments never settling. March and Olsen (1984), explain that this is especially likely to be the case in turbulent situations: "History cannot be guaranteed to be efficient. An equilibrium may not exist. Even if there is an equilibrium, historical processes can easily be slow enough relative to the rate of change in the environment that the equilibrium of the process is unlikely to be achieved before the environment, and thus the equilibrium, changes" (737).

These three objections to applying mainstream rational-choice modeling to complex and changing problems should not obscure the progress that has been made within the paradigm. In particular, contemporary game theory has lost its previous hostility to institutional analysis. Modern political economy now includes a progressive research program that has been called the positive theory of institutions (PTI) (Moe 1987). New concepts such as "structure induced equilibria" (Shepsle 1979) and methodological innovations in mechanism design and in transaction-cost theory have proved useful in understanding the institutional context of strategic action (see Alt and Shepsle 1990). Yet, despite these advances, David Kreps (1990) observes that the economic literature still "leaves open the question, Where did the institutions come from?" Indeed, "having a theory about how institutions arise and evolve could be more informative than theorizes of equilibrium within the context of a given set of institutions" but unfortunately, he says, such theories are still "over the horizon of economic theory" (530–31). This is precisely why the game-theoretic novelties have failed to attract the attention of historical scholars who

> tend to think more broadly and comprehensively about their subject matter. Implicitly, they think in terms of systems and their dynamics—about history, about process, about how the various components of the institutional system fit together. Whether their theoretical notions are correct or very promising is another matter. What is important is that PTI's general orientation to institutional questions is seen as too narrow, and too narrowly technical, to shed light on issues these writers regard as fundamental. (Moe 1987, 298)

Having located the main reasons why conventional rational-choice modeling is incompatible with the emergent-actor perspective, it is hard to avoid the conviction that tinkering with peripheral assumptions will not build any metatheoretical bridges. To satisfy the constructivist scholar takes more than minor modifications of existing theories. Exploring the possibilities of creating a model of long-term historical processes, Douglass North (1990) concludes that "devising a model of economic change requires the construction of an entire theoretical framework, because no such model exists" (112). Such a framework needs to incorporate "incomplete information and subjective models of *reality* and the increasing returns characteristic of institutions."

CONCLUSION

Motivated by a desire to understand how actors and structures emerge, such as in the post–cold war era, we set out to review the ways that actors are modeled in world politics. It soon became clear that conventional scholarship suffers from two serious shortcomings. Not only does it blur the distinction between the state and the nation, it also tends to reify the actors. In stable periods, these weaknesses would have mattered much less. As the world plunges into an era of turmoil characterized by both the creation and dissipation of states and nations, however, these restrictions threaten to bias the theory toward predicting outcomes that would only occur in stable circumstances, and thus fail to sensitize theorists and policymakers to the possibility of structural change. Clearly, such circumstances call for an extension of current modeling approaches to a dynamic perspective that allows for explicit tracing of these transient processes.

Critical theorists have long argued for richer frameworks that render this extension possible, though on a more impressionistic level than formal modeling. While their critique of mainstream IR does not lack bite, they have very little to offer beyond metatheoretical prescriptions and vague concepts drawn from social theory. In the end, their insistence on increased theoretical complexity needs to be complemented by more precise methodological devices.

Unfortunately, due to its current rigid adherence to a number of restrictive core assumptions, the modeling community has so far shown little interest in such a model-building venture. Even small changes are likely to encounter fierce technically and ideologically motivated resistance. Indeed, rational-choice modelers have good reasons for retaining some of their assumptions. Investigating how fruitful these reasons are will be the topic of next chapter. Readers who are less interested in the philosophical and methodological underpinnings of this study may want to skip directly to Chapter 4. Nevertheless, since the models presented in that and later chapters rely on rather unconventional techniques, I recommend the reader to go through at least the fourth section even if it at first blush seems less relevant to the substantive issues under scrutiny.

CHAPTER 3

Toward Richer Models

INTRODUCTION

Undoubtedly, we need more flexible ways to model actors in international politics. Yet although methodological bridge building may be a fine idea, it is not without its difficulties. Modelers generally reject the propositions of social constructivists because a contextual and history-dependent approach contradicts the core assumptions of the rationalistic paradigm. To model the complex historical processes that concern social constructivists, two methodological obstacles have to be overcome. First, as is keenly understood by rationalist theory builders, abandoning the assumption of history-independent equilibria incurs a high price. If the analysis of actors and institutions requires that attention be paid to their history, including accidental influences, how is it then possible to develop generalizable causal theories? Unless we content ourselves with narration and mere description, some way around this obstacle must be found. Second, while rational-choice modeling does not in principle presuppose self-interested individuals, most modelers adhere to narrowly individualist materialism. This position undoubtedly enhances analytical tractability, but it unfortunately excludes the possibility of analyzing intersubjectively constructed groups such as the nation.

These dilemmas are by no means new to philosophers of science. In his *The Poverty of Historicism*, Karl Popper highlighted variations on the same basic themes. According to Popper, "historicist" scholars (his label for macrosociologists) have traditionally objected that logical positivism in the social sciences neglects the higher complexity in these disciplines compared to the natural sciences. In Popper's rendering of the historicist position, this complexity arises "out of the impossibility of artificial isolation, and a complexity due to the fact that social life is a natural phenomenon that presupposes the mental life of individuals" (Popper 1957, 12). Refusing to recognize any difference in complexity between the two research areas, Popper brushed aside these objections as trivial. The absence of experimental control, he argued, can be overcome by performing quasi-experimental studies based on isolated social situations "such as a prison, or an experimental community" (see also Friedman 1953, chap. 1). Moreover, by assuming rational actors, the social sciences become "comparatively independent of psychological assumptions" (Popper 1957, 142). This chapter serves not only to highlight the errors of Popper's reasoning—mistakes that the great philosopher later acknowledged himself—but to illustrate how abandoning the restrictive positivist stance in modeling opens new ways of thinking about complex social systems.[1]

THE PROBLEM OF HISTORICAL CONTINGENCY

To realize why historical contingency poses a serious methodological problem, it is necessary to distinguish between simple and complex settings.[2] Our everyday experience of causality is based on simple situations. Everyone knows that if a ball is hit sufficiently hard and its path intersects a windowpane, the pane breaks. One does not have to be a professor in kinematics and solid-state physics to understand this basic empirical fact. Thanks to our intuitive knowledge about balls and windows, there is no need to specify the underlying mechanisms that link the cause (the bat hitting the ball) with the effect (the broken pane). Causation is easily established as a static link between the two events regardless of the historical path.

While it is tempting to regard the long-term evolution of large social systems in this way, such a view is likely to mislead. After all, humans and their societies are different from balls and windowpanes. In Friedrich Hayek's (1967) words:

> The study of the relatively simple phenomena of the physical world, where it has proved possible to state the determining relations as functions of a few variables that can be easily ascertained in particular instances, and where as a consequence the astounding progress of disciplines concerned with them has become possible, has created the illusion that soon the same will also be true with regard to the more complex phenomena.(15–16)

Despite Hayek's eloquent warning, most social scientists fail to see the difference between simple and complex phenomena.[3] As Karl Popper

---

[1] Unsurprisingly, biologists struggle with similar conceptual difficulties. In his excellent lecture "The Individual in Darwin's World," the paleontologist Stephen Jay Gould (1993) discusses two themes that closely parallel those under scrutiny in this section. The first one pertains to the temptation to overlook the role of chance in evolutionary history. The second one relates to the materialist practice of equating individuality with personhood at the expense of other, higher, levels of aggregation. See also Sober's (1983) sophisticated contribution that also distinguishes between epistemological issues such as causation and the ontological problem of levels of selection.

[2] Cederman (1996b) explores this theme at greater length.

[3] Hayek's brilliant contribution to the study of complexity deserves full notice since it anticipates many of the ideas inherent to the CAS approach. This does not mean, however,

(1972) put it, after discovering the fundamental difference between simple, clocklike phenomena and fussy, cloudlike systems, they assume that "*All clouds are clocks*—even the most cloudy of clouds" (210).

Although this Newtonian reductionism makes sense in simple settings, it confounds the fundamental difference between two types of causality (e.g., Weber 1949; McMullin 1964; Miller 1987). The first one, usually referred to as the nomothetical approach, equates causality with the establishment of empirical lawlike regularities. Originally formulated by David Hume ([1748] 1988), the nomothetical definition was elaborated and formalized by the leading logical positivist of the twentieth century, Carl Hempel. According to Hempel (1965), causal explanation (and prediction) reduces to finding a "covering law" that, in conjunction with observable initial conditions, entails the observed event. (For a useful introduction, see, e.g., Bohman 1991, 18–20.)

Despite its near dominance in contemporary social-science applications, Hempel's covering-law concept no longer coincides with the consensus among philosophers of science. As a matter of fact, even Hume realized that the nomothetical definition does not exhaust all possible conceptions of causality, since its heavy emphasis on sufficient causes overlooks necessary ones (Climo and Howells 1976, 4). The alternative, counterfactual causation, does account for them. Counterfactual explanations are claims about what would have occurred in the absence of the cause: if the causal antecedent had not happened, the consequent would not have occurred.

Unlike Hempel's covering laws, such counterfactual conditionals refer to events that did *not* occur. This is undoubtedly the reason for their limited popularity in the applied literature. While the philosophical literature abounds with analyses of counterfactual causation (see especially Lewis 1973), more practically minded social scientists and historians usually find the idea of fictitious scenarios ridiculous or even repugnant (see examples in Climo and Howells 1976, 19; and Fearon 1991). Nevertheless, there are notable exceptions from this trend. In nearly forgotten methodological essay, Max Weber (1949) not only distinguished clearly between the two types of causation but also argued that no applied scientist can do without counterfactual explanations. Half a century later, E. H. Carr (1963) brilliantly highlighted the role of counterfactuals in historiography, reaching essentially the same conclusions as the Weber, albeit reluctantly. More recent work includes an important debate in economic history (Fogel 1964, Elster 1978). This controversy and other examples

---

that I endorse his neoliberal political views. In fact, Hayek's fervent individualism clashes with the micro-macro linkage discussed below.

drawn from political science are reviewed by Fearon (1991) and Tetlock and Belkin (1996b).

In relatively uncomplicated scenarios such as the one involving the ball and the window, the counterfactual condition is straightforward. Barring earthquakes, if the ball was not hit, the window would not have broken. Thus, constructing the counterfactual contingency does not pose any problems. This fortunate state of affairs, however, may or may not apply to complex systems. In these cases everything hinges on the link between causes and effects. If the added complexity does not interfere with the hypothesized causal path, causal inference remain straightforward. On the other hand, if coincidental and random events deflect the course of events, the construction of counterfactual scenarios ceases to be trivial.

The question is whether accidents wash out in the long run or whether their effect tends to accumulate, causing history to switch onto radically different paths. In linear systems, proportionality between causes and effects is preserved. Moreover, since the explanatory factors neatly add up, their analytic separation poses no problem. This is of particular importance for tracing counterfactual contingencies. Since the independent variables are separable, it is not hard to estimate the effect should one of them change, other things being equal.

By contrast, in the presence of nonlinearity, small disturbances may spread throughout the system, rendering prediction impossible even in deterministic cases. Initially discovered by Lorenz (1963) in his attempts to simulate weather patterns, this point has given rise to an entire literature on chaos.[4] As Lorenz and his successors realized, a small perturbation of the initial conditions may lead to dramatically different outcomes in the presence of nonlinearities. More recently, the inferential problems caused by this "butterfly effect" have received attention from both philosophers (e.g., Reisch 1991; Kellert 1993) and social scientists (e.g., Richards 1990).

In addition to greater sensitivity dependence on initial conditions, nonlinearity also opens the door for complex interaction effects among the independent variables. With the loss of the additive property of linear systems, the analyst can no longer easily dissect phenomena. Other things are no longer equal. Counterfactual reconstruction of history requires tracing the entire system rather than projecting single variables linearly under the ceteris paribus assumption. Opposing physicalist conceptions of social causality as additive force vectors, Weber (1949) argued that "the totality of *all* the conditions back to which the causal chain from the

---

[4] See Gleick (1983) for a popular introduction and Stein (1983) and Kellert (1993) for more elaborate discussions. Kellert defines chaos theory as "the qualitative study of unstable aperiodic behavior in deterministic nonlinear dynamical systems" (2, italics removed).

'effect' leads had to 'act jointly' in a certain way and in no other for the concrete effect to be realized. In other words, the appearance of the result is, for every causally working empirical science, determined not just from a certain moment but 'from eternity'" (187).

Clearly such nonseparability of causes enormously complicates the logic of counterfactual causality. A counterfactual thought experiment presupposes a hypothetical change of the antecedent. But if the variables cannot be easily disentangled, any alteration could cause inconsistencies with other variables and background assumptions. If this is the case, the counterfactual ceases to be "cotenable" (Goodman 1983). Cotenability requires the connecting principles, including empirical and theoretical mechanisms, to be consistent with the counterfactual scenario: "The question, then, is not whether a factor had to occur but whether varying the factor implies changing other factors that *also* would have materially affected the outcome" (Fearon 1991, 193).

Despite its complicating consequences, the awareness of this dilemma among historians and qualitatively minded IR scholars remains weak. The temptation to pick explanations à la carte without regard for overall consistency is sometimes irresistible. To take one example, John Mueller (1988) attempts to show that nuclear weapons did not make any difference to the stability of the cold war. To establish causation, he has no choice but to rely on an explicitly counterfactual case since "we are unable to run the events of the last forty years over, this time without nuclear weapons" (66). While Mueller's study shows an unusual self-consciousness about the need for counterfactual reasoning, its results are undermined by a general failure to guarantee cotenability. This is demonstrated by his references to selected crises drawn from the postwar era. It never seems to occur to Mueller that using the Cuban missile crisis as a test case while assuming the absence of nuclear weapons entails a serious inconsistency, for it is far from obvious that there would have ever been such a crisis in first place. It is not clear that the United States would have chosen to push things as far as they did, nor that the Soviets would ever have found it worthwhile to annoy their opponent had the missiles been only conventional. By the same token, Mueller's argument that the Soviet Union would have been deterred even without nuclear weapons overlooks the possibility that the Soviets' calculation of costs and benefits would have been completely altered in the nonnuclear case. Moreover, claiming that the Soviet Union would not have had the strength to overrun Western Europe cannot be based on postwar force levels, but must take the possibility of drastically reallocated resources into account, changes that could have resulted in Soviet superiority.[5]

---

[5] This is not to say that Mueller is fundamentally wrong about the effectiveness of nuclear weapons. Scholars arguing the opposite case have made even more aggravating mis-

Given these complications, it is not surprising that social scientists do what they can to avoid getting entangled in counterfactual arguments. One way out is to concentrate on simple questions that minimize the need to rewrite history.[6] James Fearon (1991) suggests that "the cotenability requirement will be more plausibly satisfied for small causes, such as specific policy definitions, than for big causes, such as nationalism, imperialism, or a cult of the offensive" (192). Barbara Geddes (1991) echoes this advice in proposing that "we need to break up the traditional big questions into sets of specific questions that are more theoretically accessible" (68). Similarly, King, Keohane, and Verba (1994) devote an entire chapter to methods of "how to avoid endogeneity." While they are conscious of the need for well-specified counterfactuals, and propose that "they must be reasonable and it should be possible for the counterfactual event to have occurred under precisely stated circumstances" (78), they focus explicitly on relatively simple contingencies such as rerunning "the 1998 election campaign in the Fourth District in New York" (79). They thus have very little to say about how to determine whether a counterfactual is "reasonable" in more complex settings.[7]

For any project that focuses on long-term historical processes, avoidance of "big causes" appears rather meaningless. After all, "when one reaches the point of working in terms of centuries, nothing exogenous is left" (Mirowski 1988, 71). The avoidance argument seems to hinge upon a tacitly linear assumption. Yet even small causes sometimes make a big difference. Indeed, almost without exception, economic equilibrium analysis and functionalist sociology rest on the assumption that historical ac-

---

takes. In a widely cited article, John Mearsheimer (1990) asserts that the stability of the cold war was mainly due to a combination of bipolarity and nuclear weapons. It never strikes Mearsheimer as worthwhile to explore any counterfactual cases (either multipolar or nonnuclear or both), since his arguments allegedly rest on "deductive" foundations. Would it not have made some difference if the (ignored) multipolar reference case had featured Iraq or Canada as the third pole? For a more sophisticated attempt to squarely confront the problem of cotenability, see Glaser (1993), who refers explicitly, for example, to possible worlds with and without mutually assured destruction.

[6] As a way of determining the truth value of counterfactuals, philosophers have suggested various "proximity criteria." According to this logic, a counterfactual statement is true if it holds in the closest possible world (cf. Lewis's 1973 possible-world semantics).

[7] In fact, the authors never realize the fundamental difference between covering-law explanations and counterfactual reasoning. Despite their "counterfactual" definition of causality, they remain faithful to Hempelian positivism. It is therefore not surprising that they regard the identification of underlying causal mechanisms as useful but "optional" (85–87) and downplay the problems of causal complexity (87–89): "A researcher can focus on only the one effect of interest, establish firm conclusions, and then move on to others that may be of interest." Similarly, their calls for process tracing turn out to be in favor of increasing the number of observations rather than George and McKeown's (1983) original goal of *connecting* these observations into coherent patterns and processes (Tarrow 1993; see also the other critiques and the authors' response in the same volume).

cidents do wash out (Krasner 1988). History is assumed to be efficient. According to March and Olsen (1984), "an efficient historical process . . . is one that moves rapidly to a unique solution, conditional on current environmental conditions, thus independent of the historical path" (737). The analytical gains of the path-independent assumption are obvious: "By assuming quickness, theories of political behavior avoid focusing on transient phenomena that might be less predicable and more subject to effects from the details of the processes involved."

Instead of being postulated explicitly, historical efficiency often enters the analysis more indirectly as a consequence of seemingly technical assumptions. For example, economists almost always assume constant or decreasing returns to scale (Arthur 1989, 1990). Having precluded positive returns, the analyst need not bother about accidental factors threatening the desired unique predictions, because under this assumption the system will rapidly return to its equilibrium if ever perturbed. Equilibria have the welcome property of being predictable and analytically calculable.

In International Relations, neorealism, more than any other paradigm, reflects this preoccupation with stability. Neorealists assume that details on the domestic level matter little for the systemic outcomes of the system. Castigating studies factoring in the internal dynamics of countries as reductionist, Kenneth Waltz (1979) favors an equilibrium-oriented interpretation of history. Structural outcomes flow from a systemic selection process that weeds out "inefficient" actors. Given the assumed efficiency of the historical process, the historical origin of states becomes immaterial.

But what if history is not efficient in this sense? As long as the analyst studies sufficiently short periods of time, the linear approximation is likely to be helpful even in the presence of nonlinearity in the real world. But any project whose goal is to explain long-term change must make the historical paths of the counterfactual scenarios explicit (Tetlock and Belkin 1996b). The historical record is replete with cases of accidental influences with momentous consequences. Historians have provided lists of accidental chains of events that made a profound and lasting imprint on world history (Carr 1963): had Cleopatra's nose been longer, Anthony would not have fallen in love with her and thus not lost his battle; had the king of Greece not been bitten by a pet monkey and died from the wound, his country would not have found itself in war with Turkey; had Trotsky not caught a fever while shooting ducks, he, rather than Stalin, would have succeeded Lenin. In summing up the first volume of his magnum opus, Michael Mann extends the list even further:

> The "might have beens" and "almost beens" could have led into fundamentally different historical tracks. If the pass at Thermopylae had not been

defended to the death, if Alexander had not drunk so heavily that night in Babylon, if Hannibal had been resupplied quickly after Cannae, if Paul had not outorganized the "men from Judaea," if Charles Martel had lost at Poitiers, or if the Hungarians had won at Nicopolis. (Mann 1986, 533; see also Hawthorn 1991 for further examples)

Despite their slightly preposterous flavor, these "nuisance counterfactuals" refuse to go away, because they clearly influenced the course of events in momentous ways.

It is thus tempting to capitulate and announce, as do many historians, that "history is just one damned thing after another." Probably for this reason, analysts either assume away the accidents or give up all hope of detecting regularities in world history. An alternative requires finding an answer to Carr's (1963) tricky question: "How can one discover in history a coherent sequence of cause and effect, how can we find any meaning in history, when our sequence is liable to be broken or deflected at any moment by some other, and from our point of view irrelevant, sequence?" (130). Ignoring the problem of path-dependence, or concentrating on simpler, linear problems, will not provide a solution to this dilemma. We ultimately need "greater theoretical understanding of the inefficiencies in history, i.e., the historical processes that do not have equilibria, take extended periods of time, lead to non-unique equilibria, or result in unique but suboptimal outcomes" (March and Olsen 1984, 743).

As we will see below, it is indeed possible to model historical contingency without abandoning the goal of finding regularities in complex systems. Instead of excluding accidental influences by assumption, however, the modeling framework ought to let accidents generate processes along dramatically divergent historical paths, should positive feedback be present. A modeling test bench of the CAS type allows for replication of such experiments many times. If historical contingencies turn out to be unimportant, they will wash out. If not, we will learn about the limitations of postulated structural laws. But before introducing new methodology, we turn to the second conceptual hurdle on the road toward models of emergent agency.

THE PROBLEM OF METHODOLOGICAL INDIVIDUALISM
AND MATERIALISM

In addition to its commitment to optimization and equilibria, conventional modeling practice rests firmly on another professional norm, methodological individualism, which Jon Elster (1985) has defined "as the doctrine that all social phenomena—their structure and their change are in principle explicable in ways that only involve individuals—their properties, their goals, their beliefs and their actions" (5). While the assumption of individual self-interest has contributed to significant theoretical progress in identifying collective-action problems (e.g., Olson 1965; see also Udéhn 1993), it tends to reinforce a narrowly materialist perspective on politics, for self-interest entails the absence of extraindividual influences, including symbolic-group markers. Whether people or states are selected as the ultimate locus of identity, methodological individualism overlooks creative attempts to redefine the rules of the game through changes not only to the interests but also of the notion of self.

There is indeed much more collective action than the Olsonian approach to it could ever explain (see Barry 1978; Taylor 1988; Green and Shapiro 1994). To interpret all aspects of social action through the lens of self-interest is profoundly misleading since, ultimately, "identity . . . cannot be captured adequately by the notion of interest. Identity is a no more than *relatively* stable construction in an ongoing process of social activity" (Calhoun 1991, 52). Attempts to single out individuals as the "fundamental units of politics" (Geddes 1991, 68) neglect the culturally mediated and socially constructed status of individuality and leave "the existence of individuals unexamined" (Calhoun 1991, p. 61). As prisoners of their mechanist view of the world, orthodox rationalists have lost sight of the culture-bound aspects of human agency (Taylor 1985).

On the other hand, methodological individualists in the Weberian and Popperian tradition rightly react against purely holistic conceptions of social systems. The crux is to find a way of modeling collective identities without assuming the existence of a metaphysical "super-mind" existing above and beyond individuals (Toulmin 1981). Such teleological reconstructions of history fail to acknowledge that collective identities are as socially constructed as individual ones (Berger and Luckmann 1966; Calhoun 1991, 59). Clearly a dynamic concept that links individual identity with collective structures is needed.

In this connection, Norbert Elias's ([1970] 1978; [1939] 1982) historical sociology is helpful.[8] Not content with the dualism between agent and structure, Elias invented the concept of "figurations." As opposed to fixed holistic structures, figurations emerge as spatiotemporal patterns of interactions between social actors. While firmly rooted on the individual level, figurations differ decisively from developmental theories that attribute a teleological direction or postulate continuous progress. As opposed to

---

[8] I stress Elias's figuration theory because, while far from crystal clear, his concept is more clearly articulated than most alternatives. Stephen Mennell (1983) offers the best introduction to Elias's voluminous writings (though see also Abrams 1982 on figuration theory). For those interested in Giddens's structuration theory in an IR context, Wendt (1987) is a good place to start.

such "world-growth stories" (Gellner 1964), figurational processes are refreshingly free from any Hegelian *Geist*, or any other metaphysical predictions such as the "end of history" (Fukuyama 1992). Elias's ([1939] 1982) words are unequivocal: "Civilization is not 'reasonable'; not 'rational', any more than it is 'irrational'. It is set in motion blindly, and kept in motion by the autonomous dynamics of a web of relationships, by specific changes in the way people are bound to live together" (232).

Though he actually attempted a formal series of simple game models (Elias [1970] 1978, chap. 3), these frameworks are exceedingly simple and all of his other work draws on more traditional verbal analysis. To find more flexible tools, it is necessary to turn elsewhere. Interestingly, network theory has more recently received attention from social scientists as a way of modeling corporate actors. In a series of articles exploring the limits of game theory, Fritz Scharpf (1990) singles out social networks as a particularly promising model of complex social systems.

Yet standard network theory suffers from a number of drawbacks. First, since network approaches usually stress structure (Nadel 1957), it is not clear who is acting (Calhoun 1991, 59). Second, the structural bias often excludes dynamic analysis, thus making the method unsuited for capturing the inherently dynamic nature of figurational processes. Third, Scharpf (1990) notices that "there is as yet a considerable distance between purely analytical and experimental research on the one hand, and empirical social-science applications on the other hand" (38). Finally, and most aggravating for our purposes, conventional approaches focus on objective categories, and by extension, treat identities as external to the network. Even though Harrison White's (1992) innovative "catnet" concept represented a major conceptual advance over culture-neutral network formalizations, it rules out self-categorization, which makes it less well suited for modeling collective identities (Calhoun 1991, 60).

Finding a way out of this dilemma requires a more versatile type of model. What makes it so hard to grasp figurations is that they lie somewhere between the objective and the subjective.[9] To understand this distinction it is necessary to jettison the positivist dichotomization of theories into objective and normative ones. In their attempts to implement Hempel's objective criteria of rationality, social scientists have keenly urged that "positivist" science distinguish itself from "normative" judg-

---

[9] Elias himself tried to steer clear of either pure individualism or holism: "The immanent regularities of social figurations are identical neither with regularities of the 'mind', of individual reasoning, nor with regularities of what we call 'nature', even through functionally all these different dimensions of reality are indissolubly linked to each other" (Elias [1939] 1982, 231).

ments about reality. A typical such statement is the admonition of Bueno de Mesquita and his colleagues (1985): "Every student of politics is familiar with the distinction between facts and values, between the *is* and the *ought*. Scientific statements are based upon evidence about the world of experience; they are verified as true or rejected as false through empirical testing. Normative statements, in contrast, are neither true nor false" (1).

While this advice might apply in the natural sciences, life is unfortunately somewhat more complicated for social scientists. Friedrich Hayek (1952) observes that "when the scientist stresses that he studies objective facts he means that he tries to study things independently of what men think or do about them." Yet for those who set out to study humans themselves, the barrier between the "is" and the "ought" breaks down. Hayek continues:

> Until Science had literally completed its work and not left the slightest unexplained residue in man's intellectual processes, the facts of our mind must remain not only data to be explained but also data on which the explanation of human action guided by those mental phenomena must be based. Here a new set of problems arises with which the scientist does not directly deal. Nor is it obvious that the particular methods to which he had become used would be appropriate for these problems. The question is here not how far man's picture of the external world fits the facts, but how by his actions, determined by the views and concepts he possess, man builds up another world of which the individual becomes a part. (39)

This subtle blurring of the subjective and objective realms evokes Karl Popper's famous World 3. Though Popper's early writings in the positivist tradition have attracted much attention in the social sciences, his later "postpositivist" and "evolutionary-epistemological" turn have gone largely unnoticed (though see Almond and Genco 1977). In a 1967 lecture, Popper added a third category to the positivist normative/positivist dualism. In this postpositivist vision, reality consists of "first, the world of physical object or of physical states; secondly, the world of states of consciousness, or of mental states, or perhaps of behavioural dispositions to act, and thirdly, the world of *objective contents of thought*, especially of scientific and poetic thoughts and of works of art" (Popper 1972, 106). Popper elaborates on its precise meaning: "By World 3 I mean the world of the products of the human mind, such as stories, explanatory myths, tools, scientific theories (whether true or false), scientific problems, social institutions, and works of art. World 3 objects are of our own making, although they are not always the result of planned production by individual men" (Popper and Eccles 1977, 38). This definition highlights the immediate relevance of World 3 objects to our discussion. Clearly, Elias's figurations can be seen as such an entity. Other great thinkers also anticipated Popper's idea. Both Emile Durkheim's "social facts" and the less well known German bacteriologist Ludwik Fleck's "thought styles" fit into this mold (see discussion in Douglas 1986, cf. Schultz 1962).

The strong individualist bias in contemporary social science has obscured the collective nature of both scientific and social categories. Finding the idea of a "collective mind" repugnant, methodological individualists ignore the significance of World 3 objects. Responding to such doubts, Popper (Popper and Eccles 1977) explains that such entities are abstract but nevertheless real, for "World 3 objects have an effect on World 1 only through human intervention, the intervention of their makers; more especially, through being grasped, which is a World 2 process, a mental process, or more precisely, a process in which World 2 and World 3 interact" (47). Based on these observations, it is hard to deny the existence of World 3 objects "even though we may not like this admission, out of deference, say, to the great tradition of materialism" (ibid.).

Social constructivists have long been aware of the intersubjective nature of "World 3-like objects" and, most importantly for issues of agency, applied precursors of the concept to collective-identity formation. More than anyone else, the question of what constitutes a social group puzzled Georg Simmel. While Weber never managed to liberate himself from methodological individualism (cf. Gilbert 1989), Simmel ([1908] 1971) fully understood that social groups cannot be expressed solely in the language of the singular agency. In Margaret Gilbert's (1989) excellent rendering of his theory, three observations merit attention: "First, that social groups are real phenomena, as opposed to fictions or illusions of some kind. Second, that the core or essence of a social group is to be found in a specific mental state common to group members. Third, that the mental state in question involves the conception of the people concerned as linked by a certain special tie" (146). It is not hard to see a connection with both Popper's World 3 objects and our definition of the nation given in chapter 2. We will return to this parallel in chapter 6 in our discussion of nationalism.

To conclude, two ultimately philosophical obstacles prevent progress in the modeling of emergent actors in world politics. First, historical accidents magnified by nonlinear processes undermine the assumptions of conventional equilibrium approaches. Such models assume that history is "efficient" and can therefore be ignored. But this frictionless conception of historical change clashes with the inherently history-dependent character of social institutions, including states and nations. Second, the individualist and materialist bias of contemporary rationalist theories rules out any consideration of symbolically founded groups falling between the extremes of holistic objectivism and individualistic subjectivism. This flaw becomes particularly crippling for any theory that tries to come to terms with informal communities, such as nations.

Unsurprisingly, when these two dilemmas coincide, the explanatory puzzle becomes particularly vexing for traditional rational-choice theory. Despite his individualist leaning, Max Weber (1958) saw the point clearly. In his celebrated railway metaphor, he stated: "Not ideas, but material and ideal interests, directly govern men's conduct. Yet very frequently the 'world images' that have been created by ideas have, like switchmen, determined the tracks along which action has been pushed by the dynamic of interest" (280).

THE COMPLEX ADAPTIVE SYSTEMS APPROACH

Overcoming the obstacles of historical contingency and methodological individualism confronts the modeler with formidable challenges. Fortunately, the revolution in computer technology has rendered new modeling techniques possible. With the aid of these comparatively unused tools, modeling path-dependent processes and collective identities as World 3 objects becomes both tractable and rewarding. In this section, I introduce a class of models using what is commonly referred to as the complex adaptive systems (CAS) approach.[10] Originally a tool for the study of physical systems, the CAS concept has proved useful in exploring emergent macrophenomena in disciplines such as chemistry, biology, genetics, and economics (Holland 1992b; Mitchell 1993).[11] Despite the analogy between complex systems in these sciences and social systems, there have been surprisingly few attempts to employ the CAS concept in political science (though see Axelrod 1986, 1993; Axelrod and Bennett 1993; Kollman, Miller, and Page 1992; Schrodt 1993).[12]

[10] In the literature one also encounters the related terms "Artificial World" (Lane 1992) and "Artificial Life" (Langton 1988) but here I will refer exclusively to CAS.

[11] Much of the research on CAS has taken place at the Santa Fe Institute. See Waldrop (1993) for an enthusiastic informal introduction. Horgan (1993) offers a much more critical article.

[12] There is also a wider literature relying on computer simulation in the social sciences, including political science, but most of this work does not draw on the CAS concept as defined below. Alker (1983) provides a useful overview of such simulations. See also chapter 4 for a detailed comparison of such simulation-based studies to one of my own CAS models.

Defining Complex Adaptive Systems

The CAS method is a particular way of studying complex systems by computer simulation. Before offering a definition, it is necessary to discuss the meaning of the two key terms: complexity and adaptation. Complexity is notoriously hard to define unambiguously.[13] This conceptual difficulty need not bother us unduly, however, for most examples of CAS usually score high on many measures of complexity, at least compared to deductive models in the social sciences. Here it suffices to join Herbert Simon (1990) in letting a complex system stand for "one made up of a large number of parts that interact in a nonsimple way. In such systems the whole is more than the sum of the parts, not in an ultimate, metaphysical sense but in the important pragmatic sense that, given the properties of the parts and the laws of their interaction, it is not a trivial matter to infer the properties of the whole" (195).

The second concept, adaptation, concerns either the entire system or its parts. Melanie Mitchell (1993) suggests that a system, viewed as a whole, adapts if it "automatically improve[s] its performance (according to some measure) over time in response to what has been encountered previously." Other scholars stress the parts, requiring that they be adaptive (e.g., Holland 1992a, 1995). Since it is often hard to establish where adaptation actually takes place, I opt for as wide an interpretation of the term as possible, requiring it to apply to the parts, the whole, or both. Moreover, Mitchell's formulation perhaps reads too much deterministic progress into the notion of adaptation to apply to social systems, for it is often impossible to find an objective standard of performance.

Instead of relying on any particular notion of progress, my definition focuses on emergent macro properties regardless of whether they stem from narrowly or broadly conceived adaptive processes. Thus, a complex adaptive system can be defined as *an adaptive network exhibiting aggregate properties that emerge from the local interaction among many agents mutually constituting their own environment.* Each part of this rather dense definition sets CAS apart from conventional modeling methods:

---

[13] Mathematicians and computer scientists have proposed various criteria to determine how complex a system is. In his accessible review of such concepts, Heinz Pagels (1988, chap. 3) refers to algorithmic, computational, information-based, and physical definitions of complexity. In brief, algorithmic complexity is based on the size of the smallest program required to compute the abstract object to be measured. Computational measures refer to the shortest time it would take to generate the object in question. Information-based criteria look at the degree of uncertainty and incompleteness involved in the description of the object. Physical measures, finally, refer to the object's internal structure, especially the number of clusters (see Simon 1981, chap. 7; Huberman and Hogg 1988).

1. A CAS exhibits *emergent properties*, by which we understand phenomena that "(i) can be described in terms of aggregate-level constructs, without reference to the attributes of specific [micro-level agents]; (ii) persist for time periods much greater than the time scale appropriate for describing the underlying micro-interactions; and (iii) defies explanation by reduction to the superposition of 'built in' micro-properties of the [CAS]" (Lane 1992, 3). Based on analytical nontransperancy, this definition of emergence emphasizes the importance of not hard-wiring the desired outcomes into the process (Holland et al. 1987, 350).[14] Interpreted this way, emergence provides the key to making phenomena problematic in the sense referred to in chapter 2. Emergent properties may refer to any temporal or spatial patterns in the agents' behavior, their internal models, or their internal and external structure.[15]

2. A CAS presupposes *local interaction* among agents rather than globally managed behavior. The emphasis of local-level rules draws heavily on the bounded-rationality paradigm in organization theory (Simon 1955; Cohen, March, and Olsen 1972; March 1978). Instead of assuming agents equipped with unlimited calculative capacity and complete knowledge of their strategic environment, the focus on local interactions postulates actors driven by rules of thumb that help them satisfice. Out of this web of local relations, macrolevel patterns emerge. Thus, these systems are fundamentally self-organizing (Hayek 1973).

3. A CAS features a *large number* of agents. Recent work in computer science suggests that the properties of large computational networks differ fundamentally from the toy problems studied by game theory and mainstream artificial intelligence. In their study of macro level "phase shifts" in computational ecologies, Huberman and Hogg (1987) assert that "as local parameters are varied they may show sudden changes in overall performance which cannot be generally inferred from investigations of corresponding small-scale systems" (170; see also Huberman and Hogg 1988). Like wave phenomena in physics, emergent patterns of this type usually require a large number of microlevel elements (Hayek 1967, 25). In addi-

---

[14] Thus, this subjective definition entails unpredictability of results compared to the observer's knowledge. Model output is thus found surprising, or at least nontrivial, compared to input. Alternatively, emergence can be defined historically as novelty (Nagel 1973; Salthe 1991, 1993). While the former definition depends at least partly on the observer of a system, the latter is entirely objective. As we have seen, Herbert Simon (1981) adopts a similar observer- dependent approach to complexity. In his view, simulation serves a useful purpose even when we know all the underlying premises, for in complex systems "it may be very difficult to discover what they imply. All correct reasoning is a grand system of tautologies, but only God can make direct use of that fact. The rest of use must painstakingly and fallibly tease out the consequences of our assumptions" (19).

[15] A particularly important type of emergence pertains to the formation of composite, hierarchical actors (Buss 1983; Fontana and Buss 1993; for a review see Lane 1992).

tion, the large size of CAS models reinforces the previous point about local interaction since it is unrealistic and impractical to expect the agents to devise elaborate action plans with respect to all other agents. In complex systems, game-theoretic approaches suffer from a combinatorial explosion of strategies that can only be avoided by reliance on bounded rationality (Scharpf 1991). It is also worth noting that despite its being related to CAS research, chaos theory focuses on behavior of simple rather than of complex systems (Kellert 1993, 5).

4. A CAS is *adaptive* because of the microlevel agents' capacity to change their behavior or because of ecological effects that influence the development of the entire system. The system evolves over time, usually far from any global equilibrium, and produces perpetual novelty (Holland 1992a, 184). In some cases, the agents' internal models also allow for anticipation, which means that the agents try to anticipate the consequences of their actions, but this is not a constitutive feature of a CAS. Although their internal models may be quite elaborate in some cases, as in a game of chess it is impossible to predict the final outcome. Moreover, these agents, as opposed to perfectly rational ones, do not possess complete or almost complete knowledge about their strategic situation. CAS systems are far removed from the state of common knowledge in the game-theoretic sense (Aumann 1976; see also Binmore 1990).[16] The limitations imposed on internal models correspond to the focus on bounded rationality. Friedrich Hayek (1973) stresses that "the necessary and irremediable ignorance on everyone's part of most of the particular facts which determine the actions of all the several members of human society" (12). To accept the "Cartesian assumption of complete rationality" leads to an untenable position:

> The fact of our irremediable ignorance of most of the particular facts which determine the processes of society is, however, the reason why most social institutions have taken the form they actually have. To talk about a society about which either the observer or any of its members knows all the particular facts is to talk about something wholly different from anything which has ever existed—a society in which most of what we find in our society would not and could not exist and which, if it ever occurred, would possess properties we cannot even imagine. (13)

Thus there is no choice but to model the acquisition of knowledge explicitly (Simon 1986; North 1990). Modeling long-term and large-scale social pro-

---

[16] Thanks to a clever trick, game-theoretic models can be applied to uncertain situations. Yet to salvage the assumption of common knowledge this type of uncertainty must be restricted to a few well-defined dimensions (see Rasmusen 1983). It is important to see the difference between this approach to modeling incomplete information as a deviation from perfect knowledge (as in Popper's 1957 zero method of rationality) and Hayek's assumption of entirely ignorant agents.

cesses rests on agents endowed with dynamic internal models whose choices and preferences may evolve over time (cf. Lindgren 1992).

In essence, the CAS method differs from conventional modeling techniques in two respects. First, while relying on computer-guided deduction to generate results, it uses induction rather than deduction as the main method of exploration.[17] This is because attempts to derive equilibria would contradict the inherently innovative and open-ended character of CAS models. Although stable patterns often emerge, these are usually metastable and may dissipate suddenly. Also, the emergent properties are a function of history, an assumption that defies deductive analysis. Therefore, the "mathematical ploy" of constructing highly simplified models will often not work, which leaves the modeler with no choice but to rely on induction (Lane 1992). The emphasis on inductive reasoning and experimentation is, however, more than a last resort. Notwithstanding the brilliant scientific discoveries in mathematics and physics, there are good reasons to believe that induction rather than deduction provides the key to understanding and deciphering complex systems (Holland et al. 1987).

Nevertheless, the emphasis on induction does not imply that the underlying assumptions always need to be complex. Whereas CAS models are more often than not based on extremely simple microlevel principles, they exhibit complexity in terms of their emergent behavior. A good example of CAS is the Game of Life, defined by exceedingly parsimonious rules, yet capable of generating limitless emergent phenomena of great complexity (Gardner 1970; see also chapter 4 below).[18]

The second major difference from conventional modeling approaches pertains to the working style of CAS researchers. Instead of emulating the analytical method of natural scientists, which aims at separating and isolating various parts of complex systems, students of CAS stress synthesis and engineering: "One of the main themes of the revolution is that the pure scientist needs to behave like an engineer: designing and testing *working* theories. The more complex the processes studied, the closer the two must become" (Sloman 1978, 14; see also Simon 1981, 7). It is by definition impossible to understand emergent macro-properties by reducing complex systems to their smallest components. There is no alternative to "constructing large aggregates of simple, rule-governed objects

[17] By induction, I mean induction of patterns and other regularities within the artificial world rather than generalization from real-world evidence.

[18] Note that the Game of Life fails a restrictive definition of CAS since adaptation occurs on the macrolevel. This is so because the rules of the agents are entirely invariant. The wider definition adopted in this study, however, includes simple cellular automata such as the Game of Life.

which interact with one another nonlinearly in the support of life-like, global dynamics" (Langton 1988, 2).

Having outlined the main ingredients of the CAS concept, we will see that it can help us deal with historical contingency and methodological individualism. The reason for our positive assessment relates to the flexibility of CAS modeling in two respects. Not only does the CAS approach enable us to perform controlled thought experiments that filter out historical accidents, it also offers a way of escaping methodological individualism by explicitly modeling collective identities as World 3 objects.

Modeling Historical Contingency

Contrary to the persistent optimism of positivist social scientists, the lack of opportunities to perform controlled experiments in their disciplines constitutes a serious handicap. Much of the progress in the natural sciences is precisely due to the feasibility of experimentation. Only truly randomized experiments provide a robust way out of the thorny methodological difficulties afflicting quasi-experimentation (Campbell and Stanley 1966). The social-scientific awareness of these dilemmas, often further compounded by history dependence, is usually alarmingly low: "Virtually all social scientists believe that useful knowledge can be drawn from non-randomized designs. The history of their efforts to do so, however, suggests that their credo derives more from faith than from reason" (Achen 1986, ix).

Fortunately, the CAS approach offers an alternative to quasi-experimental analysis of the real world and single-case thought experiments by providing the means to replicate systematic and controlled thought experiments in artificial computer worlds. The idea is hardly new. Writing about the need to infer historical laws despite the accidental role of individuals, Leo Tolstoy (1931) appreciated the heuristic value of experimental replication:

> The founder of a sect, of a party, or the inventor impresses us less when we understand how and by what the way was paved for his activity. If we have a large range of experiments, if our observation is continually directed to seeking correlations in men's actions between causes and effects, their actions will seem to us more necessary and less free, the more accurately we connect causes and effects. (1129)

Understandably, Tolstoy had no means beyond his own imagination to perform a "large range of experiments." Today's social scientists are luckier. To check the validity of counterfactual claims "a system may be devised, and run off on a computer, for judging the soundness of any set of propositions put forward as argument" (Climo and Howells 1976, 4).

Realizing this potential, W. Brian Arthur (1990) applies computer simulation to the problem of path dependence and increasing returns to scale in economic markets:

> With this strategy an increasing returns market could be re-created in a theoretical model and watched as its corresponding process unfolded again and again. Sometimes one solution would emerge, sometimes (under identical conditions) another. It would be impossible to know in advance which of the many solutions would emerge in any given run. Still, it would be possible to record the particular set of random events leading to each solution and to study the probability that a particular solution would emerge under a certain set of initial conditions. (94)

Computer simulation not only lets us manipulate theoretical parameters, it also renders experimental randomization and replication possible, thus circumventing the dilemma of inference in quasi-experimental settings. This reliance on randomization sets CAS studies apart from conventional equilibrium analysis, which rules out accidental influences, positive-feedback processes, and multiple equilibria by assumption. In the presence of path-dependent mechanisms, repetition is indispensable. While historically efficient models help us derive causal effects in simple systems through comparative statics analysis, such local measures of causality fail if the causal paths fluctuate wildly with small perturbations. Nevertheless, Tetlock and Belkin (1996b) remark that "many game theorists, neoclassical economists, and structural realists display impressive confidence in their counterfactual claims. They know that, if one changes the incentives confronting rational actors, those actors will quickly identify the new utility-maximizing course of action."

To distinguish the counterfactual reasoning of CAS models from more conventional types of thought experiments, I call the former *complex* thought experiments and the latter *simple* thought experiments. As opposed to their simpler counterparts, complex thought experiments are stochastically repeated to filter out historical contingencies. Whereas such scenarios are implemented as computer programs, simple thought experiments lend themselves to deductive expression as intuitive or formalized arguments. The inductive nature of CAS modeling is ideally suited to perform complex thought experiments: "In short, a computer model is more an embodiment of a theory than a theory in itself. A particular run of a computer model gives only one specific outcome of the theory—it is more an experiment than an inference" (Holland et al. 1987, 347).

A simple graphical presentation may help clarify what is at stake (see fig. 3.1).[19] Typically a counterfactual argument attempts to establish causation between an independent variable X (the antecedent) and a depen-

---

[19] This illustration draws on the more extensive presentation in Cederman (1996b).

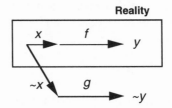

Figure 3.1. A graphical representation of a simple counterfactual

dent one *Y* (the consequent) by showing that the actual outcome *y* would not have occurred in the absence of the antecedent *x*. This requires the analyst to construct an alternative causal path starting with ~*x* and leading to ~*y* (with ~ denoting logical negation). In the diagram, the "reality box" shows the actual course of history. The counterfactual scenario, however, lies entirely outside reality since ~*x* never occurred. In addition to the antecedent and consequent, causal links or processes labeled *f* in the real case and the *g* in the counterfactual case, are needed.

Returning to our simple baseball example, it is now possible to represent the situation graphically (see fig. 3.2a). In this case, *x* stands for the status of the ball, and *y* for the status of the window at some later point in time. Here *x* can be interpreted as a ball hit by the bat, and ~*x* as the ball in rest. Furthermore, *y* symbolizes a broken window and ~*y* a whole one. Realizing that the window has already been broken, we look back at the chain of events from *y*. The ball's trajectory *f* is well described by classical mechanics, so there is no difficulty tracing the ball's movement back to its being hit at *x*. In the absence of impact ~*x*, the ball will not move and Newtonian mechanics *g* (i.e., the principle of inertia) assures that the window remains intact. Under these circumstances, it seems straightforward to attribute the cause of the broken pane to the bat hitting the ball.

The simple counterfactual story of the ball and the window can be compared to a causal explanation drawn from International Relations. Figure 3.2b replaces the two physical-state variables by an *x* pertaining to

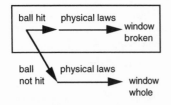

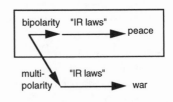

(a) Simple counterfactual   **(b) Complex counterfactual**

Figure 3.2. Contrasting two causal scenarios

the structure of an international system and a *y* to collective behavior within the same system. Some theorists argue that bipolarity *x* promotes peace *y*, whereas multipolarity ~*x* fosters instability and war ~*y* (e.g., Waltz 1979). Others claim the opposite (e.g., Deutsch and Singer 1964; see review in Levy 1989a). Here International Relations laws, to the extent that they exist, play the role of Newtonian mechanics.

While the importance of counterfactuals in causal analysis has received some, though far from sufficient, attention in the applied social-science literature, most scholars tend to identify the counterfactual method with simple thought experiments at the expense of more complex scenarios.[20] For example, Milton Friedman (1953) observes that pool players behave *as if* they calculated complicated mathematical formula in their heads. En passant he then draws the crucial analogy to economics: "It is only a short step from these examples to the economic hypothesis that under a wide range of circumstances individual firms behave *as if* they were seeking rationally to expected returns" (21).[21]

Thus, it is often argued that, unlike large-n statistics, counterfactual thought experiments cannot establish the causal weight of independent variables or measure the risks of accepting explanatory hypotheses (Fearon 1991, 178). Furthermore, within the framework of simple thought experiments, the question of cotenability remains highly problematic (ibid., 192–94). As opposed to replicated, complex methods, this approach relies upon changing one independent variable at a time, holding all other factors constant.

Although the philosophical literature on counterfactuals has concentrated almost entirely on deterministic contingencies (e.g., Lewis 1973), counterfactual hypotheses do not in principle presuppose deterministic causation; they refer to nonactual states of affairs that may be probabilistic: "Appeals to counterfactual states can and should allow terms such as 'might have been' and 'probably'" (Humphreys 1989, 12). Unlike linear mathematical modeling, the CAS technique opens the door for stochastic influences and forks. Properly performed, complex experimental replication is less vulnerable to the weaknesses of simple counterfactual thought experiments. First, testing many parameter combinations allows for assessment of causal importance based on frequency. Second, nothing prevents statistical analysis of the CAS results from exploiting the power of conventional hypothesis testing and confidence measures. Third, and

---

[20] See also the simulation studies of Stuart Thorson and Donald Sylvan (1983) and David Sylvan and Stephen Majeski (1993) for examples of counterfactual exploration in foreign-policy analysis.

[21] In a conveniently updated analogy applied to IR, Achen and Snidal (1989) refer to the skills of tennis player Martina Navratilova.

most importantly, the flexibility of the CAS method allows for a much higher degree of endogenization. This is of particular importance for avoiding inconsistent counterfactuals. In fact, since CAS modeling allows the analyst to specify well-defined microlevel rules, cotenability follows automatically for all complex thought experiments.[22]

The logic of computerized complex thought experiments follows that of traditional experiments closely (see fig. 3.3). The process starts with random assignment, continues with treatment, and ends with observation. The difference is that the objects of assignment, treatment, and observation are not people, as in medical experiments, but historical paths, or artificial worlds if you wish. Randomization creates the needed variance to test the robustness of the systematically manipulated treatment variables.

Having generated the required series of worlds, denoted $W(1)$ through $W(N)$, experimental treatment is introduced with respect to a small set of theoretically interesting parameters. This is where counterfactual logic enters the picture.[23] Each world $W(i)$ now bifurcates, one path corresponding to the positive antecedent $x(i)$, another to $\sim x(i)$. If necessary, the number of treatment (or independent) variables can be increased, al-

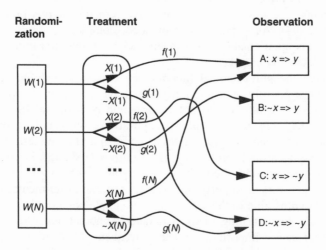

Figure 3.3. The experimental method of counterfactual simulation

[22] Of course, models do not always deliver cotenability in the real-world scenarios they represent.

[23] Since, strictly speaking, counterfactual analysis presupposes the existence of a "factual" case, it may be to stretch the term somewhat to apply it to artificial worlds. Yet if one takes some particular artificial world (e.g., $W(i)$ exposed to treatment $x(i)$) as the reference case, it becomes meaningful to talk about a counterfactual scenario (e.g., $W(i)$ exposed to $\sim x(i)$).

though one must keep in mind that each new binary variable raises the number of runs to the second power.

Now the counterfactual scenarios are unwound along the bifurcated causal paths. While the positive antecedents $x(i)$ trigger trajectories denoted $f(i)$, those associated with negative antecedents are called $g(i)$. As can be readily seen, these paths do not have to be "parallel" but may vary in a highly nonlinear and contingent fashion. Even if two paths $f(i)$ and $g(i)$ *develop almost identically for some time, an accident may occur suddenly along path* $f(i)$ that deflects this process from $g(i)$. In this sense, stochastic influences continue to influence the entire simulation.[24]

The final step involves observing what difference the treatment makes with respect to the dependent variable Y. Again, this cannot be done for a single fork but by comparing the whole set of possible worlds simultaneously. For simplicity, suppose that both the independent and dependent variable are dichotomous. Then observation amounts to classifying each simulation run as belonging to one of four categories (labeled A, B, C and D in the figure). Once the observations within each category have been added up, the causal effect can be derived by comparing two ratios. The first one is the ratio between the number of outcomes belonging to groups A and C, which represent the y and $\sim y$ outcomes generated by positive antecedents $x(i)$. The second ratio refers to groups B and D, which stand for the outcomes given negative antecedents $\sim x(i)$.

While figure 3.3 describes the logic of the experimental sequence, much has been left unexplored. An important decision facing the simulation analyst is what to randomize and what to manipulate experimentally. In addition, there is also a third category: those elements of the model that will remain hard-wired into the very framework and thus left unchanged throughout the tracing of the counterfactual thought experiments. Obviously this question cannot be answered in the abstract, but the present focus on long-term, structural change makes the need for endogenization pressing.

Interestingly, biologists also have started to experiment with CAS-like systems. Inspired by Stephen Jay Gould's (1989) cautioning words about historical contingency in biological evolution, Walter Fontana and Leo Buss (1994) have created an advanced simulation platform that enables them to "play the tape twice." The ultimate purpose of their experiments is to breed an "artificial chemistry" with lifelike properties as emergent phenomena (Fontana 1991; see review in Lane 1992). The behavior of

---

[24] Computers are unable to create true randomness. Therefore, the initial randomization amounts to the selection of a random seed that defines a given string of random numbers unique to a particular simulation run. Thereafter, the causal paths unfold deterministically, although the actual effect is that of producing a perfectly stochastic process.

their highly stylized model universe suggests that emergence of life may be less accidental than Gould claims.[25]

Modeling Collective Identities

In addition to showing how artificially replicated thought experiments may help us unfold historical trajectories, the Fontana/Buss experiments illustrate that CAS techniques have the potential to transcend methodological individualism. Going far beyond low-level selection, Fontana and Buss (1994) are able to generate higher-order self-maintaining "organisms" synthetically and show how selection operates directly on these compound entities in an hierarchical fashion (see Buss 1987).

Evidently the flexibility of CAS modeling opens the door for a fundamentally revised ontology that shuns causal one-way streets of either individualist or holist natures. Although biology is the first discipline to have benefited from these methodological advances, the social sciences are not lagging far behind. For example, in a paper on "emergent hierarchical organizations," David Lane (1992) is able to survey the state of the art in economics.[26]

Unlike thermodynamics and solid-state physics, biological systems show great variety on the microlevel (Weisbuch 1991). This insight extends even more readily to the question of individuality and culture in the social sciences. Indeed, many complex systems in general, and social ones in particular, combine physical and symbolic aspects (Simon 1981, chap. 1; Salthe 1985, chap. 3). John Holland's (1992a, 1995) genetic algorithms and classifier systems represent successful attempts to introduce fundamental complexity on the microlevel. Though clearly inspired by biological evolution, Holland formalizes the generic logic of evolutionary systems in the widest sense. By assuming chromosomes to be vectors of dichotomous genes (i.e., bit-vectors), Holland invented a manageable representation of diversity. Genetic algorithms are simple routines that search these vast multidimensional bit-spaces both locally and globally by applying various genetic operators including mutations and crossover.[27] Essentially elaborate genetic algorithms, classifier systems carry the logic further by allowing for searches of the rules themselves. The condition part of the rules consists of schemas that are bit-strings

[25] This is not to say that Gould's thoughts about historical contingency have been refuted. Much of the progress in the study of path dependence in due to Gould (e.g., Krasner 1988).

[26] So far, there are fewer examples in political science, although see Bremer and Mihalka (1977) and Axelrod (1993).

[27] For a similar representation, see Kaufman and Johnsen (1991).

that also allow for wild cards, denoted as question marks (see Holland 1992a; 1995, 57–62; Holland et al. 1987, 146–50).

To illustrate, suppose each chromosome contains three genes. Then any string of zeros and ones can be used as a representation, such as "101" or "001." In this three-dimensional space, there are eight possible strings. A schema denotes a subspace of these strings. For example, the schema "1?0" refers to "100" and "110" since these are the only two strings that match the pattern. The more wild cards a schema contains, the greater the corresponding set of chromosomes, "???" being the most general schema.

Although social evolution differs fundamentally from its biological counterpart, Holland's chromosomes and schemata provide a simple but powerful way to express culture and identity differences. By replacing the genes by cultural traits (or "memes" to use Dawkins's 1989 term), we can treat the entire chromosome as a culture vector. Furthermore, identities, viewed as subjective self-representations, can be modeled as schemata that highlight the traits that define the individual or group identities. For example, in our three-dimensional space, an actor with culture chromosome "101" and identity schema "???" is essentially unconscious of its culture. If it becomes aware of its first cultural trait, however, the identity changes to "1??". An actor with identity "101" is completely conscious of its culture. In chapter 5 we will return to the issues of culture and identity.

Even though culture vectors of this type have found their way into the social-science literature (e.g., Axelrod 1987, 1995; Arthur 1991; March 1991; Schrodt 1993), the applications have not extended to the issue of identity. Instead, these contributions have focused on how culture influences behavior through norms. By including such "tags" as a constitutive feature of actors, however, Holland (1995) deals explicitly with issues of identity.[28] There are two reasons why this representation entails important conceptual gains. First, the difference between schemata and chromosomes mirrors the difference between identities and culture. With this distinction, it becomes possible to model shifts in political identification *without* corresponding changes in culture. To a large extent, identity politics concerns the manipulation of political symbols for political purposes. Second, the representation of identity as schemata facilitates the analysis of hierarchical identities. This useful notion highlights the contrast between particular and universal identifications, a topic we will return to in chapter 6 in the context of nationalism. Third, and most importantly, schemata allow for categorically defined "imagined communities" (An-

---

[28] In his most recent project, ECHO, Holland (1992a, 1995) introduces the notion of a tag as an extension of schema concept in precisely this function.

derson 1991) that transcend the direct links holding together hierarchical corporate actors. This symbolic representation facilitates understanding decentralized but highly effective human groups of World 3 type, such as the nation.

In conclusion, the CAS modeling tradition opens a third route between highly formalized, deductive frameworks and rich verbal descriptions. This combination of rigor and flexibility can be exploited to circumvent the dilemmas of historical contingency and methodological individualism. John Holland and John Miller (1991) sum up the advantages of CAS modeling:

> Models based on pure linguistic descriptions, while infinitely flexible, often fail to be logically consistent. Mathematical models lose flexibility, but gain a consistent structure and general solution techniques. The [CAS] models, specified in a computer language, retain much of the flexibility of pure linguistic models, while having precision and consistency enforced by the language. (366)

The Weaknesses of CAS Modeling

No methodology is without its problems. Unsuprisingly, the CAS approach does not escape this rule. Because of their heavy reliance on simulation, models belonging to the CAS family often come under attack from skeptics who prefer purely deductive frameworks. While sometimes overdrawn, this critique is worth taking seriously because it does point to a series of important shortcomings. These attacks usually center on four related points:

1. *Ad hoc assumptions.* As opposed to the axiomatic foundations of rational-choice theory, simulation models, especially those assuming bounded rationality, rest on ad hoc assumptions (e.g., Kreps 1990b). The flexibility of simulation techniques can encourage intellectual sloppiness as modelers succumb to the temptation to add bells and whistles without proper appreciation of the results (e.g., Kreutzer 1986, 6).

2. *Failure to yield unique predictions.* The emphasis on path dependence leads to ambiguous or even chaotic results that cannot be falsified. Neoclassical models generally avoid this trap by producing unique equilibria (see Green and Shapiro 1994, 23–30).

3. *Fragility of results.* Even when simulation models yield unique results, there is no guarantee that these are not an artifact of specific parameter configurations. Closed-form mathematical models generate findings that are verifiable for the entire parameter space. Moreover, it is often possible to study the effect of each parameter with comparative statics, an option that is absent in simulation research since analytically differentiable expressions are lacking (see Lane 1992).

4. *Lack of cumulation.* As opposed to mathematical models, simulation models are usually implemented as hundreds of lines of computer code. Not only is it harder to understand what a simulation system really does on the micro level, it is also nearly impossible to replicate the results. Consequently, scientific progress is seriously impaired (see Lane 1992, 157).

These points pertain more to the way that simulation research has been practiced than to the potential value of CAS modeling. Here I will respond to each criticism and outline the steps that can be taken to mitigate the most serious disadvantages.

(1) The accusation of arbitrariness does not lack justification as long as it is targeted against gadget-laden simulation studies. Yet this criticism tends to obscure the less-than-obvious status of assumptions in neoclassical economics. In the words of a leading game theorist:

> Even if a particular model is based on an *ad hoc* prescription of behaviour and is analysed with simulations only, this does not mean that one cannot learn a great deal from the exercise. Economic theorists (and I include myself) too often lose sight of the fact that while we may not be too restrictive in the behavioural assumptions we make . . . we make enormously strong *ad hoc* assumptions in the range of actions we allow the actors in our models. The excuses we offer are often that we can use intuition guided by experience to factor in those things omitted from our model and, in the end, the test must be empirical. Why not employ the similar open-minded skepticism about simulations of *ad hoc* behaviour? (Kreps 1990b, 169)

Kreps is well aware of the tacit assumptions inherent in model specifications, including game forms and common knowledge (see also Binmore 1990; Rubinstein 1991). Some of these assumptions have become so accepted by the profession that they appear to have lost their questionable status.

The open-endedness of simulation modeling can still undermine the intellectual discipline of the CAS analyst (Kreutzer 1986, 6). I have adopted two measures to counteract this risk. First, as much as possible, I rely on substantive theory to motivate the choice of mechanisms and assumptions. Second, the project was developed step-by-step, something that is reflected in the modeling chapters to follow. By restarting the analysis from scratch from time to time, and adding theoretical features incrementally, this design strategy makes it easier to manage overwhelming complexity.

(2) The complaint about ambiguous predictions reflects a metaphysical

obsession with unique predictions rather than an inherent shortcoming of CAS modeling, for multiple equilibria are inevitable consequences of path dependence and historical lock-in effects. The CAS approach cannot be faulted for addressing harder problems than neoclassical theory. Besides, it is well known that many games lack unique equilibria, a "problem" that refuses to go away despite stubborn attempts to invent new solution concepts where intuitive equilibria do not exist by relying on mixed strategies or to weed them out where they are not wanted by means of abstruse "equilibrium refinements" (Binmore 1990).

More profoundly, those who criticize CAS models for their inability to generate unique predictions confuse two types of simulation. In its traditional function, simulation research assists decisionmakers in producing forecasts in specific policy settings. The prime use of CAS modeling, however, relates to a second type of research that serves a heuristic rather than predictive purpose: "Simulation is used at a prototheoretical stage, as a vehicle for thought experiments. The purpose of a model lies in the act of its construction and exploration, and in the resultant, improved intuition about the system's behaviour, essential aspects and sensitivities" (Kreutzer 1986, 7; see also Sloman 1978; Hayek 1967). Similarly turning against misplaced demands for accuracy, Herbert Simon (1981, 20) observes that "we are seldom interested in explaining or predicting phenomena in all their particularity; we are usually interested only in a few properties abstracted from the complex reality."

(3) Parameter sensitivity poses the most serious threat to CAS-based research. Critics are right in pointing out that closed-form mathematical models are always preferable if such tools are available. Unfortunately, this is usually not the case for the reasons pointed out above. Few researchers stick to simulation because of their affection for this method. The alternative would be to assume away the problematic elements, including the complexities associated with path dependence and collective identities, which is precisely what most orthodox deductivists do. But to avoid important research questions just because they are not amenable to elegant theoretical formalization cannot possibly advance our understanding of the world.

This said, the Achilles' heel of fragile results remains, but its consequences can fortunately be mitigated. First, if the goal is to establish possibility of certain outcomes, rather than their probability or certainty, the critique loses its bite (cf. Sloman 1978; Sylvan and Glassner 1985).[29] The goal of probing plausibility requires above all translating the findings back into a more intuitive formulation. Such heuristic insights can usually

---

[29] Deductive modelers are sometimes forced to content themselves with proving possibility rather than sufficient and necessary causation. See Niou and Ordeshook (1991).

be grasped *independently* of the simulation framework, and are thus less likely to be vulnerable to accusations of parameter sensitivity.[30] Second, game-theoretical models often fall short of the robustness that their creators and supporters call for. There is, as we have argued above, often a fair amount of arbitrariness hidden in deductive-model specifications. Formal elegance comes at the price of considerable rigidity that implicitly discourages sensitivity testing since mechanisms and functional forms are usually hard-wired into game forms and utility functions.[31] Ironically, thanks to their greater flexibility, CAS models allow for easier sensitivity testing than deductive frameworks, and can even cast light on the robustness of neoclassical equilibrium results (e.g., Kollman, Miller, and Page 1992). Chapter 5 exemplifies how robustness testing can be performed. That chapter introduces a series of modeling extensions and alterations designed to probe parameter and mechanism sensitivity of the basic version of the Emergent Polarity Model as specified in chapter 4. Third, it is not always the case that we need to know everything about the entire parameter space. Again, substantive theory may be of great help in cutting down the range of parameter values to a smaller set. Fourth, the contribution of "intuitive" calibration should not be underestimated. Since CAS models allow the analyst to observe the system as it unfolds, it becomes possible to check whether the results make qualitative sense.[32] In addition, artificial parameter randomization for each replication helps improve the robustness of the results. (See fig. 3.3 for the principle and chapters 4, 5, and 8 for applications.)

(4) While it is true that greater complexity of CAS models renders scientific communication and replication harder, it does not mean that cumulation is impossible. To some extent the lack of cumulation in simulation research is due to the unwillingness of orthodox modelers to deviate from their deductive tools. Whereas the latter constitute a self-contained research community that benefits from the critical mass of Kuhnian "normal science," the "upstart" CAS paradigm has to fight an uphill battle.[33] Yet this does not prevent the burden of proof from falling

---

[30] According to Friedrich Hayek (1967), this class of models "enables to predict or explain only certain general feature of a situation which may be compatible with a great many particular circumstances." (28).

[31] Moreover, some equilibrium criteria, especially those supported by mixed strategies, have a knife-edge quality that makes them unstable (e.g., Binmore 1990). Robustness testing is actually more widespread in econometrics (e.g., Achen 1986 on selection bias, and the discussion of omitted variable bias in King, Keohane, and Verba 1994).

[32] For examples of graphical computer output, see the modeling chapters to follow. John Holland (1992b) emphasizes the need to equip CAS systems with user-friendly and intuitive interfaces.

[33] Although there are cumulative debates within a rather narrow circle of professional economists, the extrascientific communication is unfortunately less impressive. Perhaps the

on those who argue that simulation can be a useful complement to mathematical modeling. So far, simulation researchers have spent far too much time figuring out clever algorithms and too little time interpreting and communicating the results. Of course, there are notable exceptions from this trend, such as Robert Axelrod's (1984) famous computer tournament. In this case, simulation has generated significant interdisciplinary progress that goes well beyond the initial experiment, advances that would have been impossible without the help of computational modeling (for a review, see Axelrod and Dion 1988). There is no reason why such cumulation could not happen in other fields.

Having defended CAS modeling, I concede that there is no substitute for parsimonious, mathematical modeling (Kreutzer 1986, 6). Whenever possible, inductive and deductive exploration should proceed in parallel (Holland and Miller 1991; Holland 1995, chap. 5). In chapter 7, I draw heavily on deductive formal results derived in the appendix to that chapter. Before doing that, however, a few words on external validity are in order. The highly abstract nature of modeling makes both CAS and mathematical approaches vulnerable to accusations of irrelevance when compared to the complexities in real social systems. These complaints usually come from empiricists and historically minded scholars rather than from neoclassical modelers, who are even less reluctant than CAS researchers to resort to drastic simplifications. Indeed, these concerns address an important problem. Friedrich Hayek (1967) captures the dilemma:

> Of course we can never be certain that what we know about the action of those forces under simpler conditions will apply to more complex situations, and we will have no direct way of testing this assumption, since our difficulty is precisely that we are unable to ascertain by observation the presence and specific arrangement of the multiplicity of factors which form the starting point of our deductive reasoning. (10)

In our specific context, the question is whether we can "infer emergence as a 'causal mechanism in the real world, once we have identified it in the [CAS]." There are reasons to be skeptical, because "it is possible that the causal mechanism hinted at in the [CAS] is swamped by the addition 'turbulence' in the real world, and some entirely different sets of interactions of direct effects drive the formation of the feature of interest" (Lane 1992, 9).

How is it possible to find out whether the postulated processes operate in the real world? Clearly, the solution does not lie in positivist tests of

---

less abstract flavor of CAS modeling could help counteract this retrenchment to the ivory tower.

specific predictions. Such a viewpoint confuses the nature of CAS processes with simple empirical laws. Koslowski and Kratochwil (1994) point out that "large-scale historical change cannot be explained in terms of one or even several causal factors but through an analysis of conjunctures" (227). This does not mean, however, that all hope for systematic observations should be abandoned: "Although a covering law for this historical process is unlikely to be found, elements within that process do form patterns that can be perceived and analyzed, since even chaotic processes are not random" (ibid.). The CAS approach produces "pattern predictions" (Hayek 1967) or "robust processes" (Goldstone 1991) rather than pointlike predictions of single events. Goldstone defines a robust process as "a sequence of events that has unfolded in similar (but neither identical nor fully predictable) fashion in a variety of different historical contexts" (57). The persistent attempt to view robust processes as if they were Hempelian covering laws has produced considerable confusion and disappointment (58).[34] It is thus not understood that the chief obstacle in disciplines concerned with complex phenomena is

> one of in fact ascertaining all the data determining a particular manifestation of the phenomenon in question, a difficulty which is often insurmountable in practice and sometimes even an absolute one. Those mainly concerned with simple phenomena are often inclined to think that where this is the case a theory is useless and that scientific procedure demands that we should find a theory of sufficient simplicity to enable us to derive from it predictions of particular events. (Hayek 1967, 27)

If the external validity of robust processes cannot easily be checked by tests of lawlike predictions, what then? The focus on causal mechanisms in CAS studies implies a partial shift from cross-sectional "variable-oriented approaches" (Ragin 1987) to detailed reconstructions of historical processes, a method described by George (1979) as "process-tracing." The contextual nature of CAS processes defy isolated and punctual observations. To engage in such context-free testing of theories is "to wrench each single state from the context in which it was formed; the state is seen in isolation, exclusive in itself, without raising the question whether its peculiar character is co-determined by its relation to its surrounding" (Hintze 1975, 159).

---

[34] It has even led some philosophers of science to doubt whether Darwinian evolutionary theory is scientific (e.g., Popper 1959; see also discussion in Sober 1993, 46–52). But, as Hayek clarifies, Darwin's account of natural selection "is a theory which neither aims at specific predictions of particular events, nor is based on hypotheses in the sense that the several statements from which it starts are expected to be confirmed or refuted by observation" (12). For a recent, equally eloquent philosophical account of the role of prediction in the sciences, see Kellert (1993).

Instead, CAS-like research turns the attention to generic processes and phenomena that emerge despite, yet in the presence of, historical idiosyncrasies. This comes close to what Stephen Kellert (1993) calls "dynamic understanding" (114) though uncovering the philosophical underpinnings of chaos theory rather than CAS research, Kellert's account parallels ours in that it emphasizes the importance of "understanding that is holistic, historical, and qualitative, eschewing deductive systems and causal mechanisms and laws." Since there is a significant risk that the popular scientific literature, which already abounds with flimsy and faddish speculations about chaos and complexity theory, will make more traditionally minded researchers mistake these new fields for nonscientific mysticism, Kellert's sobering words are particularly welcome. Rather than offering a decisive break from the Western scientific tradition, new sciences such as "chaos theory can reveal the limits of standard methodological approaches to understanding the world and impel a reconsideration of the metaphysical views that undergirded them. But any expectation that chaos theory will re-enchant the world will meet with disappointment" (116).

A brief look at the work of the pioneers of complex-systems modeling should convince the skeptic that the absence of formal proofs and detailed empirical predictions does not make this mode of research any less scientific than more conventional research approximating the narrow criteria of logical positivism.[35] Prominent examples include Thomas Schelling's (1978) segregation models and Robert Axelrod's (1984) computer tournaments. Using an extremely simple checkers-like setup while adding his own rules, Schelling was able to create segregation between two "ethnic" communities represented by white and black tokens. This phenomenon appeared regardless of the specific initial configuration. While drawing on computer experiments, Axelrod also investigated the robustness of a generic process. Pitting a wide range of computer programs against each other, he was able to demonstrate a stunning result: faced with much more elaborate competitors, the simplest algorithm, submitted by Anatol Rapoport, won the entire tournament. Because this program followed a very simple rule of reciprocity, dubbed Tit For Tat, Axelrod was able to gain useful insights about the nature of cooperation in a broad range of contexts, including interstate bargaining (see especially Axelrod and Keohane 1985). These examples illustrate that, to be of substantive value,

---

[35] In fact, the question of what should be classified as science and what should not appears to be a red herring. Contemporary philosophers of science have largely given up attempts to define a "demarcation criterion" of this type. I am grateful to George Reisch for reminding me of this point.

social science does not have to revolve around the theory-hypothesis-test cycle prescribed by empirical positivists.

AN INTRODUCTION TO THE MODELS

My effort to develop models that deviate from conventional methodological practice follows two paths. Reusing the three-by-three classification from chapter 2, figure 3.4 places each model in its proper two-dimensional context, factoring in both state formation and nation building. Offering further details on the model specification, table 3.1 could profitably be consulted simultaneously. The table presents the status of the main modeling features, including the representation of the actors and their contextualization. The actor category refers to both states and nations, breaking up the former into those governed by internal and external sovereignty. Furthermore, there are columns indicating temporal and spatial contextualization.

Taking conventional IR models as its starting point (cf. cell 2), the first excursion moves horizontally into the absent/emergent cell (labeled 3) by endogenizing the states themselves. The Emergent Polarity Model (EPM)

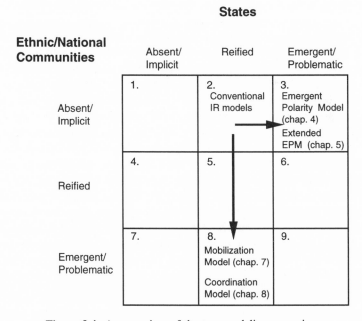

Figure 3.4. An overview of the two modeling excursions

TABLE 3.1
A Guide to the Four Modeling Chapters

	Model	Actors			Context		Model Type	Illustration
		States (ext.)	*States (int.)*	*Nations*	*Time*	*Space*		
	Conventional IR Models	R	—	—	—	—	rational choice	
Chap. 4	Emergent Polarity Model	E	R	—	x	x	CAS	Italy
Chap. 5	Extended EPM	E	E	—	x	x	CAS	—
Chap. 7	Mobilization Model	R	R	E	x	—	modified Markov chain	Habsburg, USSR, EU
Chap. 8	Coordination Model	R (E)	E	E	x	(x)	CAS	Yugoslavia

Key
E = emergent feature
R = reified feature
— = absent/implicit
x = explicitly modeled
( ) = possible extension

of chapter 4 is the fruit of this endeavor, a model that clearly belongs to the CAS tradition. Within this framework, states are viewed as a corporate actors consisting of microlevel agents and emerge spontaneously as a consequence of power competition. This setup explicitly captures the spatiotemporal environment as a network of agents locally interacting. Chapter 5 follows up this modeling exercise with a series of extensions, culminating in a two-level version that allows for internal collective action. While the original version of the Emergent Polarity Model focuses on external aspects of sovereignty, this addition deviates from the reification of internal sovereignty, thus opening the black box of the state. The table reflects this shift by displaying an 'E' for emergent rather than an 'R' for reified in the internal state column.

Whereas the horizontal shift endogenizes many dimensions that are usually absent, or at least held constant, in conventional IR models, it leaves the actors' identities implicit. In doing so, it fails to apply to cases in which identities not only matter but also change. This is especially likely to be the case in the world dominated by explicit nationalist ideologies. The remaining two models are both intended to elucidate various aspects of this complex historical process. To this end, it is necessary to treat the nation explicitly as an emergent entity. This is the goal of the second excursion that moves down from the conventional-models box down to cell 8.

Chapter 6 provides a substantive introduction to the concept of nationalism as well as a comparison of the two models to follow. Here we will only consider the methodological tools involved in building these models. Instead of leaping directly to a full-fledged CAS model of nationalism, the "vertical" deviation from mainstream modeling is made incrementally. The Mobilization Model thus abandons the full-fledged CAS framework of chapters 4 and 5 in favor of a simpler, partly deductively derived dynamic model. It does so by applying a dynamic stochastic process of Markov type to the question of assimilation and nationalist mobilization within multiethnic empires. Table 3.1 indicates that this simplification implies reification of the internal and external aspects of state sovereignty, since the multinational state is held constant throughout the analysis.

The last chapter returns to the agent-based CAS framework introduced in chapter 4. Though it also belongs to the same category as figure 3.2, the Coordination Model differs from the previous framework in its reliance on two-dimensional representation of identity and its spatial representation. While technically implemented drawing on the results of the extended Emergent Polarity Model, the latter feature is not fully explored in chapter 8, which means that at least external sovereignty remains reified for the purposes of the analysis.

To conclude, the two deviations from orthodox modeling take us some way toward the goal of integrating conventional IR theory with more constructivist and critical interpretations of world politics. Yet it should be remembered that while the current contribution represents a clear extension beyond traditional modeling techniques, it still falls well short of the double emergent perspective present in the most advanced work in the constructivist tradition. While such extensions are beyond the scope of the book, the tools explored here provide an excellent starting point for such extensions. In chapter 9 we will discuss some of these possibilities. But before that, it is time to turn to the models themselves.

CHAPTER 4

Emergent Polarity

INTRODUCTION

The end of the cold war served as a healthy reminder that states constantly form, disintegrate, and change. Having focused on the exceptionally stable postwar environment of superpower relations, International Relations scholars were ill prepared to account for the events triggered by the fall of the Berlin Wall. This is particularly true of the dominant paradigm in International Relations, neorealism. Delegating the responsibility of explaining "unit change" to historical sociologists, neorealists focus on the question of why power politics persists among the "great powers." From where these great powers arise remains an issue well beyond the traditional neorealist research agenda.

The present chapter challenges this division of labor. As Charles Tilly (1975, 1985, 1990) suggests, state formation and war are two sides of the same coin. Drawing on the work of constructivist scholars, I have already pointed out that any general theory of international politics needs to explain the origin of its main actors (e.g., Ashley 1986; Wendt 1987; Ferguson and Mansbach 1988). Instead of rejecting neorealist logic, however, I want to put it on a dynamic footing by bringing it to bear on the process of state formation. This perspective requires the theory not only to explain why balance-of-power systems maintain themselves, but why an initial system with many small political units tends to crystallize into stable rivalry among a small number of great powers. Thus, rather than to refute neorealism, I want to apply its logic to a wider historical context and establish the conditions under which its main tenets hold.

To conceive of power politics as a historical process presupposes that some states disintegrate, other states grow territorially, and system structure, especially its polarity, emerges from what actors do, rather than being fixed beforehand by modeling assumptions. Such an exploration requires an explicitly dynamic and spatial framework that allows for a higher degree of complexity than neorealist models in the microeconomic tradition can offer. To that end, I present an artificial geopolitical system, here referred to as the Emergent Polarity Model, that

1. provides an explicit spatial representation of the international system
2. involves a large number of actors

3. endogenizes the outer boundaries of these actors as well as the polarity structure of both the regional and global structure

4. endows these agents with a bounded and historically contingent decision scope.

As part of the CAS category, the Emergent Polarity Model thus sets the stage for controlled experiments that are impossible to perform in real social systems. As opposed to traditional models, the framework allows for explicit analysis of geopolitical systems featuring a large number of actors with emergent outer boundaries.

This chapter extends the neorealist logic to the phase preceding great power rivalry by asking the historical question: From where do the great powers come? The extension to state formation poses a greater challenge to neorealism than its current static focus does. Not only does the theory have to explain why the process of power politics does not degenerate into unipolarity, but it also needs to account for the reduction of polarity implied by state formation. The simulations suggest that in order for the structural core of neorealism to apply, the state system needs to remain highly competitive. Under these conditions, power politics, defined as competition among a small number of great powers, emerges almost regardless of states' motives.

To guarantee this structural effect, however, it is necessary to postulate a self-feeding predatory process that reduces polarity in the state-building phase. This means that multipolarity is constantly threatened by "hegemonic takeoffs", that is, predatory quests for global domination. As long as the geopolitical expansion of the strongest states is well balanced, a balance of power will prevail. Yet this outcome requires competition to be free from intervening disturbances, such as excessive strategic defense-dominance or regional alliances. These defensive mechanisms widen the window of opportunity for potential hegemons, increasing the likelihood of unipolarity. Thus, contrary to what most realist thinkers assert, there is a potential contradiction between global-system stability on the one hand and defense dominance and defensive alliances on the other. Against the backdrop of the market analogy on which neorealism is based, this should not come as a surprise. Economists believe that cartels, or any other attempt to inhibit competition, disturb the operation of the invisible hand in economic markets.

As the model building proceeds, several simplifying assumptions become inevitable. In order to test whether some of these often technically motivated decisions drive the results rather than the suggested explanatory mechanisms, the next chapter takes the simulation exploration further by relaxing and changing the specification of the basic version of the model. To prepare the reader for what will follow, the present discussion makes several references to the relevant sections of chapter 5 where these alterations are introduced and analyzed.

Before turning to these elaborations, however, let us see what the present chapter offers: the first section outlines the theoretical arguments to be evaluated and refined. This is followed by a brief overview of the Emergent Polarity Model, then a more detailed description. The next section presents the comparative results of the simulations of the basic system. The discussion then adds the alliance mechanism and provides a historical illustration focusing on regional balancing in Renaissance Italy. The last section sums up the theoretical conclusions and discusses some policy implications.

POWER POLITICS AND EMERGENT POLARITY

Neorealists study the interaction among given actors, commonly referred to as great powers, forming a system of power politics. These scholars usually seek to explain the occurrence of war by reference to the distribution of power in the system, most notably system polarity. The literature has attempted to resolve whether bi- or multipolarity is conducive to system stability (for a review see Levy 1989a). Structural change, by contrast, usually falls outside the explanatory scope of neorealist analysis. This does not prevent these theorists from referring to evolutionary mechanisms (Waltz 1979, 118), but as in neoclassical economics these references are implicit (cf. Friedman 1953). Like microeconomics, neorealism lacks a convincing theory of institutional change. Consequently the identity of the actor as well as system structure are treated as given, which makes it hard to study historical change of the type that the international system is currently undergoing (Kratochwil 1993).

Instead of treating system behavior, such as war, as the only dependent variable, this chapter focuses on the development of system polarity over time. In this perspective, war and conquest are side effects of the more fundamental process of integration and disintegration. Figure 4.1 illustrates this dynamic graphically, plotting system polarity as a function of time. Most historical balance-of-power systems emerged from a large number N of small political units. As a rule, the emergence of power politics involves two phases. First, in the initial contraction phase, repeated conquest reduces polarity dramatically. Second, after the state-building process, a consolidation phase follows in which the system may or may not stay within the bounds of power politics. For the purposes of the present analysis, power politics is defined as a system of great-power competition that has significantly reduced polarity (i.e., a low N of say at

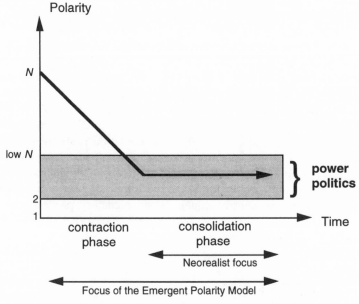

Figure 4.1. The emergence of power politics

most 10 percent of the original number of states) but that does not degenerate into universal empire.

This development corresponds to an important historical pattern. The European state system followed a similar path as it contracted from about five hundred units in 1500 to some twenty states in 1900 (Tilly 1975, 24). Other examples include Italian and Greek systems of city-states, ancient India and China, and other early examples of empire and state building (see Cusack and Stoll 1990).[1]

Conventional neorealist accounts of power politics tend to center on the consolidation phase only. Tacitly assuming that the process of integration has already taken place (and that it has not already degenerated into unipolarity), neorealist analysts focus their attention on why the system equilibrium maintains itself. This static "problemsolving" approach makes explanation easier, but only at the price of assuming away impor-

---

[1] This depiction of power politics entails two important simplifications. Though wider, the time scope is still bounded because the explanation does not account for the multitude of small states that emerges. A more complete theory needs to account for both state formation and imperial collapses. In fact, the European state system emerged as a result of Roman Empire's disintegration. Moreover the current analysis assumes that, though states' outer boundaries change, the nature of the units is constant. See Ruggie (1993) and Spruyt (1994) for more nuanced discussions of how the modern nation-state was selected from a number of alternative organization forms including empires, city-states, and city leagues.

tant historical processes (Cox 1986). As Henry Nau (1993) points out, a system characterized by large numbers of small actors is qualitatively different from one composed of a small number of great powers.

To provide a full account of the emergence of power politics, an extended, dynamic theory needs to explain both why polarity decreased and why it did not result in unipolarity. Figure 4.2 offers a conceptual guide to this puzzle. A complete theory needs to go beyond structuralist causation by relying explicitly on at least two causal mechanisms.[2] The first one is predation and constitutes the unit-level "engine" driving the process of system integration. If not stopped, predation is likely to reduce system polarity. The second mechanism, balance of power, slows down the first process through deterrence based on defensive alliances or unfettered power competition. In addition to these mechanisms, some realists argue that a third mechanism influences the predatory process, namely the defense/offense dominance of military technology (e.g., Jervis 1978; Van Evera 1984; Snyder 1984, 1991).

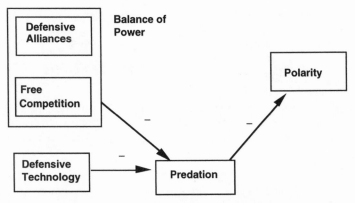

Figure 4.2. Static scheme explaining the emergence of power politics

[2] It is clear that anarchy does not by itself account for variations in system polarity. Anarchy, or more precisely the absence of international enforcement, explains why states have to be ready to counter aggression, but it does not by itself reduce polarity, and it has little to say about why unipolarity can be avoided. Waltz (1979) is aware of the flaws of primitive structuralism: "Agents and agencies act; systems as wholes do not. But the actions of agents and agencies are affected by the system's structure. In itself a structure does not directly lead to one outcome rather than another. Structure affects behavior within the system, but does so indirectly" (74). Though he specifically refers to "socialization" and "competition" as the primary "transmission-belts" between structure and agency, the argument remains mainly implicit on this point. Jon Elster (1985) offers a clear discussion of the need to specify the underlying mechanisms to support functionalist and structuralist explanations. See also Wendt (1992) for an interesting attempt to uncover the explanatory mechanisms of neorealist theory.

This simple causal scheme calls for clarification on two points. First, how many states have to be predatory in order for the system to contract? The neorealist assumption that actors are self-regarding and selfish does not tell us whether their ambition is mostly to survive or to expand (Keohane 1983; Schweller 1993). Focusing on systemic determinants of action, Waltz (1979) glosses over this important distinction by declaring that states are "unitary actors, who, at a minimum, seek their own preservation and, at a maximum, drive for universal domination" (118).[3]

Second, despite its celebrated role in realist thought, balance of power is a notoriously diffuse term (Haas 1953; Claude 1964; Levy 1989a). The question is whether power politics requires alliances to prevent unipolarity. Here the realist views range from a completely decentralized, alliance-free system automatically stabilized by "internal balancing" to a more coordinated system relying on "external balancing" through defensive alliances (Claude 1964; see Cusack and Stoll 1990, 40–53, 138–40 for a review). The latter category encompasses a wide variety of cases including local ad hoc alliances, formed to block the expansion of threatening neighbors, as well as more centralized balance-of-power strategies such as collective-security arrangements and great-power concerts (cf. Kupchan and Kupchan 1991). Generally, the neorealist literature does not disentangle the effect of internal and external balancing, thus doing little to dispel "a more general failure to identify the conditions under which alliances are stabilizing and the specific conditions under which they are destabilizing" (Levy 1989a, 235).

We shall explore a set of neorealist propositions associated with a decentralized notion of power management rather than the more conscious or "manual" types of balancing common in classical realism. Drawing heavily on the microeconomic market analogy, the neorealist approach to power politics has been labeled "relaxed realist" since it downplays the difficulty of achieving balance (Claude 1989). The actors are animated by narrowly selfish motives rather than a concern for global stability. It is assumed that international stability emerges as an unintended consequence of the states' "micromotives" (Schelling 1978). The most prominent exponent of this view is Kenneth Waltz (1979):

International-political systems, like economic markets, are formed by the coaction of self-regarding units. International structures are defined in terms of the primary political units of an era, be they city states, empires, or nations. Structures emerge from the coexistence of states. No state intends to participate in the formation of a structure by which it and others will be

[3] It should be noted that Waltz is not entirely consistent. At other places he leans toward characterizing states as predominantly status quo oriented: "The first concern of states is not to maximize power but to maintain their positions in the system" (126).

constrained. International-political systems, like economic markets, are individualist in origin, spontaneously generated, and unintended. In both systems, structures are formed by the coaction of their units. (91)

The Emergent Polarity Model contains three independent variables.
First, the *proportion of predators* refers to the density of predator states at
the outset of the analysis. Second, *defense dominance* stands for how
difficult predators judge attacking to be. To be more precise, I follow
Scott Sagan (1986) in defining this variable as the required superiority in
order to achieve victory expressed as a force ratio. Finally, the presence
of *defensive regional alliances* entails the possibility of external balancing against immediate threats from neighboring states. In their absence,
all states are forced to rely on their own means to ensure survival. Again
it should be emphasized that I am *not* investigating the influence of globally managed alliances (though great powers will automatically be more
concerned about system stability since they share borders with more
states than do lesser powers).

Having specified the explanatory factors, it is now possible to state the
propositions to be evaluated. Each proposition relates one of the independent variables to the likelihood of power politics. The first proposition,
which represents the most orthodox form of neorealism, is the most
sweeping one. The other two assertions constitute refinements of the first
one drawn from contemporary realist scholarship:

1. *Anarchy implies power politics.* This structuralist proposition means
that power politics will follow regardless of unit-level factors such as predatory frequency or defense dominance. As we have seen, Waltz (1979) dis-
counts unit-level factors such as the offensive nature of the states: "Balances
of power tend to form whether some or all states consciously aim to establish and maintain a balance, or whether some or all states aim for universal
domination" (119). Thus the locus of causation is firmly rooted on the systemic level, consistent with Waltz's famous "third image."

2. *Defense-dominance increases the likelihood of power politics.* Jack
Snyder (1991) calls this modification of P1 "defensive realism" since it suggests that defensive action contributes to system stability. As an example of
particularly disruptive behavior, Stephen Van Evera (1984) explains the outbreak of World War I as a consequence of the "cult of the offensive" dominating military establishments prior to 1914 (see also Jervis 1978; Christensen and Snyder 1990; Sagan 1986 offers a useful review and critique).

3. *Defensive alliances increase the likelihood of power politics.* Most realists count alliances as one of the main instruments to maintain system
stability. Though Waltz is less convinced of the general stabilizing impact of
alliances, he contends that "balancing" rather than "bandwagoning" is likely
to produce this result. Elaborating on this theme, in an influential study,

Steven Walt (1987) argues that in a "world of balancing" power politics prevails.

A NONTECHNICAL OVERVIEW

The easiest way to introduce the main components and rules of the simulation system is to start by displaying a picture of the territorial system's initial state. Figure 4.3 shows an artificial world consisting of four hundred actors arranged in a square grid. The figure illustrates a number of important points that distinguish the geopolitical model from conventional, nonspatial approaches. First, the actors are territorially defined, each of them surrounded by up to four neighbors. Second, they interact only with their neighbors and have no global knowledge of the system. Third, there are two types of actors, "predator" and "prey," corresponding to status quo and revisionist states, the latter denoted by the shaded areas.

These units' interactions animate the system and drive structural change. In every time period, all territorial neighbors interact locally. Both the predator and prey states follow a simple rule of reciprocity with the difference that the predators sometimes launch unprovoked attacks if they find themselves in superior positions. The criterion is called the superiority ratio and governs the defensive orientation of the system. Since both actor types reciprocate, the result of an attack is always war, which

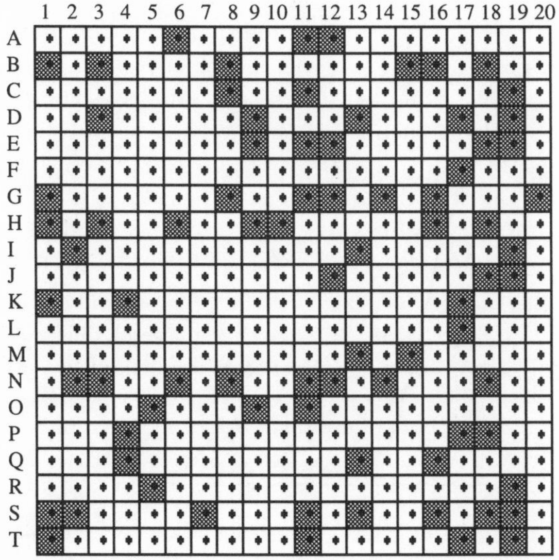

Figure 4.3. A 20 × 20 geopolitical system with 20 percent predator states

is costly for both sides. When the logical force balance tips decisively in favor of the stronger party, conquest results, implying that the victor absorbs the targeted unit. This is how hierarchical actors form. If the target already was a part of another multiprovince state, this state loses its province. Successful campaigns against the capital of corporate states leads to their collapse.

These rules imply three things: First, the number of states is going to decrease as the predators absorb their victims. Second, as a consequence of conquest, the predatory actors increase in size, their territory expanding into the conquered areas. Third, the surviving units will be predominantly predators, the more peaceful prey states having been eliminated in the selection process.

To illustrate these points, I present the results of a sample run of the twenty-by-twenty system. Figure 4.4 plots the number of sovereign states against time. The dynamic process resembles the two phases of contraction and consolidation illustrated in figure 4.1 above. The number of sovereign units decreases dramatically as soon as the predatory process is set in motion. After fifty time periods, system polarity has shrunk to about a tenth of the initial population. After this point, the behavior of the system stabilizes except for some occasional "jumps."

The discontinuities stem from imperial collapses. It is illustrative to investigate the result of the largest of these events. Figure 4.5 depicts the

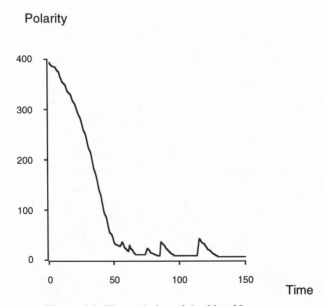

Figure 4.4. The evolution of the 20 × 20 system

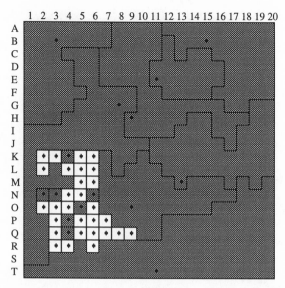

Figure 4.5. The 20 × 20 system after the collapse of actor R5

situation immediately after the collapse of the empire whose capital was R4 (the code refers to row R and column 4). The small squares in the lower left corner of the figure are the newly independent states. Within the next few time periods, these states will be absorbed by their more powerful neighbors. Except for the temporary fragmentation, the trend is clearly toward a smaller number of large predator states. These hierarchical units are controlled by a capital (marked by a dot) and have emergent outer boundaries as a result of conquest.

In its most basic form, the model does not include alliances. With the alliance option activated, however, states have the possibility to balance against threats by forming regional defensive alliances. In this world of balancing, states single out the most threatening state in their proximity. If several states are threatened by the same potential aggressor, an alliance forms against the threatening actor. Alliances enable their members to coordinate collective defense against regional hegemons.

TECHNICAL SPECIFICATION

Before presenting the results, it is useful to go through the system in greater detail. Readers who are less interested in the technical specification can skip directly to the next section.

Relation to Existing Simulation Models

Unlike conventional rational-choice models, the proposed framework incorporates an explicit spatial representation of CAS type somewhat akin to the Game of Life (Gardner 1970) and other cellular automata (e.g., von Neumann 1966; Burks 1970; Wolfram 1986). My simulation framework is not the first simulation model to be applied to realism. In a pioneering contribution, Bremer and Mihalka (1977) developed a geopolitical model to study the consistency of realist thought (see also Dacey 1974; Schrodt 1981). Because of the limited computational resources, their analysis did not reach beyond a series of suggestive sample runs. A decade later, Cusack and Stoll (1990) created a closely related, though significantly more efficient, model, and explored its behavior systematically through statistical analysis. More recently, Duffy (1992, 1993) has gone even further in enhancing computational performance by running similar experiments on a parallel machine.

These pioneering studies belong to the most promising attempts to go beyond the loose metaphors that dominate traditional realist scholarship. I found Cusack and Stoll's (1990) analysis particularly useful as a conceptual guide. While these models proved instrumental as a source of inspiration, I built up my own system in order to implement three far-reaching technical innovations. First, the original design suggested by Bremer and Mihalka (1977) relies on sequential execution that singles out pairs of initiator and target states.[4] This solution requires an exogenously defined selection rule that distributes the opportunities for action among the states. Bremer and Mihalka (1977, 309), as well as Cusack and Stoll (1990, 78–79), programmed their systems to give powerful states proportionally more opportunities to act than weaker actors. While his parallel algorithm allows for the selection of several initiators per round, Duffy (1992, 252–53) retains a similar rule of power allocation. My system differs from this design by giving all sovereign states the chance to act simultaneously in every period. The fact that powerful states happen to be those that attack more often is an emergent result rather than a hard-wired feature.[5]

Second, Bremer and Mihalka (1977) let interactions proceed as isolated campaigns according to a prespecified sequence of moves and countermoves between the initiator and the target. By contrast, the current

[4] In this context, sequential and parallel execution pertain to the flow of the program and not to the computer architecture.

[5] This truly parallel implementation raises a number of important theoretical questions pertaining to resource allocation and strategic management with respect to multiple fronts, questions that cannot be addressed within a sequential framework. The most important of these is the issue of regional balancing, to which we will return below. In chapter 5 I treat civil wars as "internal fronts" forcing the central government to allocate resources to maintain internal peace as well.

framework limits the actions to one move per state and time period. Instead, the move sequences may span over several simulation cycles. Behavioral continuity is assured by endowing the actors with a short-term memory rather than forcing them follow a predetermined game tree. This design produces more realistic protracted warfare than the reified campaigns of the Bremer/Mihalka-type models.[6]

Third, I have also simplified the rules of structural change following combat. Since state interactions in the Bremer and Mihalka architecture potentially involve a large number of states, complicated rules to determine war outcomes, including the division of spoils and territorial gains, are needed (316–17; see also Cusack and Stoll 1990, 81–91; and Duffy 1992, 258–59). My decentralized notion of combat solves this problem by having initiators target and attack provinces rather than entire multi-province states. Again, this means that the outcome is an endogenous consequence of the power struggle itself rather than a result of complicated and potentially arbitrary computational rules. As a further advantage, the desired contiguity becomes easier to assure.[7]

In conclusion, I argue that my parallel and incremental design philosophy has several advantages that compensate the loss of compatibility with the Bremer/Mihalka family of models: It leads to conceptual simplification by eliminating several complex algorithms; the behavior of my system exemplifies a higher degree of realism in that the actors' behavior is not limited to fixed move sequences; and the computational performance increases thanks to these simplifications.[8]

The State System

The system consists of a square grid of user-defined proportions. All the findings presented below were generated in a ten-by-ten system.[9] The

---

[6] Duffy's (1993) incorporation of learning and reciprocity is a move in this direction, but he does not change the underlying combat model.

[7] The disadvantage of the parallel design is the possibility of computational conflicts. However, it is easy to circumvent this difficulty by locking the units that have already been modified in the same time period, a common trick in time-sharing operation systems. To make the execution unbiased, the order is randomly determined in every time period. See Duffy (1993, 14–15) for a similar solution.

[8] The code was developed in THINK Pascal on a Macintosh and subsequently ported to Unix running on Hewlett Packard and Sun workstations as well as Turbo Pascal for Windows on a Pentium platform. Despite the conventional implementations, the computational performance under Unix was sufficient for the purposes of this study. Nevertheless, the synchronous algorithms are particularly well suited for future implementation on a parallel machine. Duffy (1992, 1993) carried out a full parallelization of his system and reports important speed gains.

[9] Bremer and Mihalka (1977) and Cusack and Stoll (1990) use a hexagonal map consist-

basic building blocks are the primitive units, the "social atoms" that constitute the most finely grained picture of social reality that the model can
offer. At the start of the simulation, each unit is endowed with resources
drawn from a normal distribution. For the purposes of this study, the mean
was set to fifty and the standard deviation to ten. Once conquest takes
place, corporate units form, each consisting of a hierarchy subordinating
the conquered units as dependent provinces under the capital. To limit the
complexity of the system, the hierarchical depth of the corporate actors is
limited to two levels, the one of the capital and the one of the provinces.[10]

Sovereignty is formalized as a specific authority structure by which the
transfer of control from the subordinated units to the heads is both direct
and absolute (Coleman 1990). The assumption of absolute rule implies a
pure command structure devoid of any sense of democracy. The sovereignty principle deprives the conquered units of their actor capacity in
two respects: the responsibility to manage foreign relations is handed
over to the head, and internal peace is automatically guaranteed by ruling
out revolutions and civil wars.[11] In essence, this conceptualization of the
state comes close to Max Weber's (1962) classical definition of a corporate group as "a social relationship which is either closed to outsiders or
restricts their admission by regulations, and whose authority is enforced
by the actions of specific individuals charged with this function, for example, a chief or head and usually also an administrative staff" (107).

The Dynamic Properties of the System

In its simplest form, the simulation proceeds as a sequence involving
three phases (see fig. 4.6). First, all sovereign actors make their decisions.
Second, the consequences for the resource distribution between the actors
are calculated according to the rules of interaction. Third, conquest transforms the system's structure.

DECISIONS

The synchronous design gives each state in every pair the choice between
cooperate C and defect D. Since the current model does not include trade

---

ing of ninety-eight states. Duffy's (1992, 244) rectangular lattice containing 128 actors is
closer to the present configuration, although his system is open by allowing neighbor relations to wrap around the system boundaries.

[10] The limitation to two-level hierarchies excludes explicit consideration of multilevel
structures such as feudal and federal systems.

[11] In the civil-war extension of the current model, internal sovereignty emerges gradually
(see chap. 5). For a theoretical critique of the neorealist sovereignty assumption, see Ashley
(1988), Walker (1990, 1993), and Ruggie (1993).

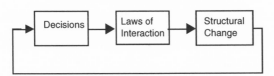

Figure 4.6. The basic simulation loop

or any other peaceful interactions, cooperation stands for little more than refraining from attack. Only bilateral encounters are considered, so the strategic situation resembles a two-by-two game. Presently, there is only one decision rule for the prey and one for the predator states, corresponding to the realist distinction between status quo and revisionist states. The status quo oriented states adhere to a very simple rule of reciprocity, dubbed Tit For Tat (TFT) (Axelrod 1984). States employing this rule always respond with the same action as the opponent played in the last round and never initiate hostilities.

The predator strategy is somewhat more involved. As the prey rule, it is also based on TFT. Yet the predator strategy sometimes includes unprovoked aggression. This is not done randomly, however, but reflects realist prudence: "The wish to acquire more is admittedly a very natural and common thing; and when men succeed in this they are always praised rather than condemned. But when they lack the ability to do so and yet want to acquire more at all cost, they deserve condemnation for their mistakes" (Machiavelli [1513] 1961, 43).

Translated into modeling language, prudence implies two things. First, a predator only considers an unprovoked attack if it is not already involved in warfare on another front. This "Schlieffen plan" rule avoids initiating costly two-front wars that might endanger the survival of the state. Second, revisionist states only attack if the relative power balance between them and their potential victim exceeds a certain ratio, referred to as the superiority ratio. It is this ratio that determines the offense-defense orientation of the system.[12] Should there be many potential victims, the aggressor selects the weakest of them.[13]

---

[12] The strategic literature often sets this ratio to 3:1. See Mearsheimer (1983). The superiority ratio usually refers to the tactical, front-related rather than strategic power balance as specified by figure 4.7. It is also worth noting that the Bremer/Mihalka family of models fixes this important parameter to one in all simulations. On the other hand, they include a probabilistic criterion that captures misperception in the attacker's power calculus (see especially Cusack and Stoll 1990, 102).

[13] This strategy corresponds to Hitler's plan to upset the international equilibrium in 1930s: "Hitler planned to overturn the tripolar system by initially devouring small and middle powers and then defeating quickly the nearest polar power (the Soviet Union) before the other pole (the U.S.) could intervene. . ." (Schweller 1993, 226). On the other hand, it is easy to find historical examples where the aggressor state turned against more powerful actors first. For example, following the Schlieffen plan, Germany attacked France before

If the predator decides to strike, a battlefield must be chosen. This is done by randomly selecting a "combat path" consisting of an agent and a target province. If both the attacker and the defender are primitive actors, they also serve as agent and target respectively. However, if one or both are corporate actors, there may be several possible angles of attack. The current implementation lets the attacker randomly choose any of its provinces (including the capital) that are adjacent to the defending state as the agent. Thereafter, the attacker selects a target randomly from the provinces of the defending actor that border the agent province.

The decision phase ends by allocating resources for the subsequent interactions. It divides the total resources evenly among all territorial neighbors regardless of local need.[14] For example, a sovereign primitive actor with four neighbors devotes one fourth of its resources to defense against each neighbor. As a corollary, great powers with long borders need more resources to defend themselves than geographically concentrated units do.

To clarify, figure 4.7 summarizes the decision phase of state i, with resources R, and n neighbors:

In its present form, the system does not support more sophisticated calculations in the game-theoretic sense. The agents' behavior is only forward looking to the extent that it takes the power ratio between the actors into consideration as a rule of thumb.[15] While some authors view the rational-actor assumption as at the core of neorealism (e.g., Keohane 1983), Waltz (1979, 118) claims that his structural theory's evolutionary logic makes it independent of this postulate. Although an extension along these lines would be of general theoretical interest, it does not seem necessary given the focus on neorealist selection arguments.[16]

In complex systems, rational computations are always bounded. As a

---

striking against the much weaker Russia in World War I. See also Bremer and Mihalka (1977, 310) for a similar rule.

[14] This is of course an unrealistic algorithm since real-world states typically reallocate their resources to where the action is. Yet it is not hard to modify this implementation. Proportional resource allocation sets the power level proportional to each opponent's power allocation in the previous period (see chap. 5 below).

[15] These decision rules resemble Cusack and Stoll's (1990) most basic styles of "power management" (71). While the predators resemble their "primitive power-seekers," the prey states follow the altruistic "collective security" strategy, though without alliances, which will be added below.

[16] Though see Cusack and Stoll (1990) for an example of simulations involving "rational" decisionmakers basing their calculations on expected utility. Another idea would be to "breed" strategies selected akin to Axelrod's (1984) tournaments (see also Axelrod 1987 and Lindgren 1992). Although it does not introduce any new basic strategies, chapter 5 analyzes strategic adaptation, which allows for more flexibility in terms of the behavioral repertoire.

> **for** each sovereign neighbor *j*,
>> **if** *j* played *D* in the previous period **then**
>>> Play *D*
>> **else**
>>> Play *C* (Tit For Tat)
>
> **if** *i* is a predator **and** there is no action on any front **then**
>> look for the weakest sovereign neighbor *j**
>> **if** $R(i)/R(j^*) > $ *superiority_ratio* **then**
>>> Randomly select own agent province and target in *j**
>>> Play *D* (i.e. launch unprovoked attack against *j**)
>
> **for** each sovereign neighbor *j*,
>> Allocate $R(i)/n$ to front *j*

Figure 4.7. The decision phase

depiction of long-term and large-scale historical processes, a rational-expectations perspective would be grossly misleading. The longer the time scope and the more complex and turbulent the social situation, the less the appeal of a pure rational-choice approach and the more of Herbert Simon's (1981) idea of satisficing. Toulmin (1981) asserts that "given the short-term character of human foresight and calculation in the social realm, it is hard to see how any sort of conscious, deliberate, calculated human decisions could have brought effective social arrangements into existence in the first place" (183; see also Duffy 1992, 242).

Assuming that interaction is confined to conventional land warfare, I further limit interactions to territorial neighbors. The endogenous nature of the corporate actors entails a similarly variable action scope by which the capital "inherits" as neighbors those of its provinces. This means that great powers may have an almost global action scope. As opposed to the unlimited rationality of game-theoretic models, however, this relative farsightedness is an emergent feature rather than an inherent property of the actors.

LAWS OF INTERACTION

Once all decisions are made, the simulation program executes the decisions for each pair of sovereign actors simultaneously. The interaction process represents the physical laws of war that govern interstate relations. Currently these conditions are fixed, but nothing prevents an endogenization of the parameter settings as a reflection of technological advances. As in a normal two-by-two game, there are four possible outcomes: *CC, DC, CD,* and *DD.* Each political interaction generates the resource differences for each pair of actors shown in figure 4.8.

This matrix depicts the very simple Richardson-like logic of combat. All the simulations reported here were performed with a destruction rate of $k = 0.05$, which means that the resource level of an actor under attack

A_j	C	D
A_i		
C	0, 0	$-kR_j$, 0
D	0, $-kR_i$	$-kR_j$, $-kR_i$

where

A_i = act of state i
R_i = local resources of state i
k = rate of destruction

Figure 4.8. The resource differences resulting from dyadic interaction

is reduced by 5 percent of the locally allocated resources of the attacking state. In opposition to standard game-theoretic models, the laws of war do not offer any immediate advantages to an aggressor other than the relative gain compared to the losses incurred in the other outcomes. Thus they differ from the conventional Prisoner's Dilemma setup in which attacking states are immediately rewarded if the defender does not respond. Each conflict must end in victory for one party. The outcome is governed by the victory ratio, which unlike the superiority ratio compares the locally allocated resources rather than the balance between the total resources of each side. Should the balance exceed the victory ratio in either direction, the stronger party has won the conflict.[17]

The resource differences produced by wars enter the calculation of each unit's new resource level. In addition to the losses incurred by combat, each actor reaps a "harvest" drawn from a normal distribution with adjustable parameters. In the present study, mean was two and the standard deviation five. A corporate state receives the sum of the harvests from its capital province and all subordinate members.[18]

STRUCTURAL CHANGE

If the resource balance exceeds the victory ratio, the superior party conquers the target province. In the current study, the victory ratio coincided with the superiority ratio. The consequences of conflict vary depending on the nature of the target unit. There are three cases:

[17] Again, see the following for an alternative rule by which decision-making is localized as well.

[18] As in the original Bremer and Mihalka (1977) design, the distribution is common for all states. This excludes the possibility of uneven growth that is sometimes said to generate instability (e.g., Organski 1968). Yet since this factor lies outside neorealism, there is no need to test it in the present study, but see Cusack and Stoll (1990, 91) for a more general implementation.

1. If it is an independent primitive actor, this unit is subordinated under the head of the conquering state. This case is illustrated by state T11 absorbing R6 in figure 4.5 above.

2. If the target is a province of a corporate actor, the subordinate unit is transferred to the attacker. To illustrate, consider an invasion by B3 of C4. The consequence would be that the disputed province becomes a subject of B3 rather than of G8.

3. If the target is the capital of a corporate actor, the entire corporate unit collapses into its primitive units when the capital falls. This is in fact what happened to the R5 empire before it fell to T11. The patchwork of small states constitute the remainders of that empire.[19]

The second case, in which the target is a subordinate province, is interesting because it sometimes gives rise to detached provinces as the vanquished corporate actor loses a part of its territory. This will be the case if there are provinces of this state that can no longer be reached from the capital province as a consequence of the loss of a newly invaded province. In this event, the truncated provinces are made independent to exclude the possibility of enclaves.[20]

When a state loses its sovereignty, it abandons control of its own resources. Upon regaining independence, a province receives an equal share of the resources previously controlled by the center. For example, if a province breaks out of a multiprovince state consisting of five subordinated members and a center prior to the secession, it will receive a sixth of the total resources. It also regains its previous strategic orientation (see chapter 5 for a more realistic rule that allows the provinces to keep their resources after conquest).

Adding Defensive Alliances

Rejecting ideologically motivated alignment patterns, the mainstream realist view suggests that alliances

---

[19] Unlike the Bremer/Mihalka-type models, the current framework does not feature immediate takeover of large states. Still, it allows the attacking state to absorb some or all of these newly independent units after imperial collapses. However, it has to do so in competition with other states that may also be both motivated and capable to fill parts of the power vacuum.

[20] The requirement of territorial contiguity derives from the realist assumption of sovereignty. Needless to say, contiguity and sovereignty were not a part of all historical systems (Ruggie 1993). The Bremer/Mihalka program also hard-wires sovereignty into their models, but since their division of spoils concerns many states and territories at a time, their algorithm is quite involved (cf. Bremer and Mihalka 1977, 316, 317; Cusack and Stoll 1990, 88–91; Duffy 1992, 258–59).

1. serve mainly to counter external security threats

2. form as a matter of expediency rather than of principle

3. are ad hoc arrangements rather than long-lasting coalitions—if the threat disappears, so does the alliance (see Holsti, Hopfmann, and Sullivan 1973 for further references).

In a recent study, Steven Walt (1987) advances his neorealist "balance of threat theory" in which alignments are reactions to security threats pertaining to four factors: aggregate power, geographic proximity, offensive power, and aggressive intentions (21–26). To extend Walt's qualitative theory to the dynamic domain, I propose a behavioral notion of threat perception based on the past behavior of expansionist states.[21] This formulation indirectly taps the capability and intentional dimensions of Walt's threat notion because actors that are both powerful and aggressive are likely to be perceived as threatening. Reflecting the analytical focus of proposition P3, only defensive, decentralized balancing is modeled, excluding the possibility of bandwagoning. Moreover, since the purpose is to investigate Walt's ideal "world of balancing," alignments should be perfectly binding and credible. Though these two assumptions deviate from the historical record, they represent the theoretically interesting case of an optimal alliance mechanism.[22]

These observations translate into a decentralized notion of alliances as independent actors that coordinate their foreign-policy actions without directly redistributing or sharing their resources. Activating the alignment option adds two additional phases to the main simulation loop (see fig. 4.9). Before the decision phase, each state updates the trust score for each neighbor, as a result of their behavioral records. This score gradually increases in the absence of unprovoked attacks or conquest. Should the latter occur, however, relations deteriorate quickly.[23] Thereafter the actor

---

[21] It is important not to confuse the term "threat" in this passive meaning from its use to denote a deterrence signal. In formal deterrence theory, the former corresponds to "belief" rather than threat. On the distinction between passive and active uses of "threat," see Cohen (1979, 4).

[22] The Bremer/Mihalka framework allows for offensive balancing and endogenously credible alliance commitments. The regional, perfectly credible alliances modeled in my system should not be confounded with Cusack and Stoll's (1990, 141, 142) "collective security" style of power management. Though automaticity is implied by both strategies, they do not coincide because in the Emergent Polarity Model states may be balancing different threats. A true collective-security system presupposes shared threat perceptions. As we will see below, the difference between regional and global balancing can have a decisive impact on system stability.

[23] The choice of parameters for updating the trust indexes is necessarily arbitrary. To rely on Bayes's rule, however, would lead to a much too fast and symmetric learning process. Instead, an alternative procedure was adopted by which the trust score T depends on a sensitivity parameter s. The latter parameter determines the impact of the change $dT =$

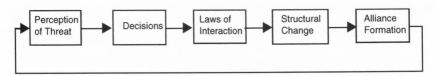

Figure 4.9. The extended simulation loop with alliance formation

singles out one of the neighbors as the prime threat. If the state perceives no aggressive behavior, there is no threat.

The second amendment is located as the last step to be executed in each iteration. Here a round of "diplomacy" follows in which every state that perceives a threat announces its willingness to counter the threatening actor. If there is more than one state that feels threatened by a given actor, an alliance automatically forms against that state. By the same token, if there are no longer at least two states that perceive a common threat, the coalition immediately dissolves.[24]

Once in place, alliances influence behavior in two ways, referred to as deterrent and defensive balancing (Cusack and Stoll 1990, 120). First, they have a deterrent function in that they enter the capability calculations of the predator states. If such a state faces a defensive alliance, its decision to launch an unprovoked attack incorporates the sum of resources of the alliance members rather than the capabilities of the chosen victim alone. Should the potential attacker itself belong to an alliance, it can only count on support from the other members if the alliance is targeted against the selected victim.

Second, the attack on an alliance member automatically creates an obligation to support the defending state by coming to its support. This means that each member of the alliance strikes against the aggressor, resulting in a collective defense. If the victim happens to be a member of the aggressor's alliance, the latter state is automatically excluded from the alliance in order to make it impossible for predators to exploit the alliance from within.

± 1000 on the new trust score: $T(t) = (1 - s) T(t - 1) + s\, dT$. The value of the sensitivity parameter differs depending on whether dT is negative or positive. In the former case, the perceptual change has a greater impact since negative experiences and threats make themselves felt more quickly than positive ones. Based on observations of the system, I calibrated the sensitivity parameter to $s = 0.5$ and $s = 0.01$ for negative and positive updating respectively. See chapter 5 for a simplified version of the threat mechanism.

[24] This solution differs from Bremer/Mihalka's one-shot alliances. In my model, alliances may persist through several time periods, but only if its members continue to feel threatened by the same aggressor.

THE IMPACT OF PREDATION AND DEFENSE:
HEGEMONIC TAKEOFF

Unlike real social systems, this CAS analysis allows for perfectly controlled experimental conditions (cf. discussion of complex thought experiments above). In this first set of runs, I explore the first two propositions by systematically varying the predatory frequency and defense-offense balance. The next section evaluates the third proposition by introducing alliances.

The first independent variable, the predator frequency, determined the number of predator states in the initial system. I ran simulations for the frequencies 0, 5, 10, 20, 40, 60, 80, and 100 percent. The second dimension, pertaining to the defense-offense balance, was modeled by setting the superiority ratio to two and three in what I will refer to as the offense- and defense-dominated systems respectively.

Due to the probabilistic nature of the model, it was necessary to generate a number of replications for each parameter setting. Each parameter configuration was replicated twenty times using different random seeds, thus ensuring that the initial power distributions and the exact location of the predators varied across the replications.[25] All simulations ran until hegemony occurred or one thousand time periods elapsed. Figure 4.10 displays state survival averaged over the twenty replications.

As can be seen immediately from the steep decrease of both curves, the number of states falls dramatically even for small numbers of predators. This effect is particularly pronounced in the offense-dominated system. A similar, though somewhat less dramatic, phenomenon is visible in the defense-dominated system as well. As would be expected, there is less attrition in the latter world.

Though an interesting statistic, the average rate of state survival does not reveal enough information to evaluate propositions about power politics. Recall that I defined power politics as a process characterized by low polarity short of universal empire. To assess the power of our three realist propositions, it is necessary to study the distribution of polarity among the replications. Figure 4.11 offers such a disaggregated view of the distributions for the defense-dominated and offense-dominated systems respectively. The diagrams display the emergent polarity of all twenty replications for each predator frequency. The number of replications for each polarity category is stacked on top of the other. The areas pertain to unipolarity, bipolarity, low multipolarity (from three to ten surviving states), high multipolarity (from eleven to ninety), and virtually no

[25] The replications resemble the use of randomization to eliminate extraneous influences in experimental research (see fig. 3.3).

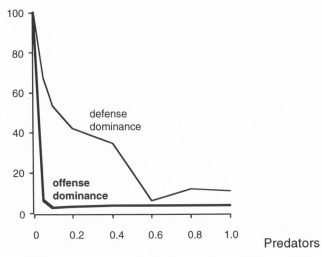

Average Polarity
at time 1000

Figure 4.10. Average state survival after one thousand time periods

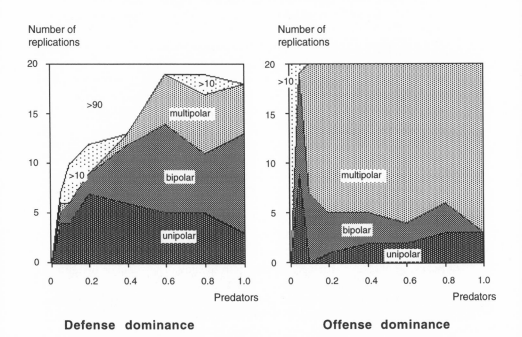

Number of
replications

Number of
replications

Defense dominance

Offense dominance

Figure 4.11. Emergent polarity without alliances

integration (from ninety-one to one hundred). For example, in the defense-dominated system at a 60 percent predator rate, among the twenty replications five were unipolar, nine bipolar, five multipolar, and one outcome exceeded ninety states.

To make things concrete, I define power politics as either bipolarity or multipolarity—that is, outcomes featuring from two to ten sovereign states. Given this operational definition, it becomes obvious that power politics completely dominates the outcomes in the offense-dominated system. It is also a common outcome in the defense-dominated world, though only for high predator frequencies. This is an intriguing result. First of all, the structural proposition P1 seems to possess considerable validity in these runs. Especially in the offense-dominated system, power politics is the structural outcome regardless of the initial frequency of predators. However, and all the more surprising, the results contradict the proposition about defense dominance P2. As anticipated, defensive attitudes tend to increase the chances of state survival, but at the same time the likelihood of unipolarity increases significantly, thus making power politics less likely in defense-dominated systems.[26]

Clearly these findings call for an explanation. At this point, it is helpful to return to figure 4.2. In light of our findings, we are now ready to refine this causal scheme. The main problem of this static model relates to the artificial separation of structural causes and consequences. In a dynamic perspective, this distinction disappears; today's structural consequence becomes tomorrow's cause. Noting the interdependence between agent and structure, Anthony Giddens (1979) emphasizes the "duality of structure": "Structure thus is not to be conceptualized as a barrier to action, but as essentially involved in its production" (70; see also Wendt 1987; Dessler 1989). This realization removes the reification of system structure. In this specific setting, it translates into a negative arrow pointing from integration back to competition. Because system integration implies that the number of states decreases, chances are that some of the absorbed states are going to be predators. But this means that there will be fewer potential competitors, thus further accelerating the process of predation.

---

[26] It is hard to compare these findings to Cusack and Stoll (1990) because they did not vary the frequency of different actor types continuously. One exception is their figure 4.5.6 (156), which displays a roughly linear response to the number of collective-security states at the outset. Since states rely on the alignment option, however, it is not comparable to the system of free competition studied here. Moreover, their heavy use of regression analysis makes it hard to recognize nonlinear dependencies. Without explicit nonlinear terms, regression equations cannot directly capture the effect of hegemonic takeoff. Finally, because these authors only study a highly offense-dominated system with a fixed superiority ratio of one, their findings say little about proposition P2.

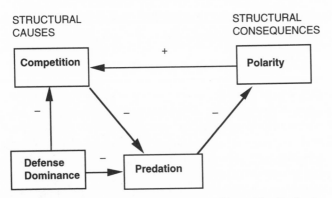

Figure 4.12. The dynamic causal model with positive feedback

The competition/predation/integration triangle constitutes a positive-feedback loop because a small disturbance in one of the variables has a tendency to multiply. It is important to note that the positive-feedback process works in both directions. A minor decrease in predation, for example, will lead to less integration and more states surviving, including predators. This raises the level of competition, thus curbing the predatory process even further. In the language of systems analysis, such an equilibrium is unstable (Kaplan 1957).

It is precisely this nonlinear effect that makes it legitimate to speak about structural phenomena. If disproportionally small disturbances invariably lead to the same outcome, the structure itself acquires a life on its own. By its nature, the snowball effect is nothing but a positive-feedback mechanism. This geopolitical process should not be confused with similar phenomena related to differential growth *within* a country (Kaplan 1957, 31–32; Organski 1968). The only thing needed to trigger the process is a somewhat uneven *initial* distribution of resources and unbiased stochastic growth rates.[27]

I label this snowballing process of conquest-induced exponential growth "hegemonic takeoff." In order for power politics to obtain, the hegemonic takeoffs need to be curbed. If the gap between the aspiring hegemon and the second most powerful state increases, the system may easily degenerate into universal empire. Robert Gilpin (1981) aptly captures this ecological dynamic:

> The operation of the balance-of-power mechanism is a function of the 'density' of an international system. International systems differ with respect to the room or space available for territorial or economic expansion. . . . As

[27] See also chapter 5 for a related snowball mechanism based on adaptation rather than on pure selection.

states expand, the open frontier shrinks, and they begin to encroach on one another. They increasingly collide, and conflict intensifies among them, raising the costs of further expansion. In time, either one state becomes dominant or a balance is established among states. (147)

This is why, paradoxically enough, offense-dominated worlds tend to remain pluralist. The greater the competition, and the more even the growth rate of the most aggressive states, the more likely a balance of power becomes. By contrast, a more defensively oriented system widens the window of opportunity for potential hegemons by thwarting the attempts of predatory rivals to catch up.

Going back to figure 4.12, defense dominance has two effects. The direct and immediate impact of this variable is to slow down further conquest by making predators more reluctant to attack. The second and more indirect link influences competition negatively as the defense orientation of the system increases. Since the arrow from competition to predation is negative, the combined effect becomes positive, thus counteracting the direct defensive mechanism. If the indirect link is stronger than the direct one, the net effect of defense dominance will be negative, thus removing the obstacles to integration, with unipolarity as the most likely outcome.

Although some realists argue that a positive-feedback mechanism in this context is a "myth" (Snyder 1991), their simultaneous adherence to the security dilemma undermines their positive evaluation of the defense. Thus this type of "defensive realism" contradicts mainstream realism, something that is vividly illustrated by Bremer and Mihalka (1977), who offer an extensive sample of statements by prominent realist scholars. For example, Waltz (1959) makes the following observation about self-help systems: "Because each state is the final judge of its own cause, any state may at any time use force to implement its policies. Because any state may at any time use force, all states must constantly be ready either to counter force with force or to pay the cost of weakness" (159). They further quote Quincy Wright (1965) who nicely captures the logic of the hegemonic takeoff mechanism: "Governments have a tendency to struggle both for increase of power and for self-preservation. Only if the latter tendency checks the first will all the governments continue to be independent. Whenever one increases its relative power, its capacity to increase it further will be enhanced. As a consequence, any departure from equilibrium tends to initiate an accelerating process of conquest" (744).

While these quotations are a bit dated, contemporary realists have not changed their minds. Robert Gilpin (1981) contends that "growth of power of a state and its expansion tend to reinforce one another, as expansion increases the economic surplus and resources available to the expanding state" (146).[28] In an even more recent contribution, Peter Liberman (1993) makes the same point:

> Since conquest pays, according to the realist view, the more you conquer, the more wealthy and powerful you become. Rulers have economic and security incentives to expand. Status-quo states must rely more heavily on threats of war to contain expansionists, and on war itself if threats fail to deter. Unless they are contained, imperial rulers will swallow up weaker nations, growing stronger and more invincible with each new conquest. (125)

Liberman goes on to provide a useful review of realist scholarship on this point, including references to prominent realists such as Halford Mackinder, Nicholas Spykman, and George Kennan.

The current model is entirely consistent with Liberman's postulate that conquest pays because the vanquished states delegate all their resources to the conqueror. While the assumption of resource cumulation undoubtedly belongs to a dynamic interpretation of realism, its empirical veracity is a far from obvious (see Hopf 1991 for a historical evaluation). Liberals point out that both modernization and nationalism tend to counteract this mechanism (see references in Liberman 1993). Later, we will replace the assumption of automatic-resource transfer to the capitals by an explicit tax mechanism.

Although hegemonic takeoffs may be rare in the contemporary world, there are several historical examples of both successful and aborted hegemonic takeoffs. Studying state formation in pre-Columbian America, the anthropologist Robert Carneiro (1970) observed an accelerating centralizing tendency driven by conquest (cf. Cusack and Stoll 1990, 47–50). Sweden's remarkable expansion in the seventeenth century is a more recent case in point. Despite its backward economy and peripheral position, Sweden succeeded in fielding an enormous army in the Thirty Years' War. The secret was Gustavus Adolphus's tactic to let war pay for itself (Van Creveld 1977, 9–12), together with the considerable revenue from the conquered territory in Balticum (Downing 1992, 196).

Another even more momentous example of hegemonic takeoff is Napoleon's famous campaigns. Though the French victories could be attributed partly to his tactical genius and the nationalist enthusiasm of his troops, there was clearly a self-feeding logic at play. Paul Kennedy (1989) quotes Napoleon as saying: "My power depends on my glory and my glories on the victories I have won. My power will fail if I do not

---

[28] This quote does not imply that Gilpin believes that economies of scale characterize all historical phases. To be precise, Gilpin posits a u-shaped cost function suggesting the existence of an optimal organizational scale beyond which decreasing returns to scale operate (see also Bean 1973). I thank Jack Snyder for pointing this out to me.

feed it on new glories and new victories. Conquest has made me what I am and only conquest enables me to hold my position" (133). Hitler's bid for Eurasian hegemony also contained important elements of positive feedback. In great detail, Peter Liberman (1993) shows that Hitlers Germany succeeded in extracting considerable economic resources from the countries it occupied, in addition to the booty, slave labor, and troops acquired through conquest.

Whether the imperialist state can hold on to its conquered territory is another question. In fact, most hegemonic takeoffs were rather transient affairs: Both Napoleon's Continental System and Hitler's Third Reich crumbled when a powerful countercoalition formed.[29] This leads us to the role of alliances in realist theory.

THE IMPACT OF DEFENSIVE ALLIANCES: REGIONAL BALANCING

Those realists who do not think that internal balancing suffices to guarantee system stability point to alliances as an extra security mechanism: "The alliance is one of the most prominent means of putting the balance of power theory to work" (Gulick 1955, 61). In its most extreme form, the "pessimistic" line of thought views alliances as a necessary condition of stability (e.g., Carneiro 1970; see also review in Cusack and Stoll 1990). The previous section has already shown that unipolarity is not inevitable even in the absence of alliances. The claim of proposition P3, however, is more modest. Having ruled out "bandwagoning" and other offensive uses of alliances (see Levy 1981; Christensen and Snyder 1990), it states that defensive alliances increase the likelihood of power politics. Given the counterintuitive results concerning defense dominance, can we expect decentralized alliances of this type to have a positive impact on system stability?

Figure 4.13 displays emergent polarity in a world of defensive balancing. A comparison of these results to figure 4.11, depicting a system without alliances, yields interesting insights. As expected, the alliance mechanism does offer some protection at least for low predation frequencies. This effect is particularly strong in the defense-dominated system where there is almost no reduction of polarity for predatory rates below 20 percent. A similar, but weaker, tendency is present in the offense-dominated world. However, contrary to the expectation of P3, defensive

[29] The short-lived nature of these disruptions does not reduce their historical importance. Moreover, it would be wrong to ignore the successful cases of hegemonic takeoff. In fact, state formation in both England and France followed a similar centrifugal path, though this process is retrospectively referred to as "internal colonization."

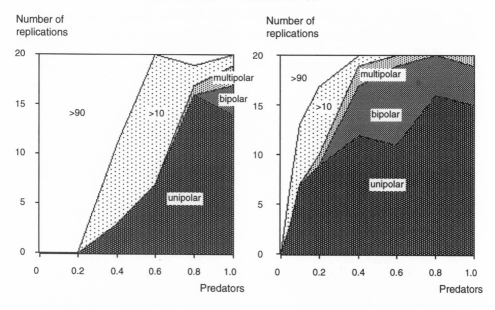

Defense dominance   **Offense dominance**

Figure 4.13. Emergent polarity with alliances

alliances lead to another important consequence. Compared to the non-aligned world in figure 4.11, figure 4.13 shows a remarkable dominance of unipolarity at the expense of power politics. From having been the most common outcome in the offense-dominated system, power politics becomes less likely than universal empire. In the defense-oriented runs, power politics almost does not appear at all except for predator rates above 80 percent.

Thus, in light of the simulation results, the proposition that defensive alliances increase the likelihood of power politics seems questionable. In analogy with the observations concerning defense dominance, the reason for this counterintuitive phenomenon is to be found in the competitive dynamics of geopolitics. One way of illustrating the effect is to replace the defense-dominance box in figure 4.12 by one that is labeled "defensive alliances." In addition to the negative, direct impact of defensive alliances on predation, there is a non trivial ecological influence that disturbs the competitive pressure. The introduction of defensive alliances reduces the level of competition by eliminating, or at least delaying, potential competitors. Without alliances, aggressor states are free to grow, which leads to a more even timing of expansionist quests.

By contrast, regional alliances tend to surround threatening states with a defensive pact, thus diminishing the encircled predators' chances to expand. Should one state manage to break out of its confinement, however, it will have more space for conquest since its competitors are prevented from joining the struggle for power. This widens the window of opportunity for the potential hegemon, making it easier for it to reach the threshold of hegemonic takeoff. Having acquired the critical size, the dominant state easily overwhelms whole subsystems of locally stable alliances. At this point, unified defenses may be formed, but as a rule, this is much too late.

While it has often been observed that collective security tends to distort the operation of the balance-of-power mechanism (Claude 1964; see also Cusack and Stoll 1990, 141, 142), it has not dawned upon realists that the decentralized, defensive alliances themselves may have a similar disruptive influence. With the exception of Waltz's (1979) reservations about uncertainty and miscalculation in multipolar systems, realists usually consider alliances to be an unproblematic addition to the balancing forces of power politics. To defend their position, some realists suggest that states need to be much more farsighted and concerned by the overall balance of the system (e.g., Kaplan 1957), but this is clearly not what neorealism is about. According to Waltz's invisible-hand imagery, power politics is an unwilled emergent phenomenon rather than a consciously managed process.

Renaissance Italy offers a striking example of how such a regional alignment system indirectly and unintendedly promoted systemic integration on a Europe-wide scale through foreign intervention. Before its collapse, the Italian city-states were entangled in a web of well-poised alignments representing a textbook example of balance-of-power logic. In his classic study of Renaissance diplomacy, Garreth Mattingly (1955) describes the emergence of the balance-of-power system:

> In the 1440s there began to form in certain Italian minds a conception of Italy as a system of independent states, coexisting by virtue of an unstable equilibrium which it was the function of statesmanship to preserve. This conception was fostered by the peninsula-wide alliances whose even balance of forces had ended every war of the past twenty years in stalemate. (83)

The equilibrium derived from the stabilizing influence of the defensive alliance formed in response to the hegemonic aspirations of Venice (Guicciardini 1969, 8). As in nineteenth-century Europe, this arrangement brought an astonishing degree of peace and stability. Satisfaction with the performance of Renaissance diplomacy was so great that, one century later, the historian Bernardino Corio looked back at the golden age with a certain nostalgia: "All over there were festivals and delights and Jupiter ruled in peace; everything seemed more stable and firm than it had been at any other time" (cited in Gilbert 1965, 261).

At the end of the fifteenth century, the external pressure on Italy mounted, but save for some aborted attempts to create an all-Italian defensive alliance, no such common defense emerged. In 1494, this fragile balance ended abruptly with the French siege and subsequent invasion of Naples. This marked the beginning of an era of foreign influence in Italy that would last until the unification of the country in the late nineteenth century. Why did the Italians fail to form a defensive alliance? In the centuries following the French intervention, this question kept a series of prominent Italian thinkers busy in a fascinating historical debate involving timeless issues of causation and blame (Gilbert 1965). In their endless search for explanations of the humiliating loss of independence, these historians typically first searched for scapegoats. Soon realizing that the reason for "this astounding instance of political shortsightedness" (259) lay deeper, the analysts later referred to luck as a shorthand for structural causes beyond human control: "the *Fortuna* which emerged as the ruler of world history in the sixteenth century was the power behind everything that happened: it was an embodiment of the uncontrollable forces determining the course of events" (269). Mattingly (1955) presents a nonteleological, structuralist answer to the puzzle, not far from my own theoretical point: "The State could think only of itself. The natural egotism of a political organization with no higher end than its own self-perpetuation and aggrandizement may come nearer to explaining the diplomacy of the 'concert of Italy' than all the more complex explanations subsequently elaborated" (91).

Although this episode serves as a mere illustration of the argument, it has both historical significance and generality. Its importance stems from the momentous consequences for the development of the modern state system. The eclipse of the Italian city-states marked not only a major shift in power from the Mediterranean to the northern states, but also the transition from the city-state as a political organization to the state. Its generality is illustrated by Gilpin's observations about historical shifts of power from the center to the periphery. Drawing on Toynbee and McNeill, Gilpin (1981) attributes this phenomenon to the diffusion of technology from the core as well as "the power struggle in the center." He elaborates on the latter process:

> The struggle both weakens them and blinds them to the threat of a Macedonia or Rome gathering strength and consolidating the land mass over the horizon. Failing to unite against the rising peripheral power, they become its victims. History is replete with examples of power struggles that exhausted

states at the center of the system and made them vulnerable to external conquest and domination. (184–85)

This point is also supported by the alliance literature. In his book on small powers and alliances, Robert Rothstein (1968) observed a tendency toward encapsulation of regional systems: "The Great Power tends to ally in terms of a threat to the balance of the whole system; the Small Power in terms of a threat to its local balance" (62). More recently, Steven Walt (1987) has elaborated the distinction between global and regional alliances in the context of postwar diplomacy in the Middle East. Among other factors explaining the trend toward autonomous alignment patterns on the regional level, he suggests that "because other regional actors present much more immediate dangers, the regional states form alliances primarily in response to threats from proximate powers" (164).

Although these authors differentiate between regional and global balancing, they treat the division between the entire system and its components as predefined. Provided that this relation remains relatively constant, as was often the case during the cold war, there is nothing wrong with this assumption. Yet in periods marked by an increasing blurring of system boundaries, the reified regional perspective is likely to distort the analysis.

The advantage of CAS models is that they treat the actors, in this case states, as emergent features rather than exogenously defined entities. By extension, the same applies to structures, including regional security systems. It follows that regional security systems are fundamentally intersubjective phenomena rather than arbitrarily defined constructs created for purely analytical purposes.[30] This conceptualization comes very close to Barry Buzan's (1991) "security complexes," each defined as "a group of states whose primary security concerns link together sufficiently closely that their national securities cannot realistically be considered apart from one another" (190).

To return to the previous example, Italian statesmen of the Renaissance regarded Italy as an isolated system: "There was Italy; and there was the indistinct mass of all the other nations of Europe which the Italians regarded as culturally inferior. The Italians of the Renaissance liked to repeat the classical adage that God—or Nature—had placed the Alps as a protecting wall around Italy" (Gilbert 1965, 255). While the current state of the model does not include any geographical discontinuities such as the Alps, regionalism emerges as a result of the territorial extension of the system. A predator surrounded by a ring of defending states, for example, corresponds to a regional security system, provided that it is spa-

---

[30] For critical evaluations of traditional definitions of regional security, see Buzan (1991) and Daase (1993b).

tially distinct from other subsystems. Emphasizing the importance of threat perceptions as the binding "glue," Buzan's definition clearly corresponds to our threat-induced alliances:

> Looked at from the bottom up, security complexes result from interactions between individual states. They represent the way in which the sphere of concern that any state has about its environment, interacts with the linkage between the intensity of military and political threats, and the shortness of the range over which they are perceived. Because threats operate more potently over short distances, security interactions with neighbours will tend to have first priority. (191)

It is the spatial nature of the modeling approach, combined with the emphasis on bounded rationality of a large number of actors, that allows us to recognize the perverse effect of defensive alliances. Models without spatial representation or those based on a hyperrational assumptions about human decisionmaking do not allow for analysis of such ecological patterns.[31]

That there are cases in which leaders have been more successful in anticipating and controlling challenges to the status quo does not necessarily contradict the assumption of the actors' limited foresight. In periods characterized by a small number of great powers, the commitments to regional and global stability coincide. The "Golden Age" of the European balance of power, so masterfully described by A. J. P. Taylor (1954), comes to mind.[32] Due to their small number and wide-ranging spheres of influence compared to the entire system, the self-interest of the major actors tended to coincide with the goal of maintaining global stability. Thus, regional balancing automatically acquires a more global quality as further states are eliminated. The model captures this effect thanks to the endogenous decision scopes of the actors: the larger the territory held by a state, the longer the external border and the more numerous the neighbor relations.

To pick an extreme example, the two objectives necessarily coincide in bipolar systems. Arguing for bipolarity, Waltz (1979) recognizes this effect: "In a bipolar world there are no peripheries. With only two powers

---

[31] The usual objection to the assumption of bounded rationality is that it forces the analyst to impose seemingly arbitrary limits on the calculative capacity of the actors. While it is true that restricting threat perceptions to neighbors implies a certain arbitrariness, the alliance literature lends support to this postulate. Moreover, to assume no limits on the human ability to forecast may appeal to the purism of the rational-expectations enthusiasts, but appears not only unrealistic but even completely misleading. The question is not whether there are perceptual limits, but how to model them in time and space.

[32] Not all observers would agree. In a recent article, Rosecrance (1992) asserts that historians have tended to exaggerate the effectiveness of the balance-of-power mechanism during this period.

capable of acting on a world scale, anything that happens anywhere is potentially of concern to both of them. Bipolarity extends the geographic scope of both powers' concern" (171). He goes on to link this observation to an argument about uncertainty being greater in multipolar systems, making war more likely than under bipolarity. The Emergent Polarity Model produces the same result without making any assumptions about uncertainty.

As in the Italian balance-of-power system, the self-operating logic of the nineteenth-century alliances ended with a disaster: "The First World War discredited the laws both of economics and of politics. The self-operating laws had failed to operate" (Taylor 1954, xx). This "market failure" put an end to centuries of European predominance in world politics and marked the beginning of the political marginalization of the Old World, culminating with the division of the continent during the cold war. Like Italy after the foreign interventions, Europe became both the prize and the potential battlefield in the new power struggle (see Dehio 1962; McNeill 1963; Buzan 1991, 202–09). It would be too speculative to attribute this shift of power uniquely to the existence of a well-functioning alliance system. Other important fragmenting factors intervened, such as the differences in economic growth rates caused by the industrial revolution and the wave of ethnic nationalism that swept over Europe during the nineteenth and early twentieth century. Yet, on a counterfactual note, had defensive alliances not stopped Napoleon and Hitler, Europe might have been more culturally and politically unified than it is today, with important consequences for the global polarity structure.

CONCLUSION

From a methodological standpoint, the Emergent Polarity Model fits well into the growing literature on complex social systems spawned by the ambiguity of the post–cold war era (e.g., Snyder and Jervis 1993; see also Richardson 1991). Instead of elevating theoretical parsimony to the unique goal, these authors emphasize themes such as complexity, non-linear dynamics, feedback loops, and the unintended consequences that result from real-world actors' insufficient capacity to grasp these phenomena. Summarizing this literature, Jack Snyder (1993a) contends that:

> complex systems like the international political systems are hard to understand. Many actors, consequently, think about only the direct effects of their behavior, overlooking feedback and indirect effects. Such failures to think in terms of systemic interconnections produce unintended consequences, many of which exacerbate conflict. (5)

As an effort to adapt realist theory to these concerns, our model provides a contextually richer and more flexible approach than the standard microeconomic analogies associated with neorealism. This explicitly dynamic and spatial reformulation confirms the neorealist expectation of emerging power politics, provided that the competitive pressure is sufficiently high. Refinements of this basic statement are potentially contradictory, at least to the extent that they impair the operation of the "invisible hand." In analogy to protectionist practices and cartels in economic markets, but contrary to the expectation of many realists, both defense dominance and defensive alliances may undermine the power of the laissez-faire interpretation of interstate relations, at least in the long run.[33]

The picture that emerges from the dynamic theory casts doubt on the ambitious, sweeping claims made by many neorealist scholars. Indeed, belief in the "invisible hand" of automatic balancing rests on a number of hidden assumptions that may not be empirically valid or even logically consistent. In particular, the prevalence of power politics depends on an explosive positive-feedback mechanism that might lead either to too little or too much integration for the realist predictions to hold. Because of their focus on a limited number of great powers, realists need to explain not only how these states emerged, but also why this integrative process prevented hegemonic takeoffs.

In the presence of defensive forces emanating from either technology, strategic beliefs, or alliance behavior, power politics does not emerge automatically. This seriously weakens the structuralist proposition that power politics prevails regardless of unit-level motivations, since its explanatory power depends on the irrelevance of predator frequencies. Purely defensive alignments on the regional level may undermine the global balance of power even in the absence of "chain-gangs" and "buck-passing" (Christensen and Snyder 1990). This stability-instability paradox stems from the tendency of states to concentrate on immediate threats to their survival.

The last point has important implications for the current situation in Eastern Europe and the former Soviet Union. The prospects for a successful balance-of-power regime in this part of the world look partic-

---

[33] See also Stephen Van Evera's (1987) thoughtful paper on the conditions under which offense dominance may be stabilizing. While Van Evera carefully separates local from systemic effects, he primarily highlights the value of the offense once the balance has broken down. Note, however, that my argument is stronger than that: not only does it postulate that "market failure" may occur in balance of power systems and that offense is indispensable in recovering from such breakdowns, but also that locally stabilizing defensive mechanisms may sometimes actively undermine such efforts. This paradox thus poses an even more serious challenge to conventional realist interpretations than Van Evera's critique.

ularly bleak: First, the collapse of communist rule opened up the possibility of extremely intense regional conflicts; second, the alignment situation remains extremely fluid, but potentially conflicting regional security complexes are currently building up; third, there are dangerous power asymmetries linked to the enormous difference in size between the smallest republics and Russia proper, fourth, the region having few norms guaranteeing peaceful resolution of conflicts, predatory incentives and behavior are rampant, as illustrated by Serbia's aggressive policy of conquest. Unfortunately, the unclear political situation in Russia does not exclude the possibility of a regime shift leading to aggressive foreign-policy behavior. Although Karl Mueller (1993) stresses the potential threat of Germany more than I would, he is right in asserting that

> the salience of intra-regional threats and territorial disputes poses a serious problem. Potential conflicts within the balance which distract its members from balancing against either Russia or Germany in order to deal with smaller but more severe local threats would make an alignment balance impossible to maintain, and such disputes are currently abundant in eastern Europe. The states in an alignment balance do not have to like or even trust each other, but they do need to fear each other less than they fear the great powers, and reaching this point in eastern Europe will require either a substantial degree of regional conflict resolution or an enormous growth in the apparent threat of Russian or German aggression. (40)

If any general policy lesson can be drawn from this reasoning, it's clearly not that offensive strategies always promote stability. Quite on the contrary, once a geopolitical system has settled, defense dominance is likely to stabilize it even further. To the extent that the proponents of "defensive realism" have this more limited policy perspective in mind, their propositions are consistent with the modeling results.[34] The more fluid historical situations under scrutiny in the present study, however, risk degenerating into unipolarity unless the level of competition is high. Given these complications, it is dangerous to place too much trust in the automaticity of the balance-of-power mechanism. After all, the market analogy is only an analogy, and not necessarily a good one. Notwithstanding the elegance of microeconomic theory, there is no a priori reason why the invisible hand should be expected to operate outside the realm of economics (especially since it does not always operate inside it).[35] Indeed, the model suggests that the automatic balancing mechanism

[34] I thank Jonathan Mercer for clarifying this important distinction.

[35] Traditional economic analysis usually presupposes decreasing returns to scale. Extensions to situations characterized by positive feedback and increasing returns to scale require a dramatically different, more history-dependent approach resembling the current simulation framework (see Arthur 1989, 1990).

may be considerably less foolproof than neorealists claim. Apart from the concert concept (Kupchan and Kupchan 1991), there are considerably less risky and probably more effective alternatives. True, regional security organizations (Ullman 1991), collective security arrangements (Betts 1992), and pluralist security communities (Deutsch et al. 1957) have their drawbacks and constraints, but to argue for a laissez-faire perspective in security affairs because neorealist models "can draw on a large and well-tested body of economic theory" (Gilpin 1981, xi) tends to exaggerate the validity of such models in their own field of application, not to mention their portability to other policy domains.

A more dynamic conception of power politics alerts us against the temptation to reify, or even ignore, regional security arrangements (Buzan 1991). The exclusive focus on three levels of analysis, corresponding to Waltz's (1959) images on the individual, societal, and systemic levels, obscures the intermediate level between the state and the system. The main reason for this omission is probably related to the mistaken belief that regional interdependencies derive exclusively from cooperative structures such as security regimes (see Jervis 1983). Obsessed by the "fact" of anarchy, realists do not believe in any type of international cooperation except for ad hoc alliances. Consequently, they fail to understand that relations of enmity may provide as strong a basis for social structure as friendship and trust do (Simmel 1955; see also Buzan 1991, 218; Daase 1993b, 81). To assume, as Mearsheimer (1990) does, that the boundaries of regional security systems can be taken for granted is likely to yield misleading and even dangerous policy conclusions, especially when applied to fluid settings lacking a clearly crystallized regional structure, as is currently the case in Eastern Europe and the former Soviet republics.

I am not claiming that the CAS framework solves all these conceptual problems. Nevertheless, it does provide a set of valuable tools that facilitate analysis of the sociotemporal phenomena. The simulation model should be seen as an artificial geopolitical world that permits us to perform counterfactual thought experiments that would have been impossible to grasp by verbal theorizing. Used in this way, simulation models are much less vulnerable to the almost ritual accusations of arbitrary specification. Such a critique is misplaced since it expects all social-science models to serve as predictive tools rather than heuristic devices. What matters here are *not* the exact results produced by the model as much as the heuristic insights and hypotheses that it generates. The latter can be understood independently of the technical implementation of the model (cf. fig. 4.11). I have made an effort to convince the reader that they make both theoretical and substantive sense.

Nevertheless, the emphasis on heuristic insights does not exclude the need for more rigorous sensitivity testing. For example, the counterintuitive results pertaining to the influence of defensive alliances may well be reversed under a different specification of the alignment mechanism. Although I randomized some factors such as the initial resource distribution for each replication, many other parameters and rules are hard-wired into the model. Therefore, the exact results should be interpreted with caution. The next chapter attempts to increase the robustness of our findings.

CHAPTER 5

Extending the Emergent Polarity Model

INTRODUCTION

The purpose of this chapter is to extend and check the robustness of the Emergent Polarity Model. While the previous chapter explored some key variables, the open-ended nature of CAS modeling invites further exploration. In doing so, we emphasize the importance of sensitivity and robustness-checking in simulation work. The main idea is thus to investigate whether the results hold up when different, more realistic, mechanisms are added. In order to study as many extensions as possible, the current exposition is briefer and more technical than that of the previous chapter. The less technically inclined reader may therefore prefer to skip the entire chapter.

SIMPLIFYING THE ALLIANCE MECHANISM: POWER BALANCING

We have already tested the influence of alliances on state formation and shown, surprisingly enough, that that particular alliance mechanism undermined the prospects of power politics. Instead of generating bi- or multipolar systems, unipolarity or large polarity followed when defensive alliances were added. The specific simulation result, however, hinges on the particular implementation, including the rather involved notion of trust indexes. How sensitive is the finding to changes in the particular specification of alliance formation?

To investigate this issue, rather than keeping track of a behavioral trust score, we will here use information about neighboring states' strategies and resource levels.[1] This formulation, which we could label power balancing, comes even closer to Steven Walt's (1987) balance-of-threat theory, for here threat is defined directly in terms of aggregate power, geographic proximity, offensive power, and aggressive intentions.

The current extension focuses on the "perception of threat" module in

---

[1] In all runs involving the extended versions of the Emergent Polarity Models, the same basic parameters were used as previously. The only change, except for those associated with the respective extensions, pertained to the laws of interaction. To prepare the ground for the PRA mechanism described below, the experiments were run without resource differences in the CD and DC exchanges (e.g., the entries in the corresponding boxes were 0,0 in fig. 4.8). Tests indicated that this change did not alter the results in any significant way.

figure 4.9, thus leaving the actual implementation of the alliances un-changed (cf. the alliance-formation phase in the same figure). In each period, the states scan their potentially threatening geopolitical neighbors, calculating a trust score that is the negative ratio between each neighbor's resource level and their own. The current mechanism assumes that each actor is able to observe the neighbors' strategic orientation. Thus all ac-tors, whether predators or prey, consider balancing against predator states only. Prey states are never seen as threatening regardless of their strength. States under attack count any attacking as an immediate, rather than po-tential, threat, and always balance against such threats before potential ones are considered. Once having listed all potential and direct threats, the most serious one is singled out as the prime threat. If this threat is sufficiently serious, the state signals interest in forming an alliance against the threatening state.

More formally, the trust score $T(i, j)$ of state i with neighboring preda-tor j is calculated as:

$$T(i, j) = - R(j)/R(i), \qquad [5.1]$$

where R stands for the total resource level of each actor.[2] The threat to balance against $j*$ is the one that minimizes $T(i, j)$, provided that $T(i, j*) < T_{min}$, where T_{min} stands for a predefined trust level over which alliance formation never takes place.

To illustrate this simple mechanism, suppose that there are four states: $R(1) = 10$, $R(2) = 25$, $R(3) = 35$, and $R(4) = 40$. Assume further that all actors, except for state 4, are predators and that $T_{min} = -3$. What is the state 1's prime threat? First, the trust scores must be evaluated:

$$T(1, 2) = - R(2)/R(1) = - 25/10 = -2.5,$$
$$T(1, 3) = - R(3)/R(1) = - 35/10 = -3.5.$$

Note that although state 4 is the strongest actor, its resource level does not enter the calculation because it is a nonthreatening prey state. Of the two threatening states, it is state 3 that minimizes the trust score. Since $T(1, 3) = -3.5 < -3 = T_{min}$, there is a prime threat. Had state 3 not been a neighbor of state 1, $T(1, 2)$ would have been insufficiently nega-tive to ensure balancing behavior against state 2. Suppose, however, that there had been combat between states 1 and 2. In that case, $T(1, 2) = -100 - 2.5 = -102.5$, which would have made state 2 a prime threat regardless of state 3's presence. Combat with both states 2 and 3, on the

---

[2] If j is already attacking i, $T(i, j) = -100 - R(j)/R(i)$, which ensures that direct threats are taken much more seriously than others.

other hand, would have made the trust score with State 3, $T(1, 3) = -100 - 3.5 = -103.5$, the lowest.

In other words, T_{min} controls the sensitivity of the alliance mechanism. A lower threshold (i.e. a more negative one) requires a lower trust score, and thus a more drastic resource ratio, to trigger alliance formation. At $T_{min} = -1$, the states align themselves against predatory neighbors that are about as strong as they are. This is the value used in the first series of runs, the result of which is displayed in figure 5.1. According to the diagrams, unipolar and massively multipolar outcomes again dominate almost all parameter combinations. A comparison with figure 4.13 reveals that, for this value of T_{min}, there are very few differences between the two alliance mechanisms. In the defense-dominated system, power politics is somewhat more common with power balancing than with behavioral alliances, but unipolarity continues to dominate the lower polarity outcomes except for very high predator frequencies.

What happens if the alliance mechanism were less sensitive? Figure 5.2 reports on runs in which the minimum threat has been increased to $T_{min} = -1.5$—that is the threatening predators need to be one and a half times as powerful to trigger counterbalancing. As would be expected, once alignments are delayed, power politics becomes more common. In the defense-dominated system, bipolarity and low-level multipolarity oc-

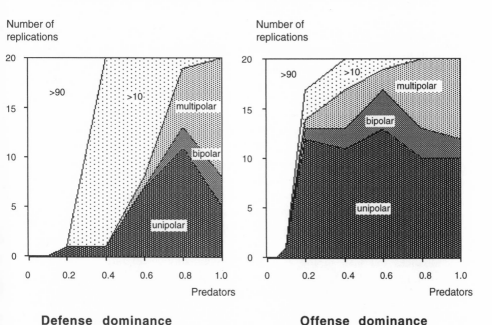

Defense dominance   **Offense dominance**

Figure 5.1. Emergent polarity with power balancing

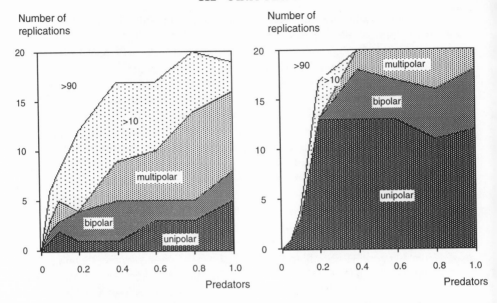

Defense dominance   **Offense dominance**

Figure 5.2. Emergent polarity with retarded power balancing

cur even for modest predator frequencies. In the offense-dominated setting, the domain of power politics is also expanded. Still, a comparison
with the nonalliance cases (cf. fig. 4.11) suggests that the impact of the
revised alliance mechanism points in the same direction as the behavioral
one. Alliances make unipolar and massively multipolar outcomes more
frequent than in their absence.

In sum, the alternative implementation of alliances should increase our
confidence in the qualitative lesson already drawn. Contrary to the expectations of mainstream realist scholarship, coalition formation may in fact
undermine the formation of balance-of-power systems rather than support it.

STRATEGIC ADAPTATION

The simplified threat definition proves useful not only in the context of
alliances but also in the analysis of socialization. So far, it has been
assumed that the agents' behavioral characteristics never change. Once
born prey, a state retains its strategic orientation regardless of its geopolitical environment. This behavioral invariance is, of course, both unrealistic and theoretically impoverished, for states anticipate future interactions and adapt their strategies to these expectations.

Fortunately, the CAS approach renders an extension along these lines possible (e.g., Axelrod 1986).[3] Before turning to this elaboration of the model, a few distinctions should be made. Simple behavioral adaptation of the type studied here belongs to the wider category of socialization. Although notoriously understudied, this class of phenomena is receiving increasing attention from International Relations scholars, especially as new states are incorporated into the international system following the collapse of communism (Ikenberry and Kupchan 1990; Schimmelfennig 1994). As opposed to selection, which operates through physical elimination of unsuccessful units, socialization involves "internationalization of institutionalized cognitive and behavioral modes" (Schimmelfennig 1994, 337, my trans.). Thus change is occurring inside the agents through some type of learning process rather than due to external ecological mechanisms such as competition.[4]

While socialization can take many forms, some of which involve comprehensive reconceptualizations affecting identities and worldviews (e.g., Nye 1987; Ikenberry and Kupchan 1990), the current focus is much more limited, evaluating realist propositions as in the previous chapter. Even a pure neorealist approach to social learning relies on some type of adaptation. Despite the brevity of his discussion, Waltz (1979) refers explicitly to both competition and socialization as two crucial microlevel processes supporting the structural logic of neorealism:

> What does rationality mean? It means only that some do better than others—whether through intelligence, skill, hard work, or dumb luck. They succeed in providing a wanted good or service more attractively and more cheaply than others do. Either their competitors emulate them or they fall by the wayside. The demand for their product shrinks, their profits fall, and ultimately they go bankrupt. To break this unwanted chain of events, they must change their ways. And thus the units that survive come to look like one another. (76–77)

The classical formulation of the security dilemma stresses the importance of geopolitical learning (Herz 1950; Jervis 1978). According to Robert Gilpin (1981), "a state is compelled within the anarchic and competitive conditions of international relations to expand its power and attempt to extend its control over the international system. If the state fails to make this attempt, it risks the possibility that other states will increase their relative power positions and will thereby place its existence in jeopardy" (86).

---

[3] The addition of strategic adaptation, albeit on a simple level, makes the system's adaptive quality more agent based.

[4] On the difference between social and biological evolution, see Harré (1979).

Thus, in this narrow sense, "socialization" can be seen as a complementary process sustaining anarchic conditions in a geopolitical system regardless of the original predatory orientation of its actors. Alexander Wendt (1992) lucidly explains why strategic adaptation sustains the security dilemma:

> For whatever reasons—biology, domestic politics, or systemic victimization—some states may become predisposed toward aggression. The aggressive behavior of these predators or "bad apples" forces other states to engage in competitive power politics, to meet fire with fire, since failure to do so may degrade or destroy them. One predator will best a hundred pacifists because anarchy provides no guarantees. (407)

Very few additions are needed to implement this "bad apple" argument in the modeling framework. Suppose that instead of forming an alliance as a response to threats, states change their own strategies in order to prepare for the worst. This requires a third strategic category, conditional predation, in addition to the pure prey and predator states. While predators always remain strategically invariant, prey states may switch to conditional predation should they feel threatened. Moreover, unthreatened conditional predators sometimes switch back to prey behavior. Two probabilities govern these adaptational changes: p indicates the likelihood (per time period) of a threatened prey state switching to conditional predation; q stands for the probability of the reverse process. Recall that $T_{\min}$ tunes the sensitivity of the threat mechanism. Thus, a state i is threatened if and only if there is no neighboring state j such that $T(i, j) < T_{\min}$. Again potential candidates for switching consider threats from predators and conditional predatory states only.

To illustrate the adaptation mechanism, I base the simulations on the defense-dominated system shown in the left panel of figure 4.11, because in that example the likelihood of power politics emerging depended strongly on the initial predator frequency. Especially for lower predator densities (say below 20 percent), unipolarity or massive multipolarity dominate. The question is whether adaptation manages to compensate for the lower level of competition in the defense-dominated system, making the occurrence of power politics less dependent on the offense-defense balance.

Figure 5.3 illustrates the effect of two adaptation mechanisms, the left panel corresponding to a weaker version and the right panel to a stronger one. In both cases, the simulations assume the same threat threshold as in figure 5.1, that is $T_{\min} = -1$, or simply parity. Here the x-axis indicates the pure predators' share of the initial population. The remaining states were all prey states to begin with, although many ended up shifting to conditional predation in the course of the simulation. In the weaker case,

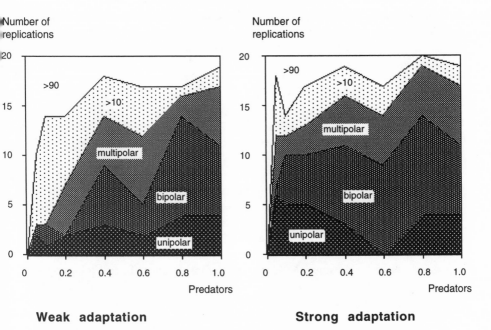

Figure 5.3. Strategic adaptation

$p = 0.5$ and $q = 0.01$, which means that there the chance of a prey state shifting strategic attitude per time step is 0.5, and 0.01 the likelihood of it changing back to prey behavior. The great asymmetry between the two probabilities reflects strategic caution: it usually takes longer to regain confidence in one's environment than becoming suspicious in the first place. The right panel displays a system with powerful and unremitting adaptation: $p = 1$ and $q = 0$. Strategic learning could not be more powerful; here the prey states immediately abandon their prey attitude and shift to predation, a strategic orientation they never abandon. This more abrupt scheme in fact goes beyond conditional predation in that the learning experience becomes permanent.

One would expect the wedgelike, predation-dependent shape of the outcomes associated with power politics (e.g., bipolarity and multipolarity) to be less narrow for low initial predator rates. A comparison with the defense-dominated system in figure 4.11 shows that the effects of both adaptation mechanisms are evident, though the right panel contains clearer evidence of this. In both cases, the power politics "wedge" is less pointed and covers more of the x-axis, thus indicating less sensitivity to the initial predator density. Special attention should be paid to the low predator frequencies since structural realism assumes power politics to follow even in such cases. This seems to be the case, for in the left panel the domain of power politics extends into the below-20-percent predator area, though only to a limited extent. Likewise, the frequency of unipolar outcomes has also gone down in the case of weak adaptation, thus reinforcing the trend in favor of geopolitical balancing. A similar, but more evident phenomenon is present in the right graph. With more powerful adaptation, a few bad apples have a tendency to generate power politics in many cases (roughly a third below 20 percent predation). Clearly, adaptation reinforces the competition mechanism by making power politics more likely.

It should be recalled that the threat mechanism presupposes that the adapting actors possess perfect information of neighboring states' strategies. Thus prey states are never perceived as threats unless they abandon their behavioral orientation conditionally. In reality, such ideal information conditions are of course rare. Realizing this, Jervis (1978) has argued that the security dilemma becomes even more severe if offensive orientations cannot be distinguished from the defensive ones. To test this proposition about "strategic blurring" within the current framework, I made the prey states respond to threatening resource balances regardless of their neighbors' strategy. This modified configuration comes very close to the classical realist stance downplaying intention while putting the stress on power resources. Indeed, this position makes more sense in a system in which the neighbors' behavioral status may shift as a consequence of adaptation.

Illustrating the influence of this elaboration, figure 5.4 displays the results of two new sets of runs, differing from those in figure 5.3 except for the addition of strategic blurring. Surprisingly enough, power politics becomes even more common under these conditions. The left panel, again representing weaker learning, now features bi- or multipolarity in at least a third of the cases for low initial predation. The bad-apple contagion is even more impressive for this strong adaptational mechanism: here more than half of the outcomes fall into the category of power politics. Indeed, due to the almost perfect stretching out of the wedge shape into a uniform, horizontal area, these runs closely resemble the offense-dominated system in figure 4.11.

In conformance with neorealist expectations, threat-induced strategic adaptation reinforces the systemic invariance by boosting predatorial behavior. This effect becomes even more pronounced if strategic separation is impossible. While Jervis's (1978) conclusions concerning the instability of such doubly insecure worlds make sense in a static perspective, adding a dynamic dimension underlines the crucial dynamic role played by the security dilemma as it is expressed through adaptation and strategic blurring. In the absence of these offense-promoting mechanisms,

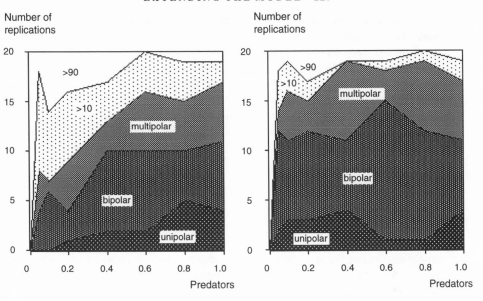

Weak adaptation   **Strong adaptation**

Figure 5.4. Adaptation in a context of strategic blurring

power politics becomes more dependent on the initial predator frequency, at least for defensively oriented systems. This undermines the theoretical power of structural realism. As pointed out in the previous chapter, it is far from obvious what to make of "defensive realism," at least from a long-term historical perspective. While one may deplore the security dilemma, taming it is easier said than done, for without it traditional power politics might not have emerged in the first place. Counterfactual cotenability of the desired pluralist scenario seems to hinge upon unsavory aspects of geopolitical competition.

PROPORTIONAL RESOURCE ALLOCATION

In the basic version of the Emergent Polarity Model, resource allocation follows a particularly simple logic. Each state divides its total resources by the number of neighboring states and allocates an equal share to each front regardless of their neighbors' behavior or resource endowment. It goes without saying that this is not a terribly realistic rule of resource allocation. Would the findings change with the introduction of a more realistic scheme that takes the strength and activities of nearby states into account?

To answer this question, we need a more refined mechanism of Proportional Resource Allocation (PRA). According to this scheme, states earmark forces proportional to their neighbors' mobilization while paying close attention to each front's status. If combat occurred in the previous time period, the front is active, otherwise it is passive. For every time step, a state i announces how many resources $r(i,j)$ it *could* commit to each front j in case of an attack, the combat status of other fronts being unchanged. There are two cases. If the front is active, the state sets off resources in proportion to the relative resistance encountered on this front:

$$r_{\text{new}}\,(i,j) = \frac{r(j,i)}{\sum_k r(k,i)}\,R(i) \qquad\qquad [5.2]$$

where the nonindexed right-hand side pertains to variables of the previous period, $R(i)$ denoting the total resources to be distributed, $r(j, i)$ the resource allocation of neighboring state j against state i, and $\sum_k r(k,i)$ the sum of all resources currently targeted against state i in combat. Obviously, if j is the only active front, the ratio is one, implying that all resources $R(i)$ go to this front.

If the front is passive, however, the calculation indicates the resource level to be allocated, should the front become active. This is done by computing the following quantity:

$$r_{\text{new}}\,(i,j) = \frac{r(j,i)}{r(j,i) + \sum_k r(k,i)}\,R(i). \qquad\qquad [5.3]$$

Here the enemy's resources $r(j,i)$, expected to be mobilized to prepare for the attack, have been added to the dominator.

In sum, the rule lets each state allocate resources to a front in proportion to the share of the enemies' allocations to that particular front. The rule seems more complicated than it is. An example helps clarify its logic. Figure 5.5 presents a simple geopolitical system with four states: i, j, k, and l with total resources 10, 30, 20, and 40 respectively. The resource allocations are indicated along each border—that is, state i allocates 10 resource units to each front, etc.

Assuming that there is no conflict at time 1, equation 5.3 suggests that each state is ready to devote all of its resources to both their fronts. For example, $r(i,j) = 30/(30+0) \times 10$. If states k and l start fighting, however, the resource levels must be recomputed as indicated by the second panel. At time 2, both states continue to allocate all their resources, that

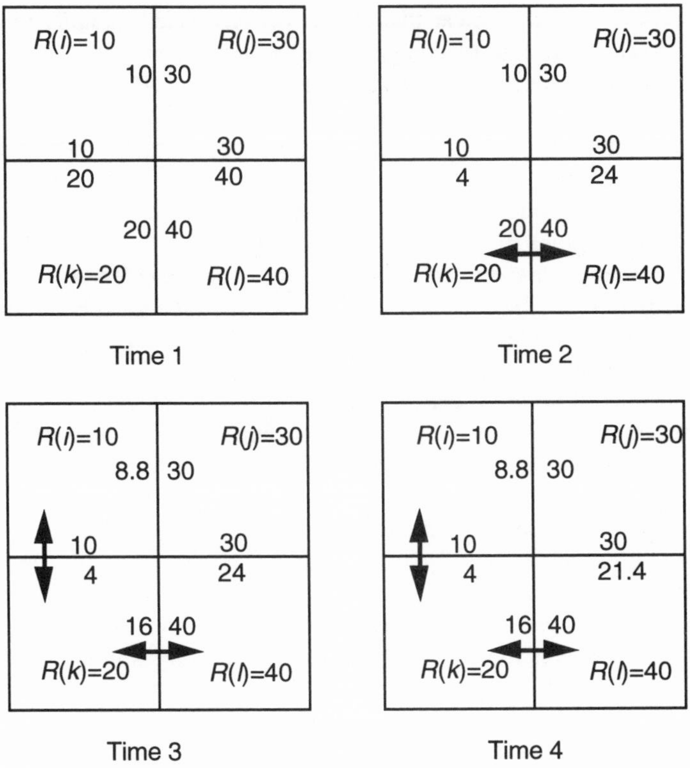

$R(i)=10$ 10|30	$R(j)=30$
10	30
20	40
20|40	
$R(k)=20$	$R(l)=40$

Time 1

$R(i)=10$ 10|30	$R(j)=30$
10	30
4	24
20|40	
$R(k)=20$	$R(l)=40$

Time 2

$R(i)=10$ 8.8|30	$R(j)=30$
10	30
4	24
16|40	
$R(k)=20$	$R(l)=40$

Time 3

$R(i)=10$ 8.8|30	$R(j)=30$
10	30
4	21.4
16|40	
$R(k)=20$	$R(l)=40$

Time 4

Figure 5.5. An example of proportional resource allocation

is 20 and 40 respectively, but they must revise the resources to be diverted to a second front should fighting break out there:

$$r(k,i) = 10 \ / \ (10+40) \times 20 = 4,$$
$$r(l,j) = 30 \ / \ (20+30) \times 40 = 24.$$

If fighting erupts between states i and k as well, state k must reallocate some of its resources from the front with state l. Instead of using all its resources on that front, it can only use:

$$r(k,l) = 40 \ / \ (10+40) \times 20 = 16.$$

As a consequence of this adjustment, in the following run (i.e., time period 4), state l is ready to devote more resources to its front with state j:

$$r(l,j) = 30 \ / \ (16+40) \times 40 = 21.4.$$

By now it should be clear that changes reverberate gradually through-out the system. In case of conquest, the invading party inherits the previous, external resource levels of the conquered state. By the same token, a newly independent unit allocates its entire resource level to all fronts.

Once having implemented PRA, the next step is to let the predators' decision to engage in unprovoked attacks hinge upon the front-related resource levels r rather than on the overall resources R. The latter was the case in the original Emergent Polarity Model. With the new behavioral criterion, a predator state i computes the power ratio $\rho(i,j) = r(i,j)/r(j,i)$ for all neighbors j, singling out the state j^* for which the ratio is minimized. If the ratio falls under the superiority threshold (governing the defense/offense dominance of the system), combat follows.

The results of all these changes appear in figure 5.6. As can be readily seen, the modification introduced by PRA and localized decision criteria have little impact on the general findings about offense and defense dom-inance (cf. fig. 4.11). Again, power politics becomes less common as the system turns more defense oriented. Moreover, a truly offense-dominated system approximates the structural invariance of power politics hypothe-sized by neorealists.

Whatever the overall robustness of the discovery concerning defense dominance, it seems to be resistant to important changes in the scheme of

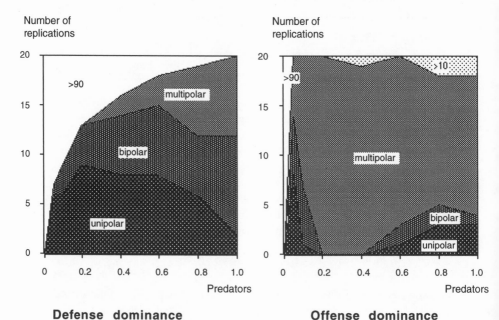

Figure 5.6. Emergent polarity with PRA

resource allocation and decision-making. The new simulation results resemble the previous ones closely, something that should give us more confidence in the general argument about defense orientation. This is an important finding because, at least in theory, PRA should make hegemonic takeoffs more difficult, especially to the extent that aggressive states become embroiled in continuous fighting on many fronts. That this did not happen is significant, thus suggesting that the monopolistic tendencies in defense-dominated systems are not necessarily an artifact of any specific resource-mobilization process.[5]

TWO-LEVEL ACTION

The current formulation of the Emergent Polarity Model presumes that conquest automatically produces great gains for the conqueror and that only external pressure can undermine states. While this idealization to some extent approximates the period of absolutism in early modern Europe, it is much less applicable to systems in which state penetration is comparably weak, as in feudal Europe (e.g., Ruggie 1983, 1993; Tilly 1990) or today's Third World (Jackson 1990). Settings characterized by high state penetration but requiring consent of the subject population also fall outside the domain of applicability. Thus, under more realistic conditions, the internal consolidation of states proceeds in a less straightforward manner than so far assumed by the Emergent Polarity Model.

If the center cannot rely on automatic support from the periphery, revolts become a serious possibility, thus producing a cyclical pattern of integration and disintegration rather than the largely unidirectional contraction traced in the original version of the Emergent Polarity Model. While that framework offers examples of imperial collapses, these are always externally induced (cf. fig. 4.5). Yet the disintegration of the Soviet Union and Yugoslavia, like so many other historical cases of geopolitical fragmentation, happened without direct intervention of external power. Sovereignty has both an internal and an external component (Bull 1977), but we focused entirely on the latter for tractability reasons. Here we extend the Emergent Polarity Model by adding the possibility of "domestic" collective action leading to secession.

Incorporating internally induced disintegration promises to uncover in-

---

[5] Note that it does not follow that alliances within the modified PRA framework still yield unipolar and massively multipolar outcomes, for the monopolistic tendencies previously observed presuppose that a hegemon remains unaffected by the multiplication of active fronts. This is, however, precisely what defensive alignments provide. Preliminary runs confirm that the previous findings related to alliances are probably dependent on resource allocation in a nontrivial way.

teresting nonlinear processes. Even a superficial look at the historical record suggests that revolutions and interstate wars tend to appear together, a pattern that is hardly due to chance. It is often forgotten that state building entails the double task of internal pacification and external territorial defense (e.g., Tilly 1985, 184–86; see also Rasler and Thompson 1989, esp. 11; Levy 1989b). Threats to sovereignty in one of these domains often spill over into the other. The rebellion of one province could invite other provinces and external enemies to join the attacks on the center, thus creating a self-feeding process leading to serious crisis and possible collapse. For example, the Spanish attempt to thwart the tax rebellion of the Dutch provinces in the Eighty Years' War led to resource depletion that created an opportunity for Catalonia and Portugal to break from the Castilian monarchy (Downing 1992, 221). The Habsburg monarchy faced a similar dilemma as it came under attack by Prussia and Piedmont in 1866. In this situation, it had no choice but to placate the Hungarians through the transformation of the Empire into the dual monarchy in 1867 (Taylor 1948). The Russian revolutions in 1905 and 1917 were also in part facilitated by the external weakening of the Tsarist regime (Szporluk 1990, 11).

It is not only the question of parsimony that has discouraged researchers from studying the interaction between domestic and interstate phenomena. Their focus on states as unitary actors, and on equilibrium conditions in balance-of-power systems, have long prevented realists from considering the possibility of political-disintegration processes. The end of the cold war has shed embarrassing light on this theoretical bias (Collins 1995).

Yet the difficulties of conceptualizing two-level action should not be underestimated. Because of the considerable complexity incurred by such an elaboration, there are few examples of formal models exemplifying what Putnam (1988) calls reverberation, that is bidirectional interaction between the domestic and the interstate levels. Game theorists have striven to formalize Putnam's metaphorical recommendations (e.g., Iida 1991). In simulation literature, there are even fewer attempts to capture true two-level interactions. Building on Bremer and Mihalka's (1977) seminal simulations Cusack and Stoll (1990) implemented a civil-war extension within their geopolitical-simulation framework. The elaboration, however, complicated their analysis to such an extent that only limited experiments were carried out.

Fortunately, the Emergent Polarity Model invites a comparatively easy incorporation of two-level action. First, the decision-making mechanism must be modified in order to allow subordinated provinces to stage revolts within states. Second, in order to model taxation and the consequences of civil war, resource transfers between the center and provinces need to be modeled explicitly.

Since the model architecture treats all relations, whether interstate or intrastate, the same way, extending action from the former to the latter realm is straightforward.[6] In the Emergent Polarity Model, each sovereign state periodically scans its "diplomatic portfolio," which contains a record of all neighboring states. The extended model adds the state's provinces (if any) to this portfolio. Dominated provinces, by contrast, only have one relationship in their portfolio, namely the asymmetric one with the center.[7]

Although the basic structure of domestic exchanges correspond to "foreign" relations, the particular parameters and strategies governing domestic and interstate interactions differ. Each province can thus be seen as a predator contemplating an attack on the center as soon as the periphery-center power balance allows. The center, on the other hand, plays a simple defensive tit-for-tat strategy. In case of an attack, it always responds by defending its internal sovereignty through combat. Civil war follows the same rules as interstate military action. While the result of successful revolts is secession, the rebellious province remains within the state in case of military failure.

Before studying the results of these extensions, a more detailed description is necessary. Figure 5.7 explains the behavioral strategies in terms of pseudocode. The center's rule is not very different from the version defined by figure 4.7. The most important differences pertain to the loops, which now include both sovereign neighbors and the own provinces. Predators consider unprovoked attacks against other states but never the regions. Note that the decision criterion use local, front-related resources r rather than total ones R, all according to the PRA scheme. This is of particular importance in the two-level setting, because the center is forced to mobilize internal as well as external fronts. Moreover, center-periphery conflict may delay the decision of predator states to launch unprovoked attacks abroad.

The provinces' decision rule is even simpler. Here there is no need to scan the relational portfolio since these subordinated actors only interact with the center. In addition to continuing combat once it has started, a provincial actor considers an unprovoked attack should the domestic superiority ratio be favorable. Since there is only one front, all of the province's resources can be used for this purpose.[8]

The laws of combat correspond closely to those stipulated for interstate conflict. In the case of civil war, a domestic-victory ratio, which may or

---

[6] By contrast, Cusack and Stoll (1990) add civil wars as a separate module.

[7] This is obviously a radical simplification compared to actual historical situations. In reality, civil war often involves conflict among provinces as well as between provinces and external actors (cf. Kratochwil 1986).

[8] This formulation overlooks that many rebellions in the premodern world were motivated by excessive taxation and scarce food supply (e.g., Ardant 1975, 167).

Center

for each sovereign neighbor or subordinated province j,
　　if j played D in the previous period **then**
　　　　Play D (respond to internal or external challenges to sovereignty)
　　else
　　　　Play C (Tit For Tat)

if i is a predator **and** there is no action on any foreign or domestic front **then**
　　look for the weakest sovereign neighbor j^*
　　if $r(i,j^*)/r(j^*,i) > $ superiority_ratio **then**
　　　　Randomly select own agent province and target in j^*
　　　　Play D (i.e., launch unprovoked attack against j^*)

for each sovereign neighbor or subordinated province j,
　　Allocate $r(i,j)$ to front j

Province

if the center j played D in the previous period **then**
　　Play D
else
　　if $R(i)/r(j,i) > $ domestic_superiority_ratio **then**
　　　　Play D (i.e., revolt against the center)
　　else
　　　　Play C

Allocate $R(i)$ to the revolutionary front

Figure 5.7. The decision phase

may not be the same its interstate counterpart, determines which side will prevail. For the purpose of the current simulation experiments, however, it is assumed that the laws of combat coincide in both cases.

As indicated above, the current extension also features a tax mechanism, which governs the transfer of resources between the center and the periphery. Recall that the basic version of the Emergent Polarity Model automatically transferred resources from newly conquered states to the conquering center. In the new version, the center is free to levy a tax on its subordinated regions, which is subject to experimental manipulation and analysis. Nevertheless, the provinces retain their own resources after conquest, although they lose parts of them through taxation.

To be precise, the tax is drawn as a given share from the province's "harvest" in each period, whether this income is negative or positive. This means that the center may gain or lose from its tax imposition, although the gains will be more important in the long run as long as the harvest mechanism's average is positive. If the province does not dispose of any resources, however, the center receives nothing.

What consequences do these alterations generate? We start by analyzing emergent polarity as a function of the tax rate. The current runs are based on the offense-dominated system with PRA from figure 5.6. In order to implement two-level action, the domestic-superiority ratio governing the occurrence of secessionist attempts is set to the same value as the external ratio—that is, two. The internal-victory ratio also coincides with its domestic counterpart, which also has the value two. This means that secessionist collective action against the center will only take place if the province is able to ensure twice the resources allocated to their common, internal front.

Given this specification, figure 5.8 reports on polarity for different tax rates. All simulations took place in purely predatorial systems (i.e., the initial predator rate was 100 percent), so the x-axis no longer represents initial predator frequency but the tax rate. Thus, at left end of the axis, the rate comes close to the automatic resource transfer in the one-level version of the system. As would thus be expected, the 100-percent-tax outcomes closely resemble the 100-percent-predator runs at the end of the x-axis in figure 5.6. In these situations there is an almost complete dominance of multipolar systems.

The main finding is that power politics appear to depend positively on the tax rate. In systems characterized by less pronounced "fiscal" centralization, unipolarity becomes more frequent. As the tax rate decreases, massively multipolar outcomes also gain in importance. Below a tax rate of 20 percent, power politics never occur, and below 10 percent the system does not converge to low-level polarity at all (at least not within one thousand time periods).

These findings fit nicely into our discussion of hegemonic takeoffs. In order for this phenomenon to occur, it must pay to conquer. The automatic and complete resource transfers following conquest ensure that this is the case. Figure 5.8 shows that if this positive-feedback mechanism slows down, power politics will not ensue, since the emergence of balancing is dependent on uninhibited predatory resource accumulation. Thus varying the tax rate reinforces the general point that traditional balance of power outcomes require a high degree of geopolitical competition. Indeed, interstate competition depends crucially on mechanisms internal to states. Thus, even structural realists rely on an implicit model of domestic resource distribution when they hypothesize that anarchy generates power politics (Liberman 1993).

Figure 5.8 also conforms a general point made in the literature on state formation. In his useful historical analysis of taxation policies, Gabriel Ardant (1975) underlines the central role played by tax collection in the emergence of the state system in early modern Europe. Given the extractive capacity of the modern state, it is tempting to take a high level of resource accumulation for granted: "We cannot understand the history of the state if we are not convinced of the idea that taxation is a very diffi-

Number of
replications

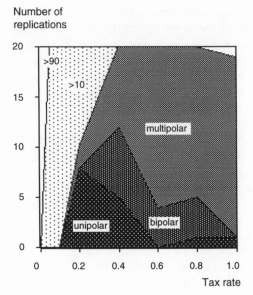

Figure 5.8. Emergent polarity as a function of the tax rate

cult operation, even under a good administration, and that this difficulty
has always weighted heavily upon the state" (165). In sum, efficient taxation may be a necessary condition of power politics. This might explain
why balancing failed to emerge in many non-European areas characterized by lower administrative efficiency than that associated with early
modern Europe.

AN EXAMPLE OF GEOPOLITICAL OVEREXTENSION

While the runs of the previous section are of theoretical interest, they do
not exploit the full power of the new specification. Because of the deterministic decision criterion, secession almost never takes place. Moreover,
taxation is unrealistically uniform, regardless of the distance between the
centers and their provinces. We can attempt to rectify these shortcomings
by introducing two changes. First, both decision-making and combat feature a probabilistic component, not unlike Clausewitz's famous remarks
about the fog of war. Second, the center's resource extraction declines
according to a distance gradient, thus emphasizing the difficulties of controlling far-flung territories.

To begin with the first modification, the predator states' and secessionist provinces' decisions to engage in combat follow a stochastic step

function. So far, the simulations have relied on a perfect knife-edge threshold criterion. This section uses a less abrupt curve, as indicated in figure 5.9. The graph plots a potential aggressors i probability of attacking another actor j as a function of the front-specific power balance $\rho(i, j)$ $= r(i,j)/r(j,i)$. As opposed to the previous criterion, which depended on a vertical step at the superiority ratio (the dashed line in the figure), the new function increases more gradually, reaching its steepest slope for the threshold value. Thus, already at a resource ratio of two, there is a 10 percent chance that the actor in question will launch an unprovoked attack. On the other hand, military action does not become inevitable except for rather high power ratios. The probability passes the 90 percent threshold when the attacker gains four times the power of its potential victim.

Mathematically, a logistic function captures the modified rule well. Suppose that the resource balance is $\rho(i,j)$, ρ_0 the threshold value (i.e., the superiority ratio) and c a tunable parameter determining the step's slope; then the probability of action takes the following form:

$$\Pr(\rho(i,j)) = \frac{1}{1 + \{\rho(i,j)/\rho_0\}^{-c}}.$$

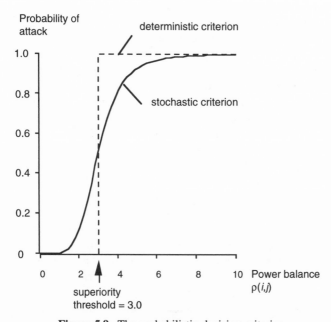

Figure 5.9. The probabilistic decision criterion

To generate the curve shown in figure 5.9, the threshold ρ_0 was set to three and the slope parameter c to five. The deterministic function corresponding to the dashed line can be obtained by letting c go to infinity. In chapters 7 and 8, we will offer a further discussion of, and substantive rationale for, this logistical function.

Note that the simulation experiments below feature not only probabilistic decision rules, but also similarly stochastic combat criteria based on exactly the same function (cf. figure 5.9). Thus, on average, an actor prevails if its field superiority surpasses the victory ratio, but since the mechanism is stochastic, victory may sometimes happen earlier or later than this threshold suggests. In practice, this means that both domestic and interstate warfare become less predictable in terms of their outcomes and often longer lasting, especially if action is triggered in the left tail of the decision function. In some cases, new fronts may open, decisively weakening the aggressor, leading to military defeat.

Having specified new decision and combat rules, it is time to turn to taxation. The experiments of the previous section employed a flat, universal tax drawn from each province's periodic harvest. To capture the logistical constraints on real geopolitical systems, the new version of the model lets the state capitals' resource extraction decrease with increasing distance to the province in question. The literature on logistical constraints is rich, and there is no need to provide a review here. Suffice it to recall Michael Mann's (1986) analysis of organizational factors in state formation, such as control, logistics, and communication. The transaction-cost literature also emphasizes the costs associated with tax collection and resource extraction in vast territories (cf. North 1981; Levi 1988). These factors do not only depend on material influences related to transportation cost, but also less tangible ones such as the loyalty of the dominated population. Ethnic fragmentation, for example, often constitutes an insurmountable obstacle to political communication and control (cf. references in Tilly 1975). For example, Bean (1973) observes that "language, religious and racial barriers and regional particularism increase the cost of administration and control" (204; see also Cederman 1996a for a simple model).

There are an infinite number of ways to implement distance dependence in the formal framework. Cusack and Stoll (1990, 73) use a rather complicated exponential function that also factors in the duration of domination. The current extension introduces a similar, though slightly simpler solution. For every unit's distance from the center, the tax contribution declines by a given fraction. The simulation runs, to follow below, feature a discount rate of 0.7, which means that provinces at one unit's distance from the center pay 70 percent of the nominal tax rate, and those at two units' distance pay $0.7 \times 0.7 = 49$ percent, etc. More precisely, given a discount rate of s and a nominal tax of τ_0, the tax rate of a province d units away from the center can be computed as:

$$\tau(d) = \tau_0 s^d$$

Figure 5.10 demonstrates the function, with the current parameter values $s = 0.7$ and $\tau_0 = 0.4$. As can be readily seen, the effectiveness of resource extraction declines rapidly for remote provinces.

Due to the model's increased complexity, the investigation of the extended system must be limited to illustrative runs. With the probabilistic criterion and the possibility of disintegration, the geopolitical system does not necessarily settle in the long run, as it did previously. Instead, geopolitical cycles of limited duration emerge. These regimes are interrupted periodically by crises, such as wars and revolutions, that undermine the stability of the geopolitical system.

As an illustration of the new features, we can trace one particular run for a duration of more than one thousand periods. Again, the simulation starts with a ten-by-ten grid. Unlike the earlier experiments, however, the initial contraction phase gives way to a more open-ended, periodically evolving historical trajectory. Figure 5.11 illustrates this behavior graphically for one particular period. The diagram plots the territorial size of the units over time. This temporal window exemplifies a double imperial

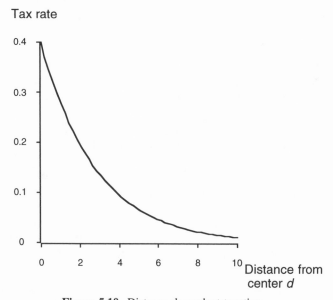

Figure 5.10. Distance-dependent taxation

Territorial size

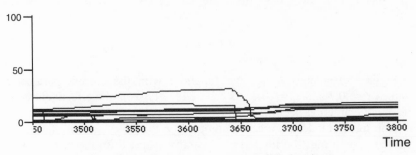

Figure 5.11. The emergence of geopolitical regimes

collapse. At the beginning of the recording, the system is unipolar. After about time period 3500, a challenger appears, creating a temporary bipolar regime. Decline affects this state at about time 3600, however, and about forty time periods later both leading powers suffer terminal fragmentation. In their place, five intermediate powers rise, absorbing the shreds of the disintegrated empires. The new multipolar regime attains a considerable degree of stability, thus radically transforming the geopolitical system.

Although this simple example does not allow us to draw any systematic conclusions, it does illustrate the impact of self-reinforcing historical processes. It is not hard to see the parallel to Niles Eldredge and Stephen Jay Gould's (1977) notion of punctuated equilibria. Developed as a response to the gradualist and determinist character of the Darwinian synthesis, their concept emphasizes the history-dependent and accidental character of biological evolution. They point out that evolutionary change tends to take place suddenly during relatively brief episodes separated by long, predominantly stable periods.

The heuristic power of Eldredge and Gould's punctuated-equilibrium approach is not limited to paleontology. Social scientists and historians have already appropriated the concept as a metaphor for historical change in human societies (e.g., Krasner 1988; Gaddis 1992/93; Rasler and Thompson 1989). Going beyond metaphorical use, however, requires a more precise way to express historical change. The extended model illustrates one way of building such a well-specified theory.

While a systematic analysis of dynamic geopolitical regimes falls outside the scope of the present study, it is useful to trace the microlevel process responsible for the observed macro events. In order to better understand this underlying dynamic, we will focus on another example of imperial collapse drawn from an earlier episode of the same run. Figure 5.12 describes the first major state collapse since the creation of the sys-

Territorial size

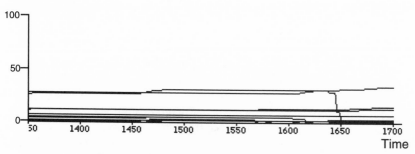

Figure 5.12. An example of imperial collapse

tem. This event terminates a rather stable period of bipolarity at about time 1650.

What causes this abrupt process of disintegration? Walking through the actual sequence in some detail tells an interesting story about the interaction between internal and external sovereignty. Figure 5.13a provides the first snapshot of what will become the crisis finishing off one of the two leading states of the system. The diagram reports on the state of the "world" at time 1630. Since all states are predators, the shading used for such actors has been suppressed. The numbers indicate the resource levels of each actor, including provinces, bold ones denoting the capitals.

As suggested by the previous figure, two states dominate the system, one located to the left, and one located to the right. The left empire,

1959	1440	2248	2260	2020	1910	2144	2330	**5033**	2462
1706	2271	2226	2433	2449	2353	1874	1562	2116	1983
1630	1858	2320	**3927**	1928	2302	2056	1855	2172	847
1490	1129	2277	1587	2110	1931	1802	1338	1430	1894
1465	2122	2002	1653	1852	2449	2599	**4384**	2436	1747
1417	1286	1505	1656	2338	1463	2455	2368	**4593**	2135
1042	1872	**3168**	1612	2351	2424	1564	1707	1796	1309
1231	2625	2277	2060	2360	1906	1966	1887	2238	1075
1854	1410	**3757**	1705	1938	1965	1958	**1768**	2427	1164
1159	1219	604	**1862**	579	1404	2077	1160	1224	1421

Figure 5.13a. The sample system at time 1630

which at that point disposes of 3927 resources, decides to launch an attack against the small state, the center of which controls 3168 resources (see the small line pointing to the right). In figure 5.13b, reporting on the state of the system at time 1634, the latter state has responded, and combat rages between the unevenly sized states. Since fighting has been underway for a few periods, the resource level of the left empire's center has been seriously eroded, down from 3927 to 3379. This invites one of the provinces (see the starred unit in the upper left corner) to launch an attack on the center. Because decision-making is probabilistic, it is not necessarily the most powerful region that takes the initiative to topple the capital. In fact, several provinces control more resources than the secessionist actor.

Three time periods later, the disintegration process gains speed (see fig. 5.13c). By this time, the center's resources have declined down to 2802. This erosion paves the way for another internal challenge (see the unit with 2428, almost as much as the center), and another external attack (see the intervention by the power controlling 5042 resources). Moving another two periods forward (see fig. 5.13d), the latter challenge has been successfully countered by the afflicted empire, but this victory comes at a high cost. The resource level has decreased down to 1812, which is in fact below that of many of the provinces. Moreover, the center has lost two provinces: one through secession, and one through external warfare.

The situation has become even more desperate at time 1645 (see fig. 5.13e). Not only have another four provinces broken loose from the state (those with resource levels 1133, 1904, 2110, and 1291), but these losses

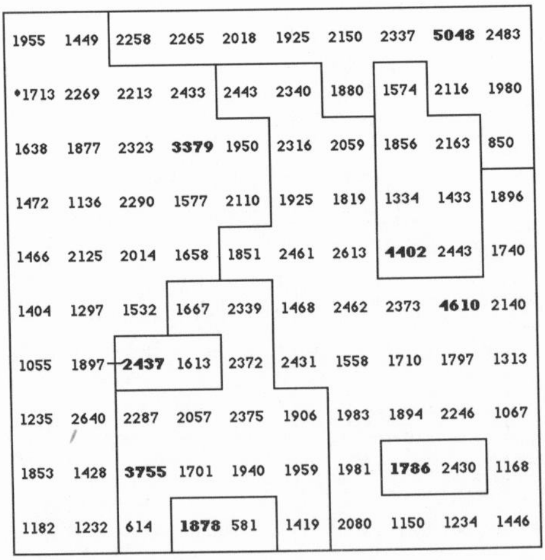

Figure 5.13b. The sample system at time 1634

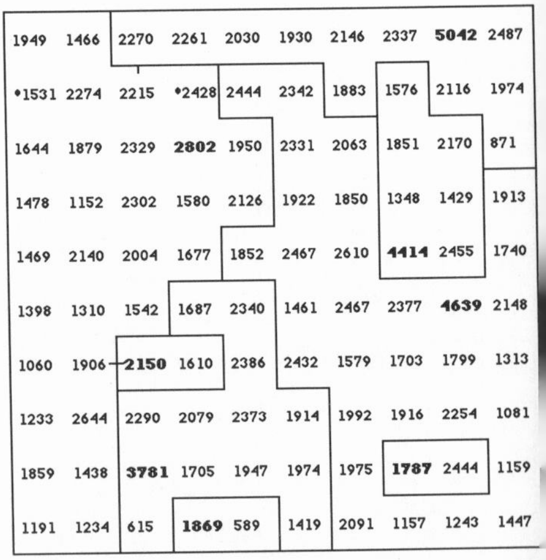

Figure 5.13c. The sample system at time 1637

1952	1468	2284	2266	2028	1937	2150	2338	**4925**	2492
♦1492	2276	2216	2373	2447	2355	1882	1574	2127	1985
1644	1885	2332	**1812**	1953	2329	2050	1861	2176	879
1469	1152	2297	1578	2139	1930	1846	1358	1426	1913
1469	2138	2010	1683	1853	2468	2613	**4435**	2464	1744
1397	1321	1550	1680	2338	1452	2473	2371	**4637**	2145
1063	1900	**2116**	1611	2387	2437	1580	1700	1799	1320
1234	2631	2292	2090	2374	1914	1994	1916	2254	1098
1858	1449	**3803**	1720	1953	1977	1974	**1800**	2451	1153
1196	1240	625	**1875**	598	1427	2085	1162	1248	1450

Figure 5.13d. The sample system at time 1639

1978	1482	2299	2282	2035	1923	2144	2336	**4956**	2505
1133	♦2268	2232	2376	2473	2379	1900	1586	2157	2007
1648	1914	2346	**907**	1904	2332	2051	1873	2162	896
♦1492	1157	2304	1584	♦2128	1946	1879	1374	1425	1909
1468	2110	2018	1703	1862	2454	2628	**4465**	2458	1761
1404	1291	1558	1674	2346	1476	2496	2397	**4664**	2139
1060	1909	**2115**	1615	2405	2454	1591	1697	1816	1324
♦1251	2664	2305	2096	2390	1948	2004	1918	2250	1135
1863	1461	**3821**	1731	1965	1970	1991	**1838**	2452	1147
1180	1256	641	**1899**	615	1423	2074	1167	1254	1460

Figure 5.13e. The sample system at time 1645

seriously threaten the territorial integrity of the state. In the next period (see fig. 5.13f), two strategically located rebellions cut off more than half of the territory in two blows (cf. the rebelling provinces with 2268 and 1492 resources in fig. 5.13e). The result is devastating for the former empire. At 556 units, its resource level is lower than all its provinces, hardly a promising situation. Ironically, the final coup de grace is dealt by newly independent states, as illustrated by figure 5.13g, which concludes the series of snapshots illustrating imperial collapse.

1978	1483	2301	2285	2033	1926	2141	2336	**4961**	2507
1135	2255	2238	2382	2476	2384	1902	1585	2153	2004
1654	1913	2343	**556**	1906	2329	2054	1867	2171	898
1489	1154	2301	1578	2113	1951	1884	1378	1420	1906
1467	2114	2024	1704	1865	2462	2625	**4476**	2463	1763
1406	1288	1552	1671	2353	1479	2497	2402	**4665**	2143
1069	1913	**2124**	1621	2406	2454	1596	1704	1819	1320
1241	2666	2304	2101	2396	1949	1998	1915	2253	1140
1866	1466	**3825**	1732	1969	1968	1993	**1849**	2453	1142
1191	1261	642	**1893**	616	1419	2075	1169	1251	1463

Figure 5.13f. The sample system at time 1646

1997	1488	2305	2308	2043	1950	2148	2355	**5005**	2509
1162	2275	2242	2397	2488	2395	1905	1598	2164	2027
1654	1925	2359	**11**	1944	2331	2076	1865	2204	913
1512	1164	2323	1591	**2106**	1954	1884	1400	1439	1914
1476	2125	2055	1725	1885	2481	2662	**4504**	2469	1798
1426	1328	1573	1709	2377	1490	2511	2422	**4706**	2156
1070	1921	**2147**	1648	2406	2465	1619	1708	1828	1333
1248	2684	2305	2117	2425	1976	2017	1937	2270	1145
1862	1491	**3841**	1738	1971	1969	1999	**1869**	2450	1144
1185	1298	636	**1914**	631	1417	2110	1208	1269	1495

Figure 5.13g. The sample system at time 1653

The disintegration process described by figures 5.13a–g clearly illustrates the interdependence of internal and external action. In the modified version of the model, states need to mobilize against both foreign and domestic threats to their sovereignty. Unlike the original scheme of resource allocation, the PRA mechanism makes the deterrent capacity dependent on active fronts only. This means that crises have a tendency to propagate from domestic to foreign policy and vice versa as deploying troops to any particular front threatens to thin out other fronts. Once set in motion, any sign of geopolitical decline has a tendency to invite further challenges, especially if protracted combat weakens the center. Again, there is a feedback mechanism, though in the opposite direction of the centralizing one discussed in chapter 4. In this section, this nonlinear process operates through power balances, giving internal and external enemies cues about when military action might pay. It should be noted, however, that feedback does not operate through formation of coalitions among these actors in the current version of the model. By contrast, we will later consider how nationalism may promote such centrifugal tendencies in multicultural states through the formation of explicit, culturally coded domestic alliances opposing the center's power.

In retrospect, it seems obvious that the attack on the small neighbor in period 1630 was a mistake. In the terminology of Robert Gilpin (1981), Paul Kennedy (1989), and Jack Snyder (1991), conquering states always risk overextending themselves. Although historical cases of unsuccessful imperial expansion appear to vindicate those who classify such behavior as irrational, the holistic character of the CAS simulation puts such judgments in their proper historical perspective. It is usually only with the benefit of hindsight that we can tell whether an expansionist policy was doomed to fail. Endowing the agents with limited cognitive foresight contributes to a more realistic assessment of the severe limits on prediction in complex systems.

Although a systematic exploration of overextension goes beyond the goal of the current project, the current episodes illustrates that such an investigation is well within reach of CAS methodology. Yet to realize that potential, many more parameters have to be systematically varied. Even more importantly, the study of long-term evolution of geopolitical systems calls for more sophisticated statistical techniques to identify the emergent macro patterns. With the exception for this section, the analysis has so far focused on raw measures of polarity in converging environments. In that sense, the current work should be seen as a mere step toward a better understanding of more open-ended settings with their own emergent dynamic.

Likewise, cautionary words against exaggerated confidence in the robustness of the results are also in order. While we have investigated a number of extensions and alternative mechanisms, we have by no means exhausted the space of theoretically relevant variations. For example, despite the introduction of strategic adaptation, the basic prey and predator strategies of the states have been constant. Moreover, the harvest mechanism is wildly unrealistic and the initial conditions were never varied (see Cusack and Stoll 1990, 172-78 for experiments of that type). Only continued research featuring important deviations from the current framework, guided by thorough empirical analysis, is likely to yield more reliable knowledge of the complex patterns of power politics. If anything, what the present experiments have shown is that some oversimplified "deductive" conclusions in the qualitative literature do not necessarily hold up when confronted with the increased complexity of stylized artificial worlds. If our theoretical intuitions do not survive such tests, there are few reasons to believe that they apply across-the-board to the infinitely more complex conditions of the real world.

CHAPTER 6

Modeling Nationalism

INTRODUCTION

So far, our attention has focused on state formation, using the Emergent Polarity Model to apply neorealist principles to a dynamic and historical context. Yet no attempt was made to extend the framework to the age of nationalism. States have been mostly modeled as internally consolidated monoliths, albeit with emergent outer boundaries. Although we did introduce some rudimentary internal state structure, the representation remained devoid of cultural idiosyncracies.

While these assumptions make some sense as an approximative depiction of the era of absolutism, in the post-Napoleonic period they lose much of their power (though see Schroeder 1994 for an even more pessimistic evaluation of neorealism). With foreign policy no longer in the hands of a small elite but crucially dependent on popular support, the realist view of equal states ceases to be a useful approximation (Claude 1986). Thus, paradoxically, nationalism undermines the realist notion of national interest. In the words of Craig Calhoun (1992):

> So long as political theory could focus its discussion of legitimate rule on arguments about divine or natural right, on questions of succession or on debates about the limits which should be imposed on monarchs, the question of national identity either didn't arise or was extremely marginal. But when questions of sovereignty began to turn on appeals to the rights, acceptance or will of "the people" this changed. The modern notion of popular will always assumed the existence of some recognizably bounded and internally integrated population. (4)

This situation presents realist scholars with a dilemma, for if sovereignty can no longer be reduced to territorial rule independent of the wishes the respective subject populations, ideology and nationalism become important resources to draw on in interstate relations. But realism in general, and neorealism in particular, continues to view world and domestic politics as qualitatively distinct arenas, governed by different laws and principles. Whereas norms and ideology are the stuff of domestic politics, interstate relations are governed by pure power competition, they claim. No one expresses this dichotomy in more uncompromising terms than Kenneth Waltz (1979), who insists on classifying internal affairs as "hierarchic, vertical, centralized, heterogeneous, directed, and contrived" and foreign affairs as "anarchic, horizontal, decentralized, homogeneous, undirected, and mutually adapted" (113).

This contrast plays an important but more tacit role in other IR theories, since it justifies the entire field of study as an intellectual enterprise distinct from other subfields of political science. Nevertheless, neorealists are the most eager supporters of this division of labor. Reserving "high politics" as their special area, they delegate "softer" issues to other social scientists. Waltz's (1986) justification is not atypical: "The theoretical separation of domestic and international politics need not bother us unduly. Economists get along quite well with separate theories of markets and firms. Students of international politics will do well to concentrate on separate theories of internal and external politics until someone figures out a way to unite them" (340). By adopting this phlegmatic approach to theoretical integration, Waltz overlooks the persistent efforts to unify economic theory. Economists have been trying to link their micro and macro analyses into one coherent theory for the last few decades, apparently finding the task of closing the micro-macro gap more urgent than Waltz implies. Moreover, these efforts have more recently been paralleled by IR theorists attempting to bring domestic politics back in (e.g., Putnam 1988; Evans, Jacobson, and Putnam 1992). In the security-related literature, there has been a continuing reluctance to analyze domestic influences (though see Snyder 1991 and further references in Walt 1991).

Because of their materialist and structuralist outlook, neorealist scholars have found it much harder to deal with cultural phenomena such as nationalism than their liberal colleagues (Lapid and Kratochwil 1996b). Responding to the changing post–cold war security agenda, realist scholars have belatedly, and perhaps somewhat reluctantly, "discovered" the field of nationalism and ethnic conflict. Because of realism's focus on instrumental power calculations, theoretical adaptation within this school has often amounted to little more than adding ad hoc factors such as "hypernationalism" to an otherwise unaltered neorealist framework (e.g., Mearsheimer 1990). On this view, ethnicity and nationalism figure as excessive and malign aberrations reinforcing hypothesized security dilemmas, rather than representing a fundamentally different organization principle at odds with the realists' core assumption of omnipresent territorial sovereignty.

Another, more drastic, response simply substitutes ethnic groups for states. According to this interpretation, realist "laws" describing interstate relations can without any serious loss of generality be applied to ethnic conflict. Barry Posen (1993) adopts precisely this approach in his study of interethnic security dilemmas in Yugoslavia and Ukraine. In his interesting study of the Yugoslav conflict, James Fearon (1994) extends this perspective to formal modeling by treating ethnic groups as if they were unitary rational actors (for a critique, see Cederman 1996c).

Nevertheless, these solutions seem unsatisfactory in that they serve a justificatory purpose in their attempt to support neorealist doctrine as well as certain methodological tools, rather than to uncover the actual influence of nationalism viewed as a process in its own right. A better understanding of world politics at the end of the millennium clearly calls for more than the addition of new "variables" or the substitution of actor types that confuse statehood with nationhood.

A TAXONOMY OF NATIONS AND STATES

The Emergent Polarity Model showed that neorealism encounters theoretical difficulties because it treats actors as given. These inconsistencies are compounded by the neorealist tendency to assume them to be nation-states. This follows as an often overlooked consequence of the Waltzian anarchy/hierarchy dichotomy. By postulating internal hierarchy, neorealists exaggerate internal cohesion as much as they underestimate the chances of external order. In reality, the processes of state formation and nationalism do not always coincide in this neat fashion. Even when both occur, one often occurs before the other. This sequence matters. If the state arrives first, nation-building acquires a completely different character than in the opposite case.

Indeed, it is often forgotten that the nation-state is a product of nationalism rather than a "natural" organization form. Inis Claude (1986) reminds us that this mistaken assumption "nourishes the illusion that the nineteenth-century ideal that nations would create states, and that states would serve their nations, has been realized" (3). Impressed by the contrast between the solidarity of the nation-state and global anarchy, he argues, neorealists fail to realize that "the solidarity of the body politic of the modern state is in considerable measure a myth. It is clearly a variable, which means that the unity of the population of some states is greater than that of others, and that the degree of solidarity within a given state changes from time to time" (ibid.).

To rectify this shortcoming, it is necessary to deviate from the Waltzian model by dissolving the conceptual glue that holds that image of the nation-state together. Abandoning the assumption that state formation and nation-building parallel each other opens the door for a spectrum of possibilities between anarchy and nation-state. Drawing on our earlier definitions of the state and the nation, figure 6.1 illustrates this by adding two new, "mixed" categories to the neorealist dichotomy. As in figures 2.1

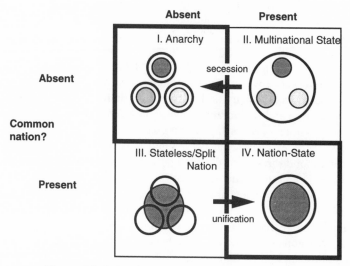

Figure 6.1 A 2 × 2 taxonomy of nationalist situations

and 3.4, we let the horizontal and vertical dimensions correspond to the state and the nation respectively, the present figure concentrates on the real-world presence or absence of the actor in question rather than its theoretical status. Thus, whereas the left column displays political systems lacking a common state, the right one represents cases with one. Similarly, the upper row shows prenational outcomes, and the lower row systems held together by a national community. This means that the horizontal dimension reflects power relationships and enforcement, while the vertical one captures more intangible aspects of politics, such as culture and identity.

The figure represents ethnic groups as shaded disks and states as bold circles. In this example, there are three ethnic categories, depicted as different shades of gray. Case 1 shows three ethnic communities (or small nation-states) that lack common political institutions and thus live in a state of anarchy.[1] In Case 2, the ethnic groups form a common, multinational state. This situation corresponds to an imperial state in which the

---

[1] The diagram can be interpreted in two ways because it does not say anything specifically about the contents of the three units in Case 1 other than that the political and cultural boundaries coincide. If they are viewed as ethnic groups without nationalist ambitions, the diagram captures the formation of nation-states from premodern conditions. The second perspective treats the three units as small nation-states, implying that save for scale, Cases 1 and 4 are identical. We will return to this issue below.

peripheral nationalities are subordinated under a foreign core, as was the case in the Habsburg Empire and the Soviet Union. In addition to imperial rule, other types of multinational cohabitation within a common state framework can be envisaged. Confederations, such as Switzerland, illustrate that culturally and ethnically diversified states do not presuppose hierarchical subordination. Case 3 differs from Case 2 in that there is cultural convergence without a common political framework. This configuration resembles Germany and Italy before their unification. Finally, in Case 4, the state and the nation converge into a large, culturally homogeneous nation-state, such as Japan or France.

It now becomes clear what neorealism overlooks. The thickly framed cases correspond directly to the Waltzian ideal types of interstate anarchy (as in Case 1) and domestic cohesion (as in Case 4). Having ruled out all other possibilities in the name of theoretical elegance, neorealists typically neglect the mixed cases (Cases 2 and 3) that symbolize situations in which popular and territorial sovereignty fail to coincide. These are serious omissions because of their historical importance in describing empires and stateless nations in the past as well as in the post–cold war era. Focusing on the horizontal power-based state/no-state dimension, neorealist scholars tend to confuse stateless national communities (Case 3) with pure anarchy (Case 1) and multiethnic states (Case 2) with cohesive nation-states (Case 4). The first source of confusion leads them to see anarchy where there is in effect potential for state-formation or at least deep-going political cooperation along the lines of Karl Deutsch and his colleagues' (1957) pluralistic security communities.[2] In the context of the cold war, this misconception ignored the possibility of the two Germaneys unifying, while the other misconception made it harder to anticipate the collapse of the Soviet Union and other communist multiethnic states.

Equipped with the full taxonomy, we are in a better position to appreciate the consequences of nationalism. Following Ernest Gellner (1983) we define nationalism as the political principle "which holds that the political and the national unit should be congruent" (1). If we interpret the units under anarchy in Case 1 as smaller nation-states (rather than mere ethnic groups), there are two cases that are compatible with nationalism, namely Cases 1 and 4. The remaining mixed cases will tend to be "unstable" in that Case 2 suffers from a deficit of states and Case 3 includes too many states. Under these circumstances, it is reasonable to expect a shift toward stability. Since culture usually changes slowly

---

[2] The sociologically and historically oriented British school of IR has also paid much attention to the concept of community (e.g., Bull 1977). Buzan (1993) provides a useful introduction to the English school and its relation to American-style IR theory.

(Smith 1986), nationalism tends to produce horizontal rather than vertical shifts, at least in the short run (see the bold arrows). Under the influence of this force, many multiethnic states are likely to disintegrate in a series of secessions, as did the Habsburg and Soviet empires. Politically fragmented national communities, by contrast, experience a trend toward political unification. Thus, nationalism is as likely to generate disintegration as it is to produce integration (Claude 1986; Calhoun 1992, 1993).

THREE TYPES OF NATIONALISM

This rather abstract account needs to be disaggregated into more context-specific processes. Whether one views it as an emergent historical trend or as a conscious ideology, nationalism was born in Europe (Kedourie 1960). Therefore, scholars have tended to base their classifications of nationalism on the ways it developed in Europe. Of course, this European perspective does not imply that nationalist movements have not existed outside Europe or that such examples are of less importance. Quite the contrary, one of the most striking facts about interstate relations on the global level is the extent to which it is influenced by nationalist rhetoric.

The German historian Theodor Schieder (1991, 87–101) identified three distinct stages of European nationalism that originated in particular geographical areas (see Alter 1989, 98–103). Drawing on the logic of figure 6.1, we trace these processes in figure 6.2. The three ideal types can be called state-initiated, unification, and separatist nationalism. Roughly speaking, they emerged in Western, Central and Southern, and Eastern Europe respectively.[3]

State-initiated   Unification   Separatist
Nationalism   Nationalism   Nationalism

Figure 6.2. Three types of nationalism

[3] These broad geographical references are controversial, especially after the end of the cold war. Counting themselves as central Europeans, for example, many people in what used to be the Soviet-dominated part of Europe now resent the putatively peripheral status conferred by the label "Eastern." Here the points of compass serve a crude heuristic purpose and should thus not be seen as an attempt to divide the continent into reified categories or to identify "good" and "bad" nationalisms.

State-Initiated Nationalism

The old Western nation-states, archetypically England and France but also Spain and Sweden, formed in a two-step process. First a period of state formation, mainly through conquest, transformed the situation from anarchy (Case 1) through a multiethnic state (Case 2). The second step involved the center's elimination of cultural differences starting at the core and proceeding slowly to the periphery (see the vertical move from Case 2 down to Case 4). Fueled by the need to raise resources for external warfare, this gradual process took English and French nationbuilders centuries (Tilly 1990). Following Henry VIII's break with the Catholic Church in 1532, the English state embarked on an early nation-building campaign that paved the way for the creation of the first full-fledged nation-state (Greenfeld 1992). The parliamentary tradition helped to solidify a popular notion of sovereignty that promoted early but slow emergence of national consciousness. By the end of the eighteenth century, England approximated the modern nation-state, though one should not exaggerate the degree of popular participation (Mann 1992, 152). Absolutism retarded nation-building in France, but when it finally followed the French Revolution of 1789, it outpaced its English counterpart in terms of both centralization and global repercussions. Even so, it took Paris at least a century to complete the national reforms such as linguistic and bureaucratic harmonization of *la province* (Weber 1976).

The two remaining types of nationalism are more clearly expressed as ideologies than the first. More than anything else, it was the French Revolution that triggered the political avalanche that came to mark most of the two centuries to follow. Unlike the gradual evolution of state-initiated nationalism, unification and separatist nationalisms appeared as "modular" meta-ideologies usually imported directly from the West.

Unification Nationalism

Due to their distinctive geopolitical backgrounds, the German and Italian nation-states developed along a very different path than the West European ones. Unlike the state-initiated variety, unfication nationalism features nation formation preceding state-building. Figure 6.2 illustrates the historical process, which started with a shift from Case 1 to Case 3, creating a culturally cohesive but politically fragmented nation consisting of various small city-states and principalities. These tiny units proved no match for Napoleon's armies. Despite its short duration, the French conquest of central Europe left deep traces. Not only did these brilliant military successes reveal the superiority of a fully mobilized nation-state over conservative and culturally fragmented states such as the Habsburg Empire, they also directly contributed to spreading the "nationalist germ" among German and Italian intellectuals (Alter 1989). Contrary to its expectations, however, France's promotion of republican government stimulated local nationalism rather than loyalty to the French state. Lacking powerful comprehensive political institutions, German and Italian nationalists had no choice but to rely on culturally mediated mobilization. Romanticism in general, and Herder's ideas of a linguistically defined nation in particular, played particularly important roles as sources of inspiration for German nationalists (Berlin 1972). Yet the final transition from a stateless nation to a full-fledged nation-state (i.e., the horizontal move from Case 3 to Case 4), which completed the state-building phase, took place as a consequence of self-interested campaigns by single core states around which the new nation-states crystallized. Prussia under Bismarck headed the German quest for unity and Italy was unified thanks to Cavour's Piedmont.[4]

Separatist Nationalism

Secession from empires sets the East European pattern of nationalism apart from the other types. The decline and final collapse of the Habsburg, Ottoman and Russian Empires gave rise to a great number of states, some of which were nation-states and others new multinational units (Hroch 1985). Stretching from Finland in the north to Greece in the south, this band of new states has continued to experience turmoil after the end of communist rule.[5] In terms of figure 6.2, these states emerged as nationalities within the multiethnic states of Case 2. Instead of following the path of centralization and nation-building, as state-initiated nationalism, the multiethnic empires broke apart as the peripheral nation-

---

[4] This stylized depiction suppresses important historical detail. In reality, the sequential order of nation formation and state-building was less clear-cut. It would be a mistake to believe that full-fledged national communities existed prior to the onset of state-building in either Germany or Italy. In fact, it is doubtful whether an Italian nation could be said to have existed even after political unification had been achieved. One of the architects of Italian unification famously quipped: "We have made Italy, now we have to make Italians" (cited in Hobsbawm 1990, 44). Still, on the elite level, the national sentiment was strong well and long before the unification process started.

[5] There were also some scattered examples of secession in northern and Western Europe starting with Belgium's divorce from the United Netherlands in 1831. Moreover, Norway left its union with Sweden in 1905, and southern Ireland broke away from Britain in 1921 (see Alter 1989, 99).

alities managed to secede from the center, thus producing a leftward shift to Case 1 rather than a downward movement to Case 4.

In some instances, this move was soon followed by further political change. To the extent that the newly independent states could be said to contain nations, as in Case 3, unification completed the metamorphosis, producing a nation-state as under unification nationalism (cf. Case 4). Irredentism is a special case of this combination of disintegration and integration since it involves a state claiming as its own a province, allegedly of the same culture, belonging to an adjacent multiethnic state that subjects the disputed territory to foreign rule (Mayall 1990). Hitler's "libreration" of the Sudenten Germans of Czechoslovakia is a paradigmatic example. Irredentism remains a potent security threat, as the civil war in Yugoslavia illustrates. In this conflict, both Serbia and Croatia have attempted to bring their supposed kin under their own political roofs by advancing and implementing irredentist declarations. Graphically, irredentism boils down to first moving leftward from Case 2 to Case 1 and then, if elements of the ensuing situation quickly transform into Case 3, a second rightward shift into Case 4.

Figure 6.2 depicts the three ideal-type nationalisms as irreversible processes. Obviously, this represents a rather crude oversimplification of the historical record. We have already seen that Western-European nationalism can turn into secession. Moreover, state-formation and geopolitics sometimes reverse the integrationist momentum. For example, after World War II, Hitler's Reich broke up into three states, the two Germaneys and Austria, reflecting a shift from Case 4 back to Case 3. In the absence of cultural exchange in Case 2, this reversal could have continued to Case 1 had it not been for the disintegration of the Soviet Empire. Indeed, there were signs of cultural and even linguistic divergence between the two Germaneys, but reunification in 1989 showed that although cultural divergence does operate, modern communication technology has made it harder than ever to break national bonds. Thus, while identity shifts can be comparatively swift thanks to modern media, cultural change continues to be a very slow process.

Even in the absence of extraneous political events, a Western path toward the nation-state may be at least partially reversed. Fringe nationalism in Brittany and Scotland suggest that state-initiated nationalism should not be interpreted in too deterministically a manner even in the old Western nation-states (see Connor 1994, chap. 7). These relapses correspond to a move from Case 4 back to Case 2, undoing the work of earlier nation-builders. Some worry that the effort to establish ethnically pluralist curricula in American schools will generate a similar relapse (e.g., Schlesinger 1992). While the nation-state represents a particularly stable outcome thanks to the cultural closure of nationalism (Brubaker

1992), its unity could be threatened from the outside as well as from the inside.[6]

While I have chosen to illustrate the typology by examples drawn from European history, it can also serve more generally as a conceptual guide to nationalism in other parts of the world. All three types of processes have occurred outside Europe, though not with equal frequency. Because modern nationalism originated in Europe and later spread to other continents as a result of colonialism, the Third World has experienced separatist nationalism before the two other types. Trapped within colonial empires (cf. Case 2), the nationalist movements in Africa and Asia drew heavily on the Wilsonian principle of self-determination and can thus be seen as an extension of the wave of imperial collapse that brought down the Eastern European empires in World War I (Mayall 1990).[7] This development was neither anticipated nor intended by Western leaders, but the global repercussions of self-determination in the Third World soon became obvious: "The promulgation of self-determination as one of the guiding principles of Allied policy [after World War I] came too early in the development of colonial nationalism to have its impact felt to the full immediately. Its inherently revolutionary implications, however, spread to every corner of the world" (Emerson 1960, 26).

Although the precolonial period featured mainly separatist nationalism, the situation after independence was more variegated. In fact, the whole spectrum of nationalist trajectories are visible in the history of newly independent states. Some early cases, especially the settler states that broke away from the British Empire, resemble unification nationalism in that a national feeling emerged before the existence of a state. Nationhood was not achieved easily, and depended at least partly on the power of a well-organized state, as the American Civil War attests, but national unity stemmed as much from civil society as from state-induced assimilation.[8] Zionism is perhaps the best example of unification nationalism since there was clearly a strong national consciousness among Jews prior to the formation of Israel. Although their state-building enterprises have

[6] Unsurprisingly, national extremists often exaggerate this threat in order to limit immigration or introduce racial segregation.

[7] Case 2 represents an oversimplification of the situation. As Breuilly (1982) points out, one should not exaggerate the extent to which colonial societies were dominated: "In fact, imperial powers were often reluctant to conquer, frequently established control by agreements with elements in the indigenous society, constantly modified their policies in response to pressure from colonial society and in many cases left because they could no longer control such pressure" (126).

[8] If one also stresses the virtual elimination of the indigenous populations in the settler states, their history has much in common with state-initiated nationalism, since conquest preceded the settlements. Yet, unlike the Western European cases, the native populations were not assimilated and incorporated into the nascent nation-state.

met with more mixed success than Zionism, the Palestinians and Kurds also belong to this category.[9]

Nevertheless, the bulk of the postcolonial experiences in the Third World correspond to separatist nationalism. While virtually all anti-colonial elites adhered to Central European nationalism rhetorically and tried to emulate Western European nation-building in practice, the result was often incomplete or aborted variants of state-initiated nationalism. James Mayall (1990) remarks that even in the absence of popular national sentiment, "anti-colonial leaders always claimed to be representing an existing nation or creating a movement whose historical task was to bring one into being" (48). The Third World elites accepted the colonial borders as a fait accompli, however arbitrary their political justification. Because of their weakness and cultural multitude, the new states could be described as multiethnic states rather than as full-fledged nation-states. In some instances, the newly independent countries managed to forge a national consciousness, but even the most successful nation-building experiences included secessionist trends. For example, after splitting into predominantly Hindu and Muslim components, the Indian nationalist movement managed to forge a national consciousness, but its achievements continue to be threatened by secessionist forces. Most of the Third World exhibits a predominantly multiethnic patchwork not unlike the conditions in Eastern Europe: "The new states turned out to be as unsympathetic to demands for self-determination from dissatisfied groups within their jurisdictions as were the Romanov, Habsburg and Ottoman rulers to the national claims that were advanced against their rule in the nineteenth century" (Mayall 1990, 49).

To sum up, all three developmental types have played a key role in both European and world history. In the non-European cases, the balance between state-initiated and separatist nationalisms is of particular importance. In the next section we will turn to nation-building conforming with these two developmental patterns.

NATIONALIST MOBILIZATION AND COORDINATION

Although the threefold historical classification serves useful purposes, understanding the logic of nationalism requires further conceptual unpacking. There is good reason to reiterate the warning against reification of the nation. The arrows in figure 6.2 do not refer to sudden magic leaps, but to specific historical processes. As we will see, these transitions are

[9] Note, however, that the Zionist and Palestinian cases differ from the original concept of unification nationalism in that unification entails migration to a "homeland" rather than territorial merger. Diaspora nationalism may therefore be a better term (Gellner 1983).

predicated upon several conditions that may or may not be present in each historical case.

Because of its centrality for the prospects of peace in postcommunist Europe, and more generally in the Third World, this section looks more closely at nationalism in multiethnic states and empires. As we saw in the previous section, the history of this part of Europe serves as a paradigmatic example and the imperial domination. Drawing similar parallels, Myron Weiner (1971) identifies a "Macedonian syndrome," defined as foreign domination, relative underdevelopment, multiethnic conditions, and newly acquired independence, and applies it to non-European cases (cf. Brubaker 1995). More recently, comparisons have been made in the other direction, using Third World examples to elucidate nationalist activities in the Soviet republics (Motyl 1992; see especially Brass 1992).

What decides whether such political organizations embark on a Western or Eastern European path? Figure 6.3 displays this puzzle graphically. Here, Case 2 is interpreted as an imperial relationship between a center and a periphery (see the small downward-pointing arrows indicating the center's hierarchical domination over the culturally distinct peripheral ethnic groups). Starting in Case 2, the question is whether the imperial government will manage to build a nation, transforming the situation into Case 4, or whether there will be a leftward move into Case 1. Of course, a third possibility is to stay at the status quo in Case 2, but in an era of nationalism this option is not always available, however much the impe-

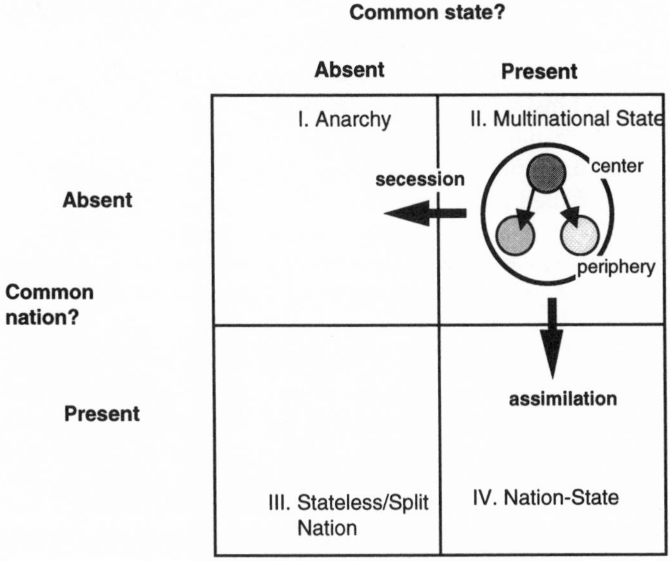

Figure 6.3. Secession or assimilation?

rial elite wishes this were the case. External and internal challenges force multiethnic states to choose between radical centralization and decentralization. These were the choices confronting the leaders of the Habsburg Monarchy and the communist elites in the Soviet Union.[10]

Since few imperial regimes hesitate to resort to repression if necessary, successful secession usually requires both excellent organization and highly motivated participants. Yet one should not exaggerate the obstacles confronting revolutionary leaders. The assumption of individual self-interest inherent in methodological individualism obscures the great possibilities of collective-identity formation. Without access to the resources of the state, few options remain for the oppositional movement because offering selective incentives or coercing its members into participating in highly risky ventures will most likely fail. But exploited in the right way, nationalism turns into a formidable weapon with great potential to transcend collective choice dilemmas. The key to success lies in the strategic use of political symbols. By drawing on the emotional power of carefully selected cultural markers such as language, religion, or other cultural dimensions, eloquent nationalist entrepreneurs are able to create a political community constituting a potent vehicle for collective-identity formation. In many cases, a de facto nation starts to exist even before independence from the imperial superstructure and acquisition of a state.

The power balance between the center and the periphery is of great importance in implementing this strategy. Everything hinges upon the amount of support that the nationalist elite can solicit from its constituency. This, in turn, depends on two conditions. First, the population must be conscious of its distinctive culture compared to the imperial center— that is, it must be politically mobilized. This presented difficulties under premodern circumstances because the parochial outlook of rural populations made them unresponsive to nationalist agitation. Second, a high degree of coordination is required, something that is far from obvious in culturally diversified areas.[11]

---

[10] Federalism has been the classical solution to the problems of governability in culturally fragmented states. Yet, one should not exaggerate the effectiveness of the federalist option. Dividing federalist states into "centralized" and "peripheralized" categories, William Riker (1964) doubts whether the latter can provide long-term stability: "Peripheralized federalisms . . . can hardly be expected to provide effective government. They fall gradually apart until they are easy prey for their enemies. Centralized federalisms, on the other hand, become more like unitary or imperial governments in time and thus render the whole federation able to function more effectively in a hostile world" (6–7). It may be that the less Darwinian environment of the modern world has made federations more viable. Fritz Scharpf (1983) has noted that both Germany and the European Union persist despite highly inefficient joint decision-making procedures.

[11] John Breuilly (1982, 366–73) adds a third condition, namely exterally induced legitimacy. See also Hardin's (1995) discussion of coordination.

Mobilization requires political communication, and thus a minimum level of literacy on the part of the masses. Ironically, this service is often rendered by the imperial center, though for very different reasons. Indeed, it is hard to imagine nationalist collective action taking place without a certain degree of modernization. Being an ultimately subjective phenomenon, a national community cannot exist in the absence of its members' political loyalty and identification. The first task of any nationalist intellectual is thus to mobilize the previously unactivated periphery. This is what constitutes the difference between an ethnic group and a nation. This metaphor, however, should not be carried too far, for awakening does not necessarily imply the existence a full-fledged nation. Instead of presupposing a neatly unitary nation waiting to be woken up from its slumber, nationalist mobilization entails a fundamentally creative act of defining boundaries and of carving out political meaning from an entangled and diffuse cultural backdrop.

Coordination, the second requirement for successful nationalist collective action, is related because if no candidate nation is waiting in the wings, this condition is not satisfied automatically. Even in the case of a fully mobilized peripheral population, cultural fragmentation within the periphery may effectively block concerted action (Breuilly 1982, 367). Little can be accomplished before the tribal underbrush has been cleared away, and should the power balance be very unfavorable, the opposition will need to resort to the conscious fabrication of myths. This was what Ernest Renan had in mind when he observed that: "Forgetting, I would even go so far as to say historical error, is a crucial factor in the creation of a nation, which is why progress in historical studies often constitutes a danger for [the principle of] nationality" (quoted in Calhoun 1993, 225).

There are few places where historical myths have played a more central role in the creation of nations than in the Balkans. The paucity of written records and the notoriously blurred ethnic map of this region set the stage for endless debates involving nationalist claims resting on scant historical evidence, debates that still rage with unmitigated force. Nevertheless, striking examples of this type should not blind us to the fact that even the most established nation-state tacitly favors the propagation of historical inaccuracies and distortions. America's glorification of its frontier men, amply supported by Hollywood, has persuaded a whole world to regard the almost total extinction of its original population as entertainment.

It is the subjective nature of nationhood that makes such disputes so hard to disentangle, because "nationalism is not simply a claim of ethnic similarity, but a claim that certain similarities should count as *the* definition of political community" (ibid., 229). It is thus futile to hope that the establishment of "historical truth" in the sense of unambiguous facts and dates will ever resolve these conflicts. Given the fluid and intangible nature of identities, it is often equally hopeless to find unequivocal evidence for any particular identification, especially in areas lacking unbiased democratic voting records. Few of the Western leaders at Versailles cared to ask the subject populations in Eastern Europe to which state they wanted to belong.

CHAPTER 7

Nationalist Mobilization

INTRODUCTION

Basing their expectations on the Western model of nation-building, analysts and policymakers alike have tended to discount the threats to the survival of multinational projects. Yet such an approach is likely to lead to unwelcome surprises. The nationalist responses to Mikhail Gorbachev's policy of perestroika surprised not only the reforms' chief architect but also most academic experts. Likewise, neither Jacques Delors nor other policymakers and observers anticipated the backlashes that stalled the European integration process, starting with the negative result of the Danish referendum in 1992.

Why this puzzlement? Indeed, the historical path is strewn with carcasses of failed multinational experiments. For example, World War I prompted the collapse of three heterogeneous states: Tsarist Russia, the Ottoman Empire, and Austria-Hungary. The imperial model suffered further blows as the old colonial empires crumbled. Nor has history been kind to attempts to erect ethnically diverse states in the postcolonial period. While most of these polyethnic state-building projects survived despite the outbreak of civil war, as was the case of Nigeria and India, others did not remain intact, as Bangladesh's secession from Pakistan attests. Even in the Western world, the stability of multinational rule cannot be taken for granted. While the nationalist tendencies have been mostly peaceful in these cases (e.g., Canada, Belgium), there are important exceptions to this pattern (e.g., Basque and Irish terrorism).

The reason for this failure to learn historical lessons is the tendency to apply context-dependent theories indiscriminately. Due to their heavy reliance on notions of modernization, Western theories and ideologies risk misleading policymakers faced with the difficult task of holding together culturally fragmented states. Unlike politicians governing nation-states, who primarily concentrate on fending off foreign threats to their states' sovereignty, leaders of multinational political units face a difficult trade-off between external challenges and internal collapse. The former, which often emanate from more cohesive competitors, force them to consider ways to mobilize their diverse populations. In an era of nationalism, the survival of states that fail to match the cohesiveness and popular commitment of nation-states is endangered. At the same time, rulers of multinational states cannot push mobilization too far or too fast, for such a policy may provoke nationalist unrest whether in the form of full-fledged secession or more modest autonomy claims.

In order to elucidate these aspects of nationalist mobilization within a multinational setting, this chapter offers a simple formal framework as a guide to the dynamics of that process. Starting at a much lower level of complexity than the full-fledged CAS models, the Mobilization Model builds on Karl Deutsch's (1953, 1969) theories of nation building. Despite its early origin, the Deutschian perspective remains one of the few well-defined attempts to grasp the interaction between mobilization and assimilation processes. Formalizing this theory shows that the mobilization rate affects the survival chances of multinational states in an era of rapid modernization. While too slow a rate leads to stagnation and possible invasion, excessive speed risks provoking nationalist secession.

The formal model consists of two steps. The first step focuses on nationality formation, while the second introduces the trade-off between internal and external collective action and spells out the consequences of different mobilization rates. As an illustration of the theoretical results, we will look at nation building in the Habsburg Empire, the Soviet Union, and the European Union.

MODELING POLITICAL MOBILIZATION

This chapter focuses on the asymmetric relationship between the center of a multinational state (or statelike organization) and its ethno-culturally distinct periphery. Assuming a process of political mobilization involving the peripheral population, the main question is whether it will adopt the center's supranational identity or whether it will create its own national movement. This difference between "foreign rule" and "home rule" presupposes the existence of an ethno-cultural distinction that can under certain circumstances be activated by nationalists.

Since this is a very general characterization, a few clarifications are necessary. For the present analytical purposes, a multinational state refers to any statelike organization containing a political center dominating its ethnically distinct peripheral areas (cf. Case 2 in fig. 6.3). While I refer to a multinational state or more generally to a multinational project, the argument also applies to imperial systems and other statelike entities falling short of complete territorial sovereignty as long as their political centers dispose of at least partial functional and territorial control over peripheral provinces.[1]

[1] According to Michael Doyle's (1986) oft-cited definition, an empire involves "effective control, whether formal or informal, of a subordinated society by an imperial society" (30).

Likewise, it is assumed that the periphery can be treated as a single unit. In reality, this assumption is often challenged by the fragmented nature of the periphery.[2] This is the case if political mobilization proceeds along more than one cultural dimension. Political identity formation involves the selection of the preexisting cultural traits to be emphasized as much as the change of the cultural raw material itself (Barth 1969; Horowitz 1975, 1985; Laitin 1986, 1988). Relaxing this assumption, the following chapter will analyze competitive nationalist mobilization in a culturally diverse system.

Setting these important complications aside, I join Karl Deutsch (1953) in concentrating on two main dichotomies. Also assuming a center-periphery setting, Deutsch divided the peripheral population along two dimensions, depending on whether or not it is mobilized and whether or not it is culturally differentiated. In the following, political mobilization designates a process by which a population acquires consciousness of its own identity through direct participation in, or exposure to, political processes. This usually requires some minimal level of political communication and participation. In this process, previously immaterial cultural distinctions become politicized (Gellner 1964). This is measured by the second dimension, which, by contrast, pertains to some potentially significant ethno-cultural trait.

Again, it is necessary to be careful with definitions. Political mobilization does not necessarily presuppose participation in democratic decision-making but could also involve the exposure to totalitarian rule (Huntington 1968). Thus, this process is closely related to, but distinct from, modernization—that is, a wide family of historical processes such as urbanization, literacy, industrialization, and other changes in social habits and institutions.[3] Thus, political mobilization can be seen as a conse-

---

Building on Watson's (1992) theory, Ole Wæver (1993, 25–26) criticizes this definition, which he finds too dependent on sovereignty. Instead, he argues for an imperial conception emphasizing radial control in the form of concentric circles. While of great theoretical importance, this distinction matters less to the current argument.

[2] Recognizing the diverse nature of many nationalist movements, Rogers Brubaker (1995, 112–13) defines a minority as a dynamic political stance rather than a static ethnodemographic condition. Such a stance is characterized by the minority's distinct notion of membership, its demand for state recognition, and its assertion of collective cultural and/or political rights.

[3] As with so many other scientific categories, "modernization" means different things to different authors. In his useful review, Piotr Sztompka (1993) recognizes three uses of the term ranging from the general to the historically specific: (1) as technological progress; (2) as "the social, political, economic, cultural, and mental transformations occurring in the west from the sixteenth century onward"; and (3) as less-developed countries attempt "to catch up with the leading, most developed countries coexisting with them" (129). Especially in the discussion of external challenges to multinational states, I follow Sztompka in focusing on the third aspect of modernization.

quence of modernization.[4] While mobilization may occur outside this context, for the current analytical purposes I mainly focus on this process as it evolves against the backdrop of modernization.

Likewise, assimilation were does not rest on the periphery's full cultural absorption into the center's culture and life-style, although this may occur, in which case a fully integrated nation-state results. Instead, I use "assimilation," or "political assimilation" more precisely, to refer to the removal of ethnic and cultural barriers to political communication, as well as a shift to the center's political identity rather than to other competing identities.[5] Obviously, this process usually entails some cultural homogenization, such as the acquisition of bilingual capacity on the part of the periphery, but again, the argument only concerns politically relevant dimensions. In the following, I use "supranational identity" to designate the center's political platform regardless of whether it is defined inclusively or tainted by the center's own cultural characteristics.

Figure 7.1 depicts a flow diagram summarizing the Mobilization Model's dynamic. To be precise, the model is a Markov process (see the appendix for details), and as such it deviates from the more open-ended Emergent Polarity Model. As we will see in the next section, however, it is possible to extend this simple stochastic design by adding contingent collective-action rules defying closed-form solution, thus moving the modeling exercise closer to the CAS tradition.

The Mobilization Model includes four probabilistic states coinciding with the four categories generated by the Deutschian dichotomies. First, there is the (for our analytical purpose less relevant) case of a nonethnic class C. This category, which comprises unmobilized but assimilated individuals, resembles the politically excluded masses of workers and peasants in nineteenth-century Western Europe prior to their incorporation in political life. Second, the absence of political mobilization can also be combined with cultural differentiation. Such an unmobilized ethnic cate-

---

[4] To use Haferkamp and Smelser's (1992, p. 2) terminology, political mobilization is particular mechanism distinct from its structural determinants and historical consequences. See also Deutsch's (1961) discussion of the conceptual relationship between social mobilization as a consequence of modernization.

[5] The current notion of assimilation resembles the one suggested by Anthony Birch (1989, 48–51) that distinguishes between its social and political aspects. Political assimilation, according to Birch, designates a situation in which ethnicity is of no political significance. Assimilation, in general, can be defined as "a deliberate policy of making similar" (Brubaker 1995, 8) but this definition is too wide for our present purpose. Moreover, as we will see below, assimilation does not have to entail any coercive, state-imposed policy aiming at the eradication of cultural differences but may involve a voluntary and evolutionary erosion of the cultural boundary between the center and the periphery. See Horowitz (1975, 1985) for a typology of assimilation depending on the underlying power balance between the two sides.

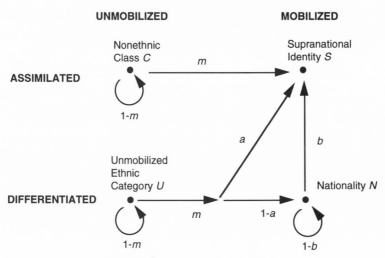

Figure 7.1. The mobilization phase

gory, here labeled U, is politically unconscious of its cultural distinctiveness (Brass 1976).[6] If this group mobilizes two things can happen: either mobilization proceeds with assimilation or it proceeds without it. In the former case, a politically assimilated population loyal to the supranational state crystallizes as S (cf. state-initiated nationalism). In the latter case, the ethnic category transforms into a nationality N.

In addition to defining all the probabilistic states, the diagram illustrates the dynamics of the process. Three main parameters govern each individual member's shift of loyalties. The first parameter, m, measures political mobilization—that is, the probability that a minority member "wakes up." If there is no awakening, which happens with probability $1 - m$, the unmobilized population remains an unmobilized ethnic category U as indicated by the loop going back to this node. Political mobilization either assimilates the ethnic group or provokes the formation of a nationalist countercoalition. The second parameter, a, refers to the probability of the former course—that is, direct assimilation. In the opposite case $(1 - a)$, direct assimilation backfires, and mobilization strengthens the nationality N. The third parameter, b, indicates the likelihood of indirect assimilation. If the center's effort fails $(1 - b)$, the nationality persists (cf. the loop going back to N).

What governs these parameters? Although a full operationalization of the three modeling parameters is beyond the scope of the current discussion, it is useful to provide some hints about their substantive interpreta-

---

[6] For a more refined scale of possibilities, see Alexander Motyl's (1987) "ethnic ladder."

tion. Political mobilization can be of either top-down or bottom-up nature. In the former case, it is usually imposed by the multinational state as a way of mobilizing the population through educational, bureaucratic, or military reforms. Bottom-up mobilization, by contrast, takes place without the aid, or even against the will, of the "home" state. In this case, mobilization follows as a consequence of the diffusion of ideas from other states or regions. Thus, mobilization can be home-made or imported or both.[7]

The interpretation of direct and indirect assimilation hinges upon less-tangible determinants. Despite his quantitative focus, Deutsch (1953, chap. 7) was well aware of the symbolic aspects of large-scale historical processes. In his view, assimilation reflects the similarity of communication habits and efficiency of political learning, and economic and material incentives, as well as compatibility of cultural values and symbols. The better the communication between the center and the periphery, the greater the periphery's incentives to shift its identities; the fewer the cultural and symbolical barriers to peripheral incorporation, the higher the level of assimilation. By extension, indirect assimilation measures the same dimensions, though the timing is different in that the individual already possesses an articulated political identity culturally distinct from that of the center.[8]

From a structural standpoint, the interaction between these parameters depends on the relationship between modernization (and by extension political mobilization) and conflict behavior. Donald Horowitz (1985) summarizes the theoretical alternatives:

> There are three ways of relating ethnic conflict to the modernization process. The first is to view ethnic conflict as a mere relic of an outmoded traditionalism, doomed to be overtaken by the incursions of modernity. The second is to regard ethnic conflict as a traditional but unusually stubborn impediment to modernization. The third is to interpret ethnic conflict as an integral part—even a product—of the process of modernization itself. (96–97)

---

[7] Thus, for mobilization to take place, the multinational state does not need to launch a deliberately mobilizational program. In introducing the concept of a "nationalizing state," Rogers Brubaker (1995) makes a similar distinction by pointing out that what really matters is whether the periphery perceives the central state to be nationalizing: "To ask whether such policies, practices and so on are 'really' nationalizing makes little sense. For present purposes, a nationalizing state . . . is not one whose representatives, authors, or agents understand and articulate it as such, but rather one that is perceived as such in the field of the national minority or the external national homeland" (114).

[8] To reiterate, political assimilation, like mobilization, does not presuppose a conscious policy on the part of the center but may emerge spontaneously in a bottom-up fashion.

In the following, I will adopt Horowitz's classifications and refer to these as assimilation theory, delayed assimilation theory, and provocation theory. Table 7.1 relates each approach to the system parameters.

Since these three theories focus on the political consequences of modernization, they all assume a high level of mobilization. The theoretical consensus, however, breaks down over the effectiveness of political assimilation. As their labels suggest, both traditional and delayed assimilation theory expect modernization to generate a higher level of loyalty with the center. Provocation theory, by contrast, anticipates a low degree of direct assimilation. Whereas traditional assimilation theory expects the nation to succumb quickly to the assimilatory pull of the supranational identity (i.e., high indirect assimilation), delayed assimilation theory predicts a more protracted process (i.e., low indirect assimilation). Finally, provocation, like the delayed assimilation perspective, emphasizes the regional nationalities' persistence. As its label suggests, however, provocation theory differs from the previous two approaches in that it stresses the tendency of mobilization, state-induced or not, to provoke resistance on the periphery (i.e., low direct assimilation).

Though the model is useful as a theoretical taxonomy, its main contribution is to allow us to trace the dynamic consequences of the theoretical assumptions. We proceed by discussing the model's behavior for each theoretical family in turn.

Assimilation Theories

As an umbrella term, assimilation theory combines a number of related theories with roots in classical sociology. Drawing on an evolutionist conception of social change, Western scholars of the 1950s and 1960s developed a set of propositions concerning social communication and postcolonial nation-building that are usually referred to as modernization

TABLE 7.1
A Comparison of Three Basic Hypotheses

	Assimilation Theories	Delayed Assimilation Theories	Provocation Theories
Mobilization m	high	high	high
Direct Assimilation a	high	high	low
Indirect Assimilation b	high	low	low

theory.[9] The main tenet of this scholarship was that "the process of building nation-states, presumably undergone by Western Europe, was destined to be repeated within the Third World" (Connor 1994, 167). Using historical analogies from European history, modernization theorists expected ethnic and tribal units within Third World states to become incorporated swiftly into the national cores through a process of social mobilization. Since modernization allegedly accounted for successful nation-building within the developed world, "the diffusion of economic and technological innovations, along with education and the spread of ideas that had originated in Europe, would lead to the rapid transformation of traditional societies and cultures into modern ones" (Geddes 1991, 47; see also Calhoun 1993).

Other scholars, belonging to the functionalist integration school, even predicted that the European nation-states themselves would smoothly merge into a supranational entity (e.g., Mitrany 1975). Like modernization theory, the functionalist approach to integration argues that peoples' material needs will prevail, and since modernization calls for larger-scale units, loyalties will shift automatically to the more efficient entities, in this case supranational organizations (see Jacobson, Reisinger, and Mathers 1986).

While Marxism differs from these modernization perspectives on crucial points, it shares their belief in Western ideas of rationality and progress. In this vision, there is no room for ethnic parochialism. Indeed, Marx expected national prejudices to wither away as a consequence of the proletarian revolution: "national differences and antagonisms are daily more and more vanishing" and socialism "will cause them to vanish still faster" (Marx quoted in Connor 1992, 32).[10]

Assimilationist perspectives expect that a high level of political mobilization and assimilation produces the emergence of supranational identity. Figure 7.2 captures such a development graphically. By employing the formal results of the appendix (see Proposition 1 and Corollary 1), we are able to plot the historical trajectory of the system given the present assumptions. To begin with, the entire population is unmobilized (cf. Assumption 1). In our particular example, mobilization is 10 percent, direct assimilation 80 percent and indirect assimilation 20 percent. To illustrate

[9] See Sztompka (1993, chap. 9) for a review of both "old" and more recent theoretical modernization work as well as related perspectives, such as convergence theory. According to Sztompka, traditional modernization theorists relied on an evolutionist conception of social change assuming it to be unilinear, irreversible, gradual, adaptive, and progressivist in character (130–31). More recent contributions to the modernization tradition, however, have largely tended to relax these assumptions.

[10] Yet, as argued by Erica Benner (1995), one should not underestimate the sophistication of Marx and Engels' approach to the nationality question.

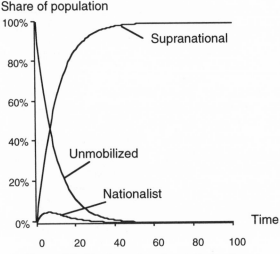

Figure 7.2. The dynamics of assimilation theory

the dynamics, figure 7.2 plots the three subpopulations' share of the entire minority population as a function of time.

Figure 7.2 shows that, whereas the unmobilized population U decreases steadily, mobilization produces a rapid surge in the number of individuals loyal to the existing state S. Within fifty time periods, the center has assimilated almost the entire population. Even at its peak, nationalist opposition N is insignificant (no more than 5 percent), whereafter it declines quickly. This pattern coincides with the basic logic of assimilation theory: there are no serious obstacles to modernization so the center succeeds in quickly assimilating the minority.

Delayed Assimilation Theories

The history of the twentieth century has clearly contradicted the optimism of assimilationist scholarship. Nation-building in the Third World proved much harder than expected. European integration stalled, and the entire field of regional integration was almost entirely abandoned. Moreover, Soviet nationalities continued to resist Moscow's repeated attempts to convert them.[11]

Unwilling to abandon their belief in the final integration of cultural minorities, some theorists responded to these anomalies by modifying the

[11] See Young (1993) for a broad overview of these developments.

foundations of assimilation theory. While retaining the assumption that modernization promotes direct assimilation, the modified perspective is skeptical about indirect assimilation. Once politically aroused, minority populations tend to resist assimilation more successfully than their unmobilized counterparts:

> An ethnic group that is politically passive and whose members do not participate in political life may more easily be assimilated or, for that matter, incorporated into political life than an ethnic group that is already self-conscious of its own identity and is already politically organized to deal with the political system in which it lives. In short, where ethnic minorities are already self-conscious participants in the political system, then the option of assimilation as a means of building national sentiment is generally not feasible. (Weiner 1971, 182)

Using the label "revised modernization theory," Barbara Geddes (1991, 49) explains how this school of thought attributed the failure of assimilation to "persistence of traditional norms and values at variance with the culture traits assumed to be conducive to economic achievement and to honest, efficient government." Still, the theorists of revised modernization "continued to see the international economy as a source of progressive innovations and to focus on explanatory variables located in domestic society." The source of the lingering traditionalism, the corruption, and the tribes' unwillingness to assimilate was certainly not to be found with the "benign" modernizer. And in the long run, these aberrations would disappear.

In a similar vein, students of regional integration refined the optimistic predictions of early functionalism. Ernst Haas (1958) qualified the automaticity of functionalist processes. Agreeing with traditional functionalism that local loyalties are likely to shift in case of "a tranquil and unmobilized people, in which mass emotions play no part and in which there is no general political participation," Haas suggested that the functionalist logic did not apply to nations with "ascriptive status patterns, traditional or charismatic leadership" (50).

Lenin's work can also be counted as delayed assimilation theory, especially his refinement and extension of Marxism to nationalist issues. Distancing himself from the imperial "prison of nations," Lenin attempted to reconcile communist ideology with the ethnic fragmentation of the empire he inherited. This difficult situation forced him to adopt a "dialectical" nationality policy that excluded forced assimilation (Connor 1992, 31). Though vague on the timing, Lenin never made a secret of his wish to integrate the Soviet Union. Nevertheless, he realized that "national and state differences . . . will continue to exist for a very, very long time even after the dictatorship of the proletariat had been established on a world scale" (quoted in Connor 1984, 388).

To summarize the logic of delayed assimilation theory, we turn to figure 7.3. As with traditional assimilation theory, this approach starts by assuming swift mobilization (again 10 percent). As long as assimilation occurs before nationality formation, the local loyalties will shift toward the center (80 percent as before). If mobilized, however, the nationality will persist for a considerable time. This assumption is formalized by reducing the rate of indirect assimilation from 20 percent down to 2 percent (cf. table 7.1).

Again, there is a steep increase in assimilation, but compared to the previous case the nationalist subpopulation rises above 10 percent and persists much longer. Since indirect assimilation is much lower in this case, the nationality is able to resist centralization and acculturation. While the delayed assimilation school tempers the optimism of the most drastic assimilationists, some scholars do not think it goes far enough. The third theoretical perspective attempts to address this problem.

Provocation Theories

Unlike both assimilation perspectives, Horowitz's third family of theories links nationalism and ethnic strife directly to modernization. Karl Deutsch (1961) first suggested relating ethnic mobilization to modernization.[12]

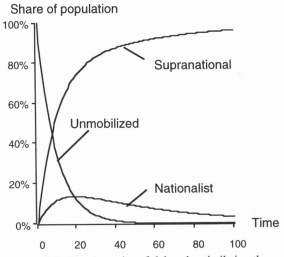

Figure 7.3. The dynamics of delayed assimilation theory

[12] Because his position changed over time, critics have often misclassified Deutsch as a naive modernization theorist (Connor 1972). This criticism fails to do justice to his sophisticated understanding of mobilization and modernization. Already in his pioneering contribution, Deutsch (1953) explicitly analyzed the trade-off between assimilation and nationalist mobilization (see also Horowitz 1985, 99–100).

A series of analyses have explored and refined Deutsch's original insight (see Horowitz 1985, 100–101, and Motyl 1991, 28–29 for references). They have in common a focus on how attempts to modernize tend to provoke unintended separatist mobilization. According to Samuel Huntington's (1968) apt formula: "modernity breeds stability, but modernization breeds instability" (41).While some of the earlier contributions, including Huntington's, avoid the pitfalls of modernization theory, their focus on macrosocial processes generally obscure more specific institutional mechanisms, in particular the key role played by the state (Tilly 1973, 1978).

More recent scholarship rectifies this shortcoming by explicitly analyzing the impact of modernizing state policies. Forced to keep up with the developed world, nation-building elites have often been tempted to accelerate political mobilization in the name of supranational loyalty. These elites are in for unpleasant surprises: "Mobilization of nationalism by a country's elite can just as easily serve to entrench ethnic schisms as newly incorporated groups become politicized" (Olzak 1983, 359). Indeed, deep-reaching state policies "often have the contrary effect to that desired leading frequently to the stimulation of ethnic feelings among the articulate segments of the minorities denied the right to use their own language or express their own cultural values in the public sphere" (Brass 1980, 47).

These findings are consistent with a rich tradition of "provocation hypotheses" in the social sciences. At the turn of the century, Georg Simmel (1955) wrote on the cohesive function of conflict. According to Simmel, conflict not only increases the cohesion of the in-group, it can also create new groups by crystallizing previously blurred boundaries.[13] The writings of George Herbert Mead echo the preoccupation with self/other relationships. Rather than reifying selfhood, Mead (1962) defined it as a consequence of social interaction. Several decades later, the Norwegian anthropologist Fredrik Barth (1969) pointed out that ethnic distinctions not only persist in the face of intensive cross-boundary communication, "but are quite . . . often the very foundations on which embracing social systems are built" (10). Similarly, the social psychologist Henri Tajfel (1981) explained how minorities form not despite but because of intergroup communication. In his view, group consciousness results from self-categorization linked to three processes:

> In the first of these, a common identity is thrust upon a category of people because they are at the receiving end of certain attitudes and treatment from the "outside." In the second case, a group already exists in the sense of

[13] Lewis Coser (1956) elaborated and qualified Simmel's hypotheses on the centralizing effect of conflict, but failed to appreciate its constitutive nature. See Sylvan and Glassner (1985) for a critique of Coser's interpretation of Simmel.

wishing to preserve its separate identity, and this is further reinforced by an interaction between the "inside" and the "outside" attitudes and patterns of social behaviour. In the third case, an existing group might wish to dilute in a number of ways its differences and separateness from others; when this is resisted, new and intense forms of a common group identity may be expected to appear. (351)

To illustrate this type of hypotheses within a formal framework, we again rely on a diagram (see figure 7.4). As the ethnic category mobilizes, assimilation does not follow automatically. Instead, awakening is more likely to be accompanied by growth in nationalist activity. This is the provocation effect. The parameters coincide with the run presented in figure 7.3 except for a reduction of direct assimilation from 20 percent to 2 percent.

As opposed to the two previous diagrams, figure 7.4 illustrates how nationalist mobilization initially outpaces assimilation. If the center succeeds in controlling the sudden outburst of nationalist mobilization, however, it will prevail in assimilating the entire population. The difference between the short-term and the long-term balance underlines the importance of adopting an explicitly dynamic framework.

MODELING COLLECTIVE ACTION

The first phase of the Mobilization Model says nothing about possible revolutionary disruptions in the short term. In fact, the previous section

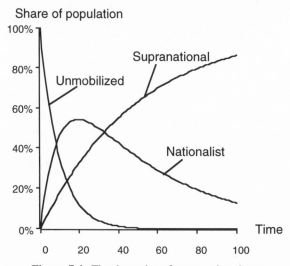

Figure 7.4. The dynamics of provocation theory

assumed that the probabilistic process has only one final state: complete assimilation and the creation of a stable and all-encompassing supranational identity.[14] Even a brief glance at the historical record reveals that this simplification is overly determinist. On the other hand, one should not interpret provocation theory too deterministically in the other direction: "Admittedly, there is a danger of countering the assumption that the process of modernization leads to cultural assimilation with an opposing iron law of political disintegration which contends that modernization results, of necessity, in increasing demands for ethnic separation" (Connor 1994, 35–36). Clearly, this calls for an extended model that specifies when assimilation processes are likely to be interrupted prematurely.

One way of modeling this possibility is to study the relationship between the main state variables. Again, Karl Deutsch (1969) provides a good starting point. According to his assessment, the key to nationalist conflict is the balance between mobilization and assimilation:

> If assimilation stays ahead of mobilization or keeps abreast of it, the government is likely to remain stable, and eventually everybody will be integrated into one people. . . . On the other hand, where mobilization is fast and assimilation is slow the opposite happens. More and more mightily mobilized and disgruntled people are held at arm's length from the politics and culture of the state, and they easily become alienated from the government, the state, and even the country to which they thus far had belonged. (27)

Formally, this criterion translates into a comparison of the strength of the nationalists and of those loyal to the multinational project. If the former exceeds the latter, or formally $N(t) > S(t)$, political instability becomes likely. This situation corresponds to the overshooting effect shown in figure 7.4—that is, where the nationalist curve crosses the supranational one in the short run. Under which conditions does overshooting occur? Proposition 2 of the appendix provides a precise answer: Overshooting takes place if and only if the direct assimilation rate a falls under 50 percent.

This result should not come as a surprise since it coincides with the provocation theory's underlying assumptions of low direct assimilation. What is less intuitive, however, is that overshooting does not vary with the rate of mobilization m. Nevertheless, as we have seen, Deutsch's account emphasizes the independent role of this process (cf. Connor 1972). Similarly, Samuel Huntington (1968) suggests that "the higher the level of education of the unemployed, alienated, or otherwise dissatisfied

---

[14] Cf. Corollary 2 in the appendix. This outcome may be identical to a culturally homogeneous nation-state but could also correspond to a multinational state endowed with a solid and working political identity, as the case of Switzerland would suggest.

person, the more extreme the destabilizing behavior which results" (48). Thus, one would expect the risk of political instability to increase together with political mobilization.

It is thus necessary to question whether overshooting itself offers the most likely indicator of nationalist collective action. Of course, this is ultimately an empirical question, but there are theoretical reasons for a reinterpretation. Instead of considering the difference between the two mobilization processes, an absolute measure of nationalist strength $N(t)$ may be more appropriate. This is because nationalist conflict usually pits government forces against nationalists, but does not necessarily involve recently assimilated minority members. Suggesting precisely this solution as a first cut, Deutsch (1953) opts for a measure exclusively based on the nationalist category: "The share of mobilized but differentiated persons among the total population . . . is the first crude indicator of the probable incidence and strength of national conflict" (104).

Graphically, this measure corresponds to the "height" of the nationality curve's peak. Mathematically, the desired quantity can be calculated as the maximum of the $N(t)$ curve (see Proposition 3 in the appendix). The timing of the highest value depends on the rates of mobilization m and indirect assimilation b. As might be expected, the maximum occurs earlier and attains higher levels as the mobilization rate increases.[15]

However interesting these findings may be, they suffer from a fundamental weakness: while measuring the maximum level of nationalist activity, they offer only indirect information about the long-term risks of collective action. For example, from the center's standpoint, it is not obvious that bringing down the peak level of nationalist mobilization is preferable to running a lower risk of collective action during a longer time period. Thus, an evaluation of a multinational state's survival chances requires a more contextual rendering of the power conditions. For instance, macro processes such as political mobilization and nationalism cannot be understood properly without reference to their geopolitical background (e.g., Breuilly 1982; Brubaker 1992). Sovereignty depends on both internal and external dimensions. According to Samuel Huntington (1968), the same applies to multinational states: "Political modernization involves assertion of the external sovereignty of the nation-state against transnational influences and the internal sovereignty of the national government against local and regional powers" (34).

This has immediate consequences for our model-building venture: it is necessary to construct a dynamic, rather than a snapshot, model of nationalist collective action. Moreover, an explicit mechanism capturing external threats to sovereignty must be added. For heuristic purposes, I refer

---

[15] This result is based on numerical comparisons rather than on analytical proof.

to these two classes of events as secession and invasion respectively, although it should be remembered that internal and external challenges to state survival may sometimes take less drastic forms. Though falling short of outright military conquest, foreign economic domination may undermine political sovereignty. By the same token, there are more subtle types of internal challenges to domestic control than secession, such as various forms of territorial autonomy and decentralization as well as functional opt-outs.[16]

The second modeling step features a superimposed probabilistic process with variable transition probabilities. These depend on the underlying mobilization model described previously. The technically interested reader is again encouraged to consult the appendix for a more detailed description.

The superimposed collective-action model features three probabilistic states: status quo, invasion, and secession (see fig. 7.5). This is an abstraction of the more involved two-level design proposed in the extended Emergent Polarity Model. The process starts in the first state and shifts to either of the latter two states, which are historial end points (or absorbing states in technical terms). Thus, there are three possible long-term outcomes. First, if the process remains in the status-quo state, the multinational project succeeds. Second, if invasion occurs, by contrast, the project fails and the state is conquered by a foreign power. Third, secession also amounts to failure, but in this case the loss of sovereignty is due to an internal nationalist challenge.

This specification begs the question about the origin of transition probabilities. As indicated above, $p_{inv}(t)$ and $p_{sec}(t)$ derive from the output of the model's first phase. More precisely, it is hypothesized that both col-

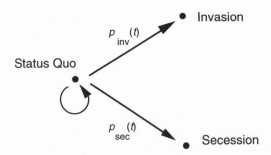

Figure 7.5. The collective-action phase

---

[16] In the following, I draw on the literature on revolutions although secession differs from this concept in that collective action serves to leave the state rather than changing its regime.

lective-action mechanisms follow a threshold logic based on the relevant power balance (again see the appendix for details). To begin with secession, this event becomes more likely the stronger the nationalist opposition $N(t)$. Thus, while the center has little to fear as long as the nationalists are numerically weak, the situation changes dramatically beyond some exogenously given threshold reflecting the center's resources. Similarly, the risk of invasion also varies with the underlying parameters, but in this case the threshold pertains to the strength of some external challenger. Since modern warfare requires a mobilized political system, whether in terms of troops or economic performance, the multinational organization's performance is a function of the supranational loyalty of its citizens $S(t)$. As long as this variable remains low, the probability of invasion by more cohesively organized competitors is considerable. If the center manages to mobilize the periphery against external challenges above a given level, however, this probability decreases significantly.

Before studying the consequences of the internal and external collective-action mechanisms, a few comments about the nonlinear threshold logic of these two processes are in order. First, secession falls into the category of revolutionary collective action. Facing a powerful center, the peripheral actors have no choice but to rely on large numbers. Secession, and other less drastic challenges to internal sovereignty, require the nationalist opposition to engage in large-scale coalition formation. Without such a policy, the nationalists are unable to transcend the Olsonian collective-choice dilemmas (Tilly 1978; Taylor 1988). As opposed to premodern, rural conditions, the modern world with its communication technology and discursive literacy makes the categorical identities potent tools of political mobilization (Gellner 1964; Anderson 1991; Calhoun 1993).

Communication among the nationalist subjects leads to secessionist chain reactions. Drawing on pioneering work by Schelling (1978) and Granovetter (1978), Timor Kuran (1989, 1991) has developed a simple threshold model of revolutionary collective action (see also Lohmann 1994 for extensions and critique). If the potential participants are able to observe the behavior of their fellow nationals, self-reinforcing processes are likely to kick in beyond a certain critical point. Once the nationalist movement acquires this critical strength, collective action acquires a life of its own (see also Macy 1990, 1991; and Goertz 1994).[17]

Similarly, a threshold logic often operates with respect to external challenges to sovereignty. The Emergent Polarity Model in chapter 4 sup-

---

[17] This threshold logic suggests that political independence is likely to be a "step good" corresponding to a sharply increasing curve of collective benefits at the critical point (Hardin 1982, 55).

posed that a successful invasion requires either a 3:1 or a 2:1 superiority ratio depending on the offense-defense balance. Whatever the exact threshold, the outcome depends nonlinearly on the force balance. The balance, in turn, hinges upon the level of mobilization, at least under modern conditions (e.g., Tilly 1975; Mann 1993a). Of course, modern technology and a professional army may to some extent compensate for a lack of popular adhesion, but one should not underestimate the underlying requirements of modern military competition in terms of economic and technological performance as well as political control and organization. These factors become problematic in ethnically, and especially linguistically, fragmented settings.

What results, then, does the second modeling phase produce? Figure 7.6 shows a typical outcome as a function of time. Here the underlying process coincides with that in figure 7.4—that is, the situation conforms with the assumptions of provocation theory ($m = 0.1$, $a = 0.2$, and $b = 0.02$). As the dynamic process unfolds, the chances of survival decrease dramatically. After about fifty time steps, however, the situation stabilizes. The long-term outcome converges on invasion in a tenth of the cases and secession in more than half, thus fixing the survival rate at about 35 percent. Even if the latter probability is rather low, should the multinational project survive the first fifty periods, its prospects are excellent.

Obviously, the figure only reports on one the outcomes of one specific parameter constellation. Having created an explicit model of state sur-

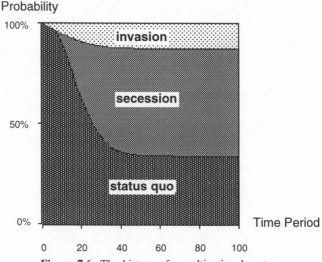

Figure 7.6. The history of a multinational system

vival, however, we are now in a position to study its behavior more systematically. In particular, the difference between assimilation theory, whether traditional or delayed, and provocation theory deserves our attention. The two panels of figure 7.7 illustrate the long-term outcomes as a function of the mobilization rate m. Note that the x-axis is logarithmic—that is, its units mark increases by a power of ten. The left graph (see fig. 7.7a), which assumes that the mobilization process corresponds to delayed assimilation theory, reveals that the risk of invasion decreases steadily as the mobilization rate goes up. In this case, the center has everything to gain from speeding up its mobilization policy since this helps reduce the probability of external challenges.

Figure 7.7b tells a dramatically different story. In addition to invasion and status quo, a third outcome appears, namely secession. Again, the likelihood of invasion falls with increasing mobilization, but state survival ceases to be the mirror image of invasion. Beyond a certain mobilization rate, in this case about $m = 0.03$, secession becomes a distinct possibility, and from $m = 0.1$, it dominates the picture.[18] This means that long-term survival does not increase unilinearly with mobilization. Instead, the relationship is curvilinear since there is an optimal level at about $m = 0.04$ beyond which the status quo is less likely. To ensure survival of their project, the central elite needs to tune the rate of mobilization

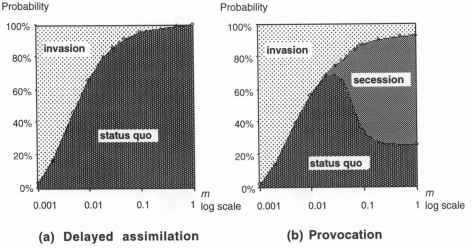

(a) Delayed assimilation   **(b) Provocation**

Figure 7.7. Long-run outcomes as a function of mobilization m

---

[18] A comparison of figures 7.6 and 7.7b shows that the long-run outcome of the former figure can be found in the latter for $m = 0.1$.

within a narrow band. While too slow a rate invites foreign intervention, too speedy a process provokes internal challenges.[19]

By now the policy implications should be clear. Mistaking an assimilation situation for one involving high risks of provocation could lead to unpleasant surprises for the center. Assimilationists, whether belonging to the traditional or delayed school, tend to care about the need for mobilization to counter external threats. In their view, thus, the world operates according to the principle of figure 7.7a. Under these circumstances, the best policy is to speed up mobilization as much as possible. If reality follows the provocation logic spelled out by figure 7.7b, however, accelerated mobilization entails a significant risk of internal collapse. To the extent that the mobilizing elite subscribes to an assimilationist perspective, such a development will come as a surprise because of their conceptual bias ruling out the possibility of provocation.

HISTORICAL ILLUSTRATIONS

Although a full validation of the Mobilization Model goes well beyond the scope of the current treatment, it is useful to illustrate the argument with a few historical examples. To limit the discussion, this section considers three supranational projects: the Habsburg empire, the Soviet Union, and the European Union. Despite important differences, all these cases fall into the category analyzed by this chapter, namely that of a culturally distinct center attempting to hold together a multinational state or statelike organization in the face of external challenges. In particular, the state-maintaining or state-building elites have had to consider to what extent, and how rapidly, their culturally distinct peripheries could be mobilized.

As the paradigmatic example of a multinational empire, the Habsburg monarchy had to deal with both internal and external challenges to its survival. These threats became particularly serious as a consequence of the French Revolution. Having barely escaped the attack of Napoleon's *Grande Armée*, in itself a creation of the Revolution, the imperial elite had to cope with a wave of nationalist activities inspired by revolutionary ideas of popular sovereignty. The latter posed a deadly internal threat to imperial survival. In his study of the post-Napoleonic period, Henry Kissinger (1957) highlights the dilemma faced by Metternich and his successors:

[19] Like the replication diagrams in chapters 4 and 5, figure 7.7 offers a counterfactual picture of parameter space. Note, however, that the figures report numerically calculated probabilities of the Markov states that only have to be computed once, rather than the outcome of repeated simulations.

The new doctrines of nationalism and rationalized administration could not but be dissolving for so intricate, indeed so subtle, a structure as this last survivor of the feudal period. Nor was it yet certain whether the pressure from the West was not about to be replaced by a similar threat from the East. How to avoid both impotence and dissolution? How to achieve both peace and proportion, both victory and legitimacy? (8)

Following the near imperial collapse in the nationalist revolutions of 1848, the Habsburg leaders had to abandon any hope of transforming the monarchy into a centralized state competing with the old and emerging nation-states in terms of cohesiveness and popular commitment. After the defeat by Prussia in war, Vienna had no choice but to accept the compromise (*Ausgleich*) with Hungary in 1867, cementing the empire's fragmented composition. With the exception of the tendencies toward Magyarization and Germanization (which happened against the will of the imperial elite), few attempts were made to increase political participation. Indeed, "after the revolutions of 1848 and the lost wars of the 1860s, [the Habsburg rulers] acknowledged the force of modern nationalism. They reversed the course and committed themselves to the theory that they might survive as rulers of a multinational world through systematic reduction of their central authority" (McCagg 1991, 50).

The low mobilization rate toward the beginning of the twentieth century helped prevent secession. Nevertheless, it caused a more serious problem, for it was not internal collapse that broke the backbone of the empire but international conflict. Alan Sked (1989) argues that, had it not been for World War I, the monarchy might well have survived. In the end, "it fell because it lost a major war. Yet almost until the very end of that war there was no question but that it would survive, even if it failed to secure victory" (264). Though demanding larger political freedom, most nationalists expected a future within an overall Habsburg framework and fought for the empire until 1918. If nationalism was the cause of the final collapse, it was primarily because it undermined the empire's financial and military performance.

In terms of figure 7.7b, the mobilization rate m probably lay well to the left of its optimal value. Well aware of the dangers of secession, the imperial elite refrained from mobilizing the population. By international comparison, the mobilization rate remained low and by the time the monarchy was put to its final test, its army proved vastly inferior to those of its more cohesive competitors, thus leading to "invasion" as the final outcome.

The Soviet supranational experiment, by contrast, was not terminated by foreign invasion. Instead, it was internal disintegration along national lines that finished off the USSR. All the same, the Soviet elite confronted a policy dilemma not unlike the one that haunted their Habsburg counter-part. Again the trade-off concerned both internal and external threats to the survival of a multinational project. Yet as opposed to Metternich and other Austrian imperialists, the Soviet leaders mobilized primarily against external threats. Drawing on imperial nationalism of the Tsarist period (Beissinger and Haida 1990) and interpreting Marxist ideology as a theory of development, Lenin and his successors embarked upon a massive campaign of modernization (Gitelman 1992). Indeed, there was no lack of foreign threats: Hitler's Operation Barbarossa confirmed these fears, only to be replaced by the specter of a superpower confrontation with the United States.

By the time that Gorbachev took over, these external concerns loomed as large as ever. Apart for the internal problems caused by severe economic decline, the Soviet Union was involved in an increasingly costly arms race with the United States. Desiring to reassert Soviet power at home as well as abroad, Gorbachev launched his reforms as an attempt to modernize the country (Åslund 1989, 15–16; Motyl 1991, 35). In contrast to the Habsburg approach, Gorbachev's reform policy, based on perestroika and glasnost, emphasized efficiency through massive and speedy political mobilization. In Dawisha and Parrott's (1994, 18) words: "In essence, his strategy was to encourage greatly expanded public participation in political life in order to generate the power needed to ram through basic reforms of the institutional structures inherited from the Stalin era" (18)

Gorbachev hoped to overcome economic stagnation by eradicating corruption and inefficiencies, especially in the non-Russian republics. Nowhere was this more urgent than in the least developed southern part of the country:

> A significant increase in the effectiveness of industry could not take place without reallocating investment from one region to another, penetrating diffuse patronage networks, integrating the excess labor resources of Central Asia, and mobilizing the non-Russian, as well as the Russian, populations and intelligentsias. (Ibid., 312)

In addition to the increased penetration caused by perestroika, the increased freedom promoted by glasnost further accelerated political participation. As an attempt to overcome the legitimacy crisis of the Brezhnev era, glasnost presupposed massive popular support (see Gitelman 1992, 235; Beissinger and Hajda 1990, 313).

The sweeping nature of Gorbachev's project ensured that its impact would be considerable. Unfortunately for Gorbachev, however, the reforms did not produce the desired direct assimilation; instead, they stimulated the nationalist periphery to mobilize against the center. The main reason for this unexpected turn of events was Gorbachev's insensitivity to

what could, and indeed did, provoke resistance in the non-Russian republics.[20] To overcome the penetration crisis and improve economic performance, perestroika had to break the local entrenched power structures
that had emerged under, and even been promoted by, the Brezhnev regime. In accordance with assimilation theory, Gorbachev did not expect
his modernization policy to have any adverse regional effects: "Seemingly assured of Soviet solidity and control, he paid scant attention to
national sensitivities, and he blithely overlooked the rules for national
representation that had been in effect since 1956" (Carrère d'Encausse
1991, 10).

Filling the country's highest cadres with Russians and intensifying the
campaigns against corruption in central Asia and in the Caucasus, Gorbachev opted for a centralization policy of a strongly Slavic bent (Beissinger and Hajda 1990; Carrère d'Encausse 1991). Nationalist unrest
soon erupted in both these areas. Yet the most serious challenge to the
Soviet state's internal sovereignty came from the Baltic republics, which
claimed the right to secession.

It was not only the provocation of perestroika that made these protests
so widespread, for glasnost also spawned nationalist protests. By launching this component of the reform package, Gorbachev hoped that pluralism would accelerate direct assimilation by creating a truly civil society
encompassing the entire country. As Ernest Gellner (1992) astutely remarks, Gorbachev overlooked the fact that "seven decades of resolute
centralism . . . have all but destroyed most potential bases for such asso-
ciations" (249). The absence of viable pluralist organizations created a
vacuum that promoted nationalist agitation, a tendency that continues to
bewitch democratization efforts in the post-Soviet period (ibid., 249–50;
see also Motyl 1990, 71).

Interestingly enough, the European debate following upon the signing
of the Treaty on European Union in Maastricht showed similar signs of
a participatory vacuum. To the integrationist elite's surprise, when the
treaty provisions were subjected to confirmation in referenda, public sup-

[20] This is not to say that other factors were not important. To avoid a monocausal interpretation, it is useful to recall that the center-periphery balance is the ratio between the
resources R controlled by the center and those controlled by the regional elite Nr, where N
is the number of nationalist adherents and r the power of each individual. Under these
assumptions, revolutionary collective action becomes possible if the ratio of forces exceeds
some threshold ρ—i.e., if $Nr/R > r$. Given the strength of the totalitarian state, it can be
safely assumed that $r/R << \rho$. The relationship, however, could be reversed for great Ns.
This analysis suggests that the disintegration of the Soviet Union depended on several
factors. I have highlighted the consequences of increases in N, but changes affecting r and
R were no doubt also important, especially the decline in the center's economic performance. To complicate things further, the decision to rebel depends crucially on each individual's expectation of future changes in N and the center's willingness to use its power
resources R.

port proved lukewarm as the Danish no and the French *petit oui* demonstrated. Of course, these nationalist backlashes have not so far threatened the Union's survival, but they did prompt the return of "Euro-pessimism" and robbed the integration process of its regained momentum.

Although a comparison with the Habsburg and Soviet cases may seem extravagant, the structural conditions of the European integration process, especially in its present state-building phase, feature important parallels to these two imperial systems.[21] As is usually the case in multinational identity politics, the European integrationists found their project challenged both from abroad and from within. Although the most-cited threats pertained to economic competition with Japan and the United States (cf. e.g., Grant 1994, 225; Ross 1995, 89), it would be a mistake to overlook the security domain. Concerned by instability in the East after the fall of communism, Commission President Delors was haunted by a vision of the community as a "big Switzerland with gigantic economic power, few diplomatic and no defense capabilities" (Ross 1995, 92).[22]

Like Gorbachev's modernization attempt, the Delorist integration strategy strove to counter relative decline compared to the main competitors, a phenomenon often labeled Eurosclerosis.[23] To improve Europe's competitiveness and assert its political clout, wide-ranging reforms were suggested. Although the immediate goal was economic, the improved market harmonization did not fail to have ethnocultural consequences (Delanty 1995, 143). Emboldened by the successes of the Single European Act (SEA), Delors went well beyond the strictly economic sphere and expressed confidence that Europe would soon be ruled by Brussels in more matters than trade (Grant 1994, 80). These statements, as well as the increasingly visible cultural side-effects of the SEA, provoked immediate nationalist reactions (See Ross 1995, 142; Wallace 1994, 64). Although no member state left the union, various opt-outs and delays slowed down the ratification process.

CONCLUSION

The double policy dilemma facing political leaders in multi-national environments can be fruitfully analyzed with a simple dynamic model. As

[21] Ole Waever (1995) even goes as far viewing the European Union as an imperial system. Whatever the merits and weaknesses of such a comparison, it has the advantage of highlighting the ethno-territorial segregation of the Union as opposed to the standard reference point, the United States.

[22] Symptomatically, Delors and other integrationists often applied military analogies to economic and cultural competition. The latter point is confirmed by Delors's statements about Hollywood's alleged "media invasions" (Schlesinger 1994).

[23] Here relative rather than absolute power matters. It goes without saying that Europe's position was not declining in the same sense as that of the Soviet Union.

opposed to purely verbal analysis, this model sheds light on the temporal repercussions of political mobilization. In a world of nationalist mass politics, popular support is the sine qua non of state survival, as the Habsburg elite realized belatedly in 1918. Today, the bases of power have shifted partly from the purely military to the economic and informational domains, but Metternichian conservatism remains as untenable as in the last century. This is because, despite the existence of new technology, the new power bases require at least as much public loyalty as the old ones.

Ever since the nineteenth century, various modernization ideologies have claimed to offer an effective alternative to conservative stagnation. Nevertheless, by downplaying the difficulties of political assimilation, these modernist paradigms fail to appreciate the full dilemma. By dramatically speeding up political mobilization, politicians such as Gorbachev and Delors provoked unintended and counterproductive nationalist reactions. Rather than improving the chances of survival, the joint reforms of perestroika and glasnost accelerated the Soviet Union's final collapse. Delors's state-building strategy also provoked serious setbacks, though less fatal ones.

In order to succeed, mobilization drives in multinational states need to be carefully tuned. While too slow a process invites external interventions, too rapid a mobilization triggers nationalist collective action with serious consequences for state survival. In his comparative study of declining empires, Alexander Motyl (1991) comes to the same conclusion:

> Resource mobilization . . . under the economically inefficient and politically fragmented conditions of a decaying empire will not only divert the energy, time, and attention of the center from its problems of the periphery, but it will also compel the center to engage in a pell-mell economic and military mobilization that is sure to aggravate the center's relations with the periphery, to inflame the nationalist passions of regional elites, and to lead to economic disruptions and perhaps even economic collapse. In turn, peripheries will respond to crises by losing faith in the authority and leadership skills of the center, by intensifying their resistance to the center's encroachments of their resources, and by rejecting the attempts of the center to extend more or less absolute rule over the polity in general and the drifting periphery in particular. (32)

While manipulation of analytical parameters appears simple in theory, such fine-tuning proves less straightforward in reality. To shake up stagnating political systems is an achievement in itself. Once the mobilization ball has been set in motion, however, it may be impossible to stop it. After an initial honeymoon, Gorbachev soon encountered severe difficulties in trying to control the speed of political mobilization. In managing the negotiations prior to the Maastricht Treaty, Delors and his collaborators experienced a similar acceleration effect. No longer in control of the integration agenda, the commission found itself surpassed by events as the integration process acquired a life on its own (Ross 1995). Thus, in opposition to neofunctionalist expectations, "spillover" cannot always be nicely exploited for integrationist purposes.

Moreover, contrary to the received wisdom of integrationist scholarship, integration may itself produce disintegration. Rather than being a premodern residual, nationalism retains its vitality, and integration may even strengthen it. Among the few to have realized this important counterintuitive point, we find Ole Wæver and Morten Kelstrup (1993) who contend that "integration might well provoke reaction against integration—and thus be the triggering cause for turning towards fragmentation" (90–91; see also Wolton 1993, 82; and Delanty 1995, 154).[24]

A more cautious approach to political mobilization may also be preferable in Eastern Europe and the former Soviet Union. Since the collapse of communism, Western scholars and policymakers have been falling over themselves to "help" these countries. It is seldom recognized that well-intended modernization programs could actually worsen an already precarious political situation. Rather than being an anachronistic remainder from the precommunist period, national-identity formation remains an active force that will hardly disappear in the immediate future. Under such circumstances, successful reforms require the driver to use both the gas and the brake, a fact overlooked by the supporters of economic shock therapy and instant democratization.

These insights should be seen as possibilities rather than predictions. To move beyond heuristic evaluation of particular multinational projects, it is necessary to consider elaborations of the modeling framework and to be much more specific about the operationalization of its parameters. First, it should be recalled that the current model presupposes a single cultural cleavage. Reality is usually more messy, especially where mobilization occurs along more than one cultural dimension. In such situations, the spectrum of assimilation policies ranges from inclusive, political platforms to narrowly ethnonational ones. Second, following Deutsch's simplified approach, the model introduces the explanatory factors as exogenous parameters rather than endogenous variables. This rules out interesting interaction and feedback effects linking the parameters.[25] Fi-

---

[24] Intergovernmentalist scholars also postulate a positive link between integration and nationalism (cf. Milward 1992; Moravcsik 1991), but because of their realist leanings they fail to offer a theory of change and political mobilization.

[25] See Deutsch (1953, 130, 137) for a discussion of various multiplier effects. In particular, such positive-feedback mechanisms stem from the interactive nature of political mobilization linking individual processes with collective outcomes (cf. Kuran 1991). One way of formalizing this would be to make the direct assimilation a a decreasing function of the already acquired strength of the nationalist movement N. The reader should also note that

nally, though more explicit than most other mobilization models, the geopolitical modeling phase suffers from a fundamental weakness. In fact, internal and external threats to sovereignty often reinforce each other (Breuilly 1982, 98), as suggested by the two-level extension of the Emergent Polarity Model In the following chapter, we incorporate some of the richness of that extension in a CAS model of competitive nationalist mobilization in a two-dimension cultural space.

APPENDIX

This appendix provides a technical specification of the dynamic model's two phases. The stochastic process was modeled as an absorbing Markov chain (for an introduction to the application of Markov processes in the social sciences, see, e.g., Olinick 1978). As figure 7.1 suggests, this process has four probabilistic states: the absorbing state S, and the transient states of nationalism N, unmobilized class C, and unmobilized ethnic category U. Furthermore, we let m denote the probability of mobilization, a the probability of direct assimilation (and consequently $1 - a$ the likelihood of provocation), and finally b the probability of indirect assimilation (and $1 - b$ the likelihood of nationalist persistence). The dynamic rules defined by the state diagram can be expressed compactly as a transition matrix, whose entries M_{ij} represent the probability of a transition from state i to state j ($i, j \in \{S, N, C, U\}$):

$$\mathbf{M} = \begin{bmatrix} 1 & 0 & 0 & 0 \\ b & 1-b & 0 & 0 \\ m & 0 & 1-m & 0 \\ ma & m(1-a) & 0 & 1-m \end{bmatrix}.$$

If the initial probability vector is $\mathbf{p}^{(0)} = [S_0, N_0, C_0, U_0]$ where $S_0 + N_0 + C_0 + U_0 = 1$ the state of the system can be computed as:

$$\mathbf{p}^{(t)} = \mathbf{p}^{(0)} \mathbf{M}^t.$$

In component form, this corresponds to $\mathbf{p}^{(t)} = [S(t), N(t), C(t), U(t)]$. We are now ready to describe the system's dynamic behavior explicitly:

Proposition 1: Assuming the nontrivial case for which $0 < m < 1, 0 < a < 1, 0 < b < 1$, the process at time t is defined by: If $m \neq b$,

---

some of the current model's constants may be anything other than constant in real cases. For example, the collapse of the Soviet Union probably depended as much on the endogenous erosion of the center's resources as on nationalist mobilization itself. More technically, this point amounts to a decrease in the constant G (cf. the appendix).

$$S(t) = 1 - (N_0 + c_1 U_0)(1 - b)^t - (C_0 - c_2 U_0)(1 - m)^t,$$
$$N(t) = (N_0 + c_2 U_0)(1 - b)^t - c_2 (1 - m)^t,$$
$$C(t) = C_0 (1 - m)^t,$$
$$U(t) = U_0(1 - m)^t$$

where

$$c_1 = \frac{b - ma}{m - b} \text{ and } c_2 = \frac{m(1 - a)}{m - b} .$$

Otherwise ($m = b$),

$$S(t) = 1 - \left(C_0 + N_0 + U_0 \left\{ 1 - \frac{m(1 - a)}{1 - m} t \right\} \right) (1 - m)t,$$

$$N(t) = \left\{ N_0 - U_0 \frac{m(1 - a)}{1 - m} t \right\} (1 - m)^t.$$

PROOF: We want to derive an explicit expression for $\mathbf{p}^{(t)} = \mathbf{p}^{(0)} \mathbf{M}^t$. The difficult part is to compute $\mathbf{M}^t$. This task is greatly simplified by diagonalizing the matrix and finding the eigenvalues and eigenvectors. Once this has been done, the transition matrix can be written as $\mathbf{M} = \mathbf{A} \Lambda \mathbf{A}^{-1}$ where $\mathbf{A}$ is the matrix of the eigen vectors and Λ the eigen value matrix. Since Λ is diagonal, calculating $\mathbf{M}^t$ is greatly simplified:

$$\mathbf{M}^t = (\mathbf{A}\Lambda\mathbf{A}^{-1})(\mathbf{A}\Lambda\mathbf{A}^{-1})...(\mathbf{A}\Lambda\mathbf{A}^{-1}) = \mathbf{A}\Lambda(\mathbf{A}^{-1}\mathbf{A})\Lambda(\mathbf{A}^{-1}\mathbf{A})...(\mathbf{A}^{-1}\mathbf{A})\Lambda\mathbf{A}^{-1} = \mathbf{A}\Lambda^t\mathbf{A}^{-1},$$

where, assuming that $m \neq b$,

$$\mathbf{A} = \begin{bmatrix} 1 & 0 & 0 & 0 \\ 1 & 1 & 0 & 0 \\ 1 & 0 & 1 & 0 \\ 1 & \dfrac{(a - 1)m}{b - m} & 0 & 1 \end{bmatrix} \text{ and } \Lambda^t = \begin{bmatrix} 1 & 0 & 0 & 0 \\ 0 & (1 - b)^t & 0 & 0 \\ 0 & 0 & (1 - m)^t & 0 \\ 0 & 0 & 0 & (1 - m)^t \end{bmatrix}.$$

Inversion of $\mathbf{A}$ and straightforward matrix multiplication yields the desired expression for $\mathbf{M}^t$:

$$\mathbf{M}^t = \begin{bmatrix} 1 & 0 & 0 & 0 \\ 1 - (1 - b)^t & (1 - b)^t & 0 & 0 \\ 1 - (1 - m)^t & 0 & (1 - m)^t & 0 \\ 1 - c_1(1 - b)^t + c_2 (1 - m)^t & c_2\{(1-b)^t - (1 - m)^t\} & 0 & (1 - m)^t \end{bmatrix}.$$

Premultiplication by $\mathbf{p}^{(0)}$ yields $\mathbf{p}^{(t)}$ as stated in the proposition. The probability vector for the case $m = b$ is obtained by calculating $\lim\limits_{k \to w} \mathbf{p}(t)$. QED.

We have assumed that the initial minority population only consists of unmobilized, culturally differentiated individuals, or formally:

Assumption 1: $S_0 = 0$, $N_0 = 0$, $C_0 = 0$, $U_0 = 1$.

This assumption yields a simpler expression for the system's dynamic behavior:

Corollary 1: Under Assumption 1 and $m \neq b$, the system at time t is defined as follows:

$$S(t) = 1 - c_1 (1 - b)^t + c_2 (1 - m)^t.$$
$$N(t) = c_2\{(1 - b)^t - (1 - m)^t\},$$
$$C(t) = 0,$$
$$U(t) = (1 - m)^t.$$

PROOF: Follows immediately by substitution of the initial probabilities defined by Assumption 1 in Proposition 1. QED.

A second corollary confirms that the Markov chain is indeed absorbing. In the long run, the process converges on state S:

Corollary 2: if $m > 0$ and $b > 0$,

$$S(t) \to 1, \ N(t) \to 0, \ C(t) \to 0, \ U(t) \to 0 \text{ as } t \to \infty.$$

PROOF: Follows directly from taking the limits of the expressions in Proposition 1. QED.

We are now ready to state a proposition about when the overshooting effect occurs—that is, when the nationalist mobilization exceeds assimilation. This phenomenon occurs if and only if the rate of direct assimilation a is less than one half:

Proposition 2: Under Assumption 1, $\exists t \geq 1$: $N(t) \ S(t)$ iff $a < 1/2$.
PROOF: To prove that $a < 1/2$ implies $N(t) > S(t)$, it is sufficient to set $t = 1$ and to show that the inequality holds:

$$S(1) = 1 - \frac{(1 - a)m}{m - b}(1 - b) + \frac{b - ma}{m - b}(1 - m) = ma$$

$$N(1) = \frac{m(1 - a)}{m - a}\{1 - b - 1 + m\} = m(1 - a)$$

If $a < 1/2$, $a < (1 - a)$, so there is a t such that $N(t) > S(t)$, namely $t = 1$.

To prove the other direction, we need to demonstrate that if $a > 1/2$, $\neg\exists t \geq 1$: $N(t) > S(t)$. This is the same as proving that $S(t) - N(t) \geq 0$, $\forall A t \geq 1$. We begin by calculating the difference:

$$S(t) - N(t) = 1 - 2\frac{m(1 - a)}{m - b}(1 - b)^t + \frac{b + m(1 - 2a)}{m - b}(1 - m)^t = 1 + T_1 + T_2$$

where

$$T_1 = \frac{m(1 - 2a)}{m - b}\{(1 - m)^t - (1 - b)^t\} \text{ and } T_2 = \frac{1}{m - b}\{b(1 - m)^t - m(1 - b)^t\}.$$

There are two cases:

Case 1. If $m \geq b$ then clearly $T_1 \geq 0$ because $m(1 - 2a)(m - b) \leq 0$ and $\{(1 - m)^t - (1 - b)^t\} \leq 0$, so it sufficient to show that $T_2 \geq -1$. For this purpose, it is helpful to rewrite the last factor of T_2:

$$b(1 - m)^t - m(1 - b)^t =$$
$$- (1 - b)(1 - m)\{(1 - m)^{t-1} - (1 - b)^{t-1}\} + \{(1 - m)^t - (1 - b)^t\}.$$

We may now write

$$T_2 = -\frac{(1 - b)(1 - m)}{m - b}\{(1 - m)^{t-1} - (1 - b)^{t-1}\} + \frac{1}{m - b}\{(1 - m)^t - (1 - b)^t\},$$

but because the first term is positive, we know that the whole expression is greater than the second term, so we know that:

$$T_2 \geq \frac{1}{m - b}\{(1 - m)^t - (1 - b)^t\}.$$

Multiplying the numerator and the denominator of the right hand side by $(1 - b)^t$ yields a new expression for the right hand side of the inequality. Under the initial assumption $m \geq b$ or $1 - b \geq 1 - m$, it follows that $\{(1 - m) / (1 - b)\}^t < (1 - m) / (1 - b)$ and $(1 - b)^t < (1 - b)$ as long as $t \geq 1$, so we arrive at a new inequality proving that $T_2 \geq -1$:

$$\frac{1}{m - b} (1 - b)^t \left\{ \left(\frac{1 - m}{1 - b} \right)^t - 1 \right\} \geq \frac{1}{m - b} (1 - b) \left\{ \left(\frac{1 - m}{1 - b} \right) - 1 \right\} = -1.$$

Case 2: If $m < b$, the proof follows the same logic as in the previous case. Again, we write $S(t) - N(t) = 1 + T_1 + T_2$ and because $T_1 \geq 0$, we need only show that $T_2 \geq -1$. Rewriting T_2 as above, we get:

$$T_2 \geq \frac{1}{m - b} \{(1 - m)^t - (1 - b)^t\} = \frac{1}{m - b} (1 - m)^t \left\{ 1 - \left(\frac{1 - b}{1 - m} \right)^t \right\} \geq$$
$$\frac{1}{m - b} (1 - b) \left\{ 1 - \left(\frac{1 - b}{1 - m} \right) \right\} = -1.$$

Having shown that $T_2 \geq -1$ for both cases, we know that the proposition holds in both directions. QED.

If the condition of nationalist collective action refers to the absolute strength of the nationalist movement rather than the difference between it and the center's resources as the previous proposition, Proposition 3 provides information about when the nationality curve has its maximum:

Proposition 3. Under Assumption 1, $N(t)$ has a maximum at t_{max}:

$$t_{max} = \frac{\ln\{\ln(1 - b) \, / \, \ln(1 - m)\}}{\ln(1 - m) - \ln(1 - b)}.$$

PROOF: To find the maximum, we differentiate $N(t)$ with respect to t and set the result equal to zero:

$$\frac{\partial}{\partial t} N(t) = c_2 \left\{ (1 - b)^t \ln(1 - b) - (1 - m)^t \ln(1 - m) \right\} = 0.$$

Solving for t_{max} yields the maximum. QED.

Proposition 3 can be used to compute the location of the maximum in figure 7.4. Given that $m = 0.1$ and $b = 0.02$, we know that the N curve has a maximum at $t_{max} = \ln\{\ln(1 - 0.02)/\ln(1 - 0.1)\}/\{\ln(1 - 0.1) - \ln(1 - 0.02)\} = 19.4$. Substitution of the closest integers ($t = 19$ and $t = 20$) into the expression for $N(t)$ given by Corollary 1 yields the maximum value $N(19) = 0.55$.

As we have seen above, the second phase of the model focuses on collective action. The flow diagram presented in figure 7.5 captures a Markov process with variable transition probabilities. This process must be numerically solved since standard Markov analysis presumes constant probabilities. Formally, the state vector $\mathbf{x}^{(t)}$ describes this process for each time step t:

$$\mathbf{x}^{(t)} = \mathbf{x}^{(0)} \prod_{\tau=1}^{t} \mathbf{P}^{(\tau)},$$

where the transition matrix has the following form:

$$\mathbf{P}^{(t)} = \begin{bmatrix} 1 & 0 & 0 \\ 0 & 1 & 0 \\ p_{\text{inv}}(t) & p_{\text{sec}}(t) & 1 - p_{\text{inv}}(t) - p_{\text{sec}}(t) \end{bmatrix}.$$

The vector's first element stands for the probability of invasion, the second one for the probability of secession, and the third one for the probability of survival. Thus, the first and second rows of the matrix represent the two absorbing states. The third row, by contrast, contains the probability of a shift from the status quo to the other two outcomes—that is, $p_{\text{inv}}(t)$ and $p_{\text{sec}}(t)$, as well as the likelihood of survival in the given time period.

The transition probabilities $p_{\text{inv}}(t)$ and $p_{\text{sec}}(t)$ are specified as logistic functions depending on the underlying power balance. According to this formalization, the probability of invasion decreases with increasing supranational loyalty $S(t)$. Beyond a certain step F, symbolizing some exogenously defined external force, the probability drops abruptly. Similarly, the likelihood of secession varies nonlinearly with the power balance between the nationalists $N(t)$ and the government's resources G:

$$p_{\text{inv}}(t) = \frac{q_{\text{inv}}}{1 + (F / S(t))^{-c_{\text{inv}}}}.$$

$$p_{\text{sec}}(t) = \frac{q_{\text{sec}}}{1 + (N(t) / G)^{-c_{\text{sec}}}}$$

While both c parameters determine the slope of the step, the q values calibrate the maximum probability of collective action for each time step. In the particular runs reported in figures 7.6 and 7.7, the following values were used: $F = G = 0.5$; $c_{\text{inv}} = c_{\text{sec}} = 10$; $q_{\text{inv}} = 0.005$ and $q_{\text{sec}} = 0.05$. Similarly, the probability of secession hinges upon the underlying mobilization dynamic.

The probability of survival until the tth time period is given by:

$$P(t) = \prod_{\tau=1}^{t} \{1 - p_{\text{inv}}(\tau) - p_{\text{sec}}(\tau)\} =$$

$$\prod_{\tau=1}^{t} \left\{ 1 - \frac{q_{\text{inv}}}{1 + (F / S(\tau))^{-c_{\text{inv}}}} - \frac{q_{\text{sec}}}{1 + (N(\tau) / G)^{-c_{\text{sec}}}} \right\}$$

Due to the complexity of this expression, no closed-form solution can easily be derived. Figure 7.6, however, suggests that the long-term probability of survival (shown in fig. 7.7), $P = \lim_{t \to \infty} P(t)$, converges.

CHAPTER 8

Nationalist Coordination

INTRODUCTION

We have found that national identities do not come in prepackaged bundles. With rare exceptions (e.g., Huntington 1993), contemporary analysts agree that ethnogenesis is a fundamentally dynamic and open-ended process (see Giddens 1984; Calhoun 1993, 214–15). Although nationality formation belongs to the past in most Western states, struggles over identity characterize newly independent states in both the Second and Third Worlds.[1] Conflicts concerning the very definition of state and society overshadow other issues in the former Yugoslavia and the newly independent post-Soviet republics.

While retaining the focus on center-periphery relations within multiethnic states, we now shift the main attention from mobilization to coordination. If the periphery consists of more than one potential nationality, identity formation ceases to be a one-dimensional process. The identity of a newly independent country depends crucially on the cultural landscape prior to independence and how it was manipulated and politicized by nationalist leaders. This argument is heavily path dependent, because the precolonial situation assumes great importance for future developments (March and Olsen 1984; Krasner 1988). In retrospect, it is tempting to obscure this essential history dependence and speak of the new state's national identity as well as of the precolonial nationalities themselves as if they were all reified entities, but this would be fundamentally misleading. A counterfactual analysis offers a less prejudged view of nationalism since it does not rule out other, potentially very different outcomes as a matter of assumption. To go back to Gellner (1983, 2), there are many more nations than there are viable states, so treating those lucky few ethnic categories that achieved nationhood, not to mention statehood, as being in any sense "natural" risks buying in to nationalist rhetoric, which usually attempts to glorify the nation as a self-evident and primordial phenomenon. Of course, such a position begs the question

---

[1] Yet it would be a mistake to treat identity politics as a secondary factor in all developed countries. The examples of Belgium, Canada, and Northern Ireland illustrate that the alleged dominance of the nation-state must be qualified (see Connor 1994). Even in the United States, immigration and differential birth rates have undermined the traditional WASP definition of national identity (e.g., Schlesinger 1992).

why any particular nation belongs to those that "made it" as opposed to the vast backdrop of unrealized candidates.

Here I apply a CAS model to the problem of nation formation in Yugoslavia. As opposed to the simple, dynamic framework presented in the previous chapter, the current model does not make any assumptions of linear behavior on the microlevel. This allows for truly path-dependent analysis including positive-feedback processes like hegemonic takeoffs. Instead of conquest, however, here the processes revolve around band-wagoning effects in nationalist mobilization. The counterfactual exercises yield important insights about the emergence of, and competition among, national identities in an imperial setting. Most importantly, among the conditions that shape mass politics in the aftermath of national liberation, I focus on the power asymmetry between the precolonial center and the periphery. In brief, I suggest that the more powerful the center compared to the periphery, the more inclusive the emergent identity of the new political unit.

The assertion that ethnic identities depend on power relations has been pioneered by ecological theorists drawing on the work of the Norwegian anthropologist Fredrik Barth (1969).[2] Reacting to traditional scholarship in his discipline, Barth rejected the idea that ethnic groups are primordially given. Instead of classifying such groups on objective criteria imposed by an external observer, he posited that identity formation is a self-ascriptive process. Rather than considering the specific contents of cultural traits, Barth focused on their form and function as boundary markers.[3]

While this perspective can be classified as an instrumentalist approach to identity formation, Barth never argued that collective identities lack stability.[4] In fact, he asserted that boundaries may persist despite considerable demographic mobility across them (Barth 1969, 9). Moreover, the Barthian perspective is not incompatible with observations concerning the significance of primordial traits in politics. It should be remembered that culture can be manipulated either through direct assimilation or by selective emphasis of certain criteria over others. Throughout this chapter, we will follow Barth in exploring the latter type of manipulation since it offers a powerful way of circumventing cultural reification. In Barth's own words:

[2] By power I mean resources rather than influence. For a clear conceptual discussion of this difference, see Baldwin (1985).

[3] For a critique of the formalist position and an argument for the explicit inclusion of cultural content, see Eriksen (1992, 1993).

[4] On the distinction between primordial and instrumental (or modernist) approaches to nationalism, see chapter 2.

The features that are taken into account are not the sum of "objective" differences, but only those which the actors themselves regard as significant. Not only do ecologic variations mark and exaggerate differences; some cultural features are used by the actors as signals and emblems of differences, others are ignored, and in some relationships radical differences are played down and denied. (14)

While Barth's insights have still not penetrated the bulk of the sociological and political-science literature on nationalism, they have given rise to sophisticated empirical generalizations and inspired important progress in organizational ecology. In an early contribution, Horowitz (1975) advocated "a fresh look at the impact of changing territorial boundaries." Anticipating the neoinstitutional turn a decade later, he insisted that "the contextual character of ethnic identity suggests that the strong links between formal and informal processes can hardly be ignored" (140). This theme resonates well with more recent attempts to connect nationalism with explicit analyses of the state as an institution (e.g., Breuilly 1982; Brass 1991; Calhoun 1993). Indeed, the current study can be seen as an attempt to develop new theoretical tools to grapple with the state-nation nexus.

As a complement to Horowitz's empirical generalizations, Michael Hannan's (1979; see also Hannan and Freeman 1989) ecological model of nationalism and modernization represents a useful starting point for formalization of ethnic mobilization. After observing that identities are frequently organized hierarchically, Hannan examines which of such multiple loyalties becomes politically consequential. In a potentially revolutionary situation involving a center and a periphery, small-scale identities within the latter act as obstacles against the formation of more widely shared identities that could serve as a basis for collective action. Paradoxically, an imperial center is bound to change the conditions of power competition among the potential elites on the periphery: "Sustained mobilization in opposition to further penetration by the center must be on a scale commensurate with that of the center. Therefore, successful penetration by the center alters the condition of competition among the various bases of collective action in a direction that favors large-scale identities" (256).

Since traditional societies are typically composed of various small units, such as tribes and ethnic communities, collective action remains impossible as the long as the center is able to deal with each premodern entity separately. Coordination of the various opposition movements constitutes the key to successful revolutions: "If an ethnic stand is to be made against the center, it must be on the basis of some identity larger than that of the premodern ethnic identities" (270). Drawing on Barth's theory, Hannan proposes that the effectiveness of an ethnic boundary hinges upon both the behavioral fitness of the boundary's cultural content and the power balance with respect to the center. In situations where the external power dynamics play a subordinate role, the cultural content itself acquires great importance. Since the asymmetric power conditions of colonial settings impose severe constraints on the periphery, local adaptation is of less consequence.

Hannan's discussion remains the only coherent attempt to develop an ecological theory of nationality formation. Still, he leaves room to articulate the mechanisms that eliminate traditional identities, for on this point his account is rather sweeping. Rather than detailing the power struggle, he attributes explanatory power to modernization as a general category. Nevertheless, Hannan clearly has a selection mechanism in mind:

> As the system becomes more connected, the size of the interacting population increases and the size of the largest competitor increases for all but the largest unit. As a result, the conditions of organization (more precisely, of selection among forms of organization at different scale levels) are altered. Attempts at organizing around larger scale cultural identities, even if no less frequent or intense, ought to be more successful. (271)

AN ECOLOGICAL MODEL OF NATIONALITY FORMATION

In order to study competition among alternative national identities, we need to generalize the situation studied in chapter 7. The current focus on competing identities renders obsolete the assumption of a dichotomous cultural difference between the center and the periphery. If, instead, identity depends on many dimensions, it is no longer possible to take the unity of the periphery for granted, not even in a relative sense when compared culturally to the center.

Because of the inherent complexity of this extended theoretical agenda, I rely on simulation methodology rather than mathematical modeling. In doing so, the current model draws heavily on the extended geopolitical framework of chapter 5. The goal is to create an artificial environment that resembles the domestic system of a multicultural state. Within this context, nationalist groups launch campaigns to overthrow the central government, or at least to gain a higher degree of autonomy. The success of these attempts depends not only on the power balance between the movement and the center but also on their power relative to competing nationalist campaigns.

Before spelling out the dynamic rules of this artificial political system, it is necessary to explain how identity is represented. As in chapter 4, I assume the system consists of several "primitive" units.[5] These social atoms correspond to small culturally homogeneous communities, such as the premodern village units or city-states (cf. Skocpol 1979), and their political identities are communal. An communal actor's identity is like a string of cultural traits akin to a chromosome.[6] To take the simplest multidimensional example, suppose that such a string consists of two dichotomous traits, each with the value 0 or 1. Reflecting Barth's formalism, it is immaterial if these traits stand for religion, language, or other cultural attributes. With two traits, there are four possible identity strings: 00, 01, 10, and 11.[7]

Revolutionary collective action usually requires coordination among several of these peripheral communities. In such cases, we speak of transcommunal identities, corresponding to social "molecules." Such groups define themselves politically by which cultural traits they choose to emphasize. Politicized transcommunal identities can be represented as cultural vectors that highlight at least one of their traits while suppressing others.[8] To continue the two-trait example, there are eight possible transcommunal identities—00, 01, 10, 11, ?0, ?1, 0?, 1? (not counting ??)— where the question mark is a wild card designating indifference. The relationship between communal and transcommunal identities defines the way political loyalty works. It is helpful to think of a transcommunal identity as the program of a political movement. We postulate that a primitive community can only share a transcommunal identity to the ex-

---

[5] These units are primitive in the sense of being the smallest, indivisible actors to be modeled, and not necessarily in the sense of being underdeveloped or culturally primitive.

[6] This representation does not imply that the model complies with sociobiological principles. Sociobiologists go even further than even the most ardent nationalists by arguing that certain social and behavioral traits are not only reified and group-specific but actually genetically hard-wired. It goes without saying that the current framework has nothing to do with such a view of human relations. To emphasize this difference, Dawkins (1989) calls the unit of social selection "meme" rather than "gene." The meme concept can be compared to the notion of a cultural trait in the current model.

[7] The focus on two rather than many traits, motivated by expositional clarity, differs from most historical situations. Generally speaking, the more dimensions among the peripheral actors, the harder collective action becomes. This is why nationalist movements rely extensively on myths and charismatic leadership to obscure internal differences. Because of its two-trait assumption, the current model may therefore downplay the difficulties of cultural coordination.

[8] Strictly speaking, this also applies to communal identities, but since the focus is on coordination rather than mobilization, I assume that the communities are always conscious of their culture. In the previous chapter the peripheral actors were initially mere unmobilized ethnic categories—i.e., endowed with a wild-card identity "?". The present model also differs from the previous one in that assimilation is ruled out by assumption. Thus, while transcommunal identities are free to vary, the cultural traits of the communities remain constant.

tent that it does not violate its own identity, although it does not have to match it fully. For example, an atomic actor of type 00 can adopt the transcommunal identities 00, ?0, and 0? only, whereas one of type 01 is restricted to the identities 01, 0?, and ?1. This implies that these two communal units could agree to share only the transcommunal identity 0?. The remaining alternatives would violate either or both of the communal identities.

The bit-string representation allows for a hierarchical conceptualization of identity. Clearly, the less specific the transcommunal identity, the more inclusive its character and the greater the chances that it will satisfy a fragmented population. More precisely defined platforms, by contrast, take on a narrower character. In the following, we will study a very simple world in which the peripheral population consists exclusively of 00 and 01 types. The center, however, has the identity 1?. Thus, the first trait corresponds to the main ethnic determinant setting the center apart from the periphery. In an imperial setting, a one denotes the status of foreign ruler. Though both the peripheral types share a zero on this first trait, they differ with respect to the second trait. This difference could be thought of as "tribal" idiosyncracies distinguishing the two peripheral types. The wild card marking the center's second trait indicates indifference with respect to the local idiosyncracies.

Figure 8.1 illustrates a system with an equal number of 00 and 01 provinces, all ruled by an imperial center of type 1?. Although the system is explicitly territorial, the location of each region is immaterial for the purposes of the simulations.[9]

00	00	01	00	01
00	00	01	01	01
01	00	1?	01	01
00	00	01	01	01
00	00	00	01	00

Figure 8.1. A 5 × 5 imperial system

[9] This ceases to be true as soon as the analysis extends into the postindependence phase. In the present version of the model, however, the simulation runs stop as soon as a coalition has gained enough power to topple the center. In "weak" empires, geographical distances also influence the power relationship between the center and the periphery. For example, as opposed to its less favorably located neighbors, the mountainous region Montenegro enjoyed de facto independence despite Ottoman claims to the contrary. See Jelavich (1983, 247–48) and Banac (1984, 271–75).

Finally, it is assumed that the center is strong enough to eliminate any interregional conflicts. Thus, each subordinate province interacts directly with the center only. As we will see, however, this does not exclude the possibility of coalition formation among the regions.

Michael Hannan's theory of nationalist collective action relies implicitly on ecological mechanisms. These mechanisms have two tasks: they must generate both variation and selection (Campbell 1969; Harré 1979; Eder 1985).[10] The role of variation and selection in nationality formation can be understood with reference to the historical generalizations of Miroslaw Hroch (1985), who studied nationalist movements in a number of small European countries. Although he framed his theory in comparative rather than evolutionary terms, Hroch provides a useful classification of nationalism's historical stages: First there is a period of scholarly interest during which intellectuals "rediscover" and systematize the vernacular language and local customs (phase A). Then follows a period of patriotic agitation, still on a rather limited, elite-based level (phase B). Finally, the nationalist movement gains massive support, paving the road for revolutionary collective action (phase C).

To return to the variation-selection dichotomy, phase A corresponds to variation in that intellectuals launch campaigns based on various ideological and cultural platforms. Then political entrepreneurs convert these mostly apolitical ideas into political initiatives. Thus, the actual selection process takes place during phases B and C. As in biological evolution, the imperial environment poses enormous challenges to the survival of opposition movements. Not only do they have to compete with each other for popular support; they also face direct resistance from the central government. Only the most successful national identities make it to phase C.

The distinction between variation and selection should help to remove some of the confusion haunting the literature on revolutionary collective action, especially the controversy regarding the role of rationality. Emphasizing the collective-choice dilemma, rational-choice theorists have argued that nationalist activities can best be understood against the background of individual self-interest. These scholars suspect that putatively selfless leaders and heroes are in fact nothing but power-hungry political entrepreneurs motivated by personal gains (Meadwell 1989; Hechter

[10] For an application in historical sociology, see Spruyt (1994). Despite the parallels to biological evolution, these processes are distinct from their Darwinian counterparts. In principle, social evolution does not need to rely on sociobioloical theories of how genetic factors influence behavior (Campbell 1969; Hayek 1973, 22–23; Harré 1979, 364; Hallpike 1983). Organizational ecology, for example, studies competition between alternative organizations rather than between genes. In our context, the unit of selection is the transcommunal identity of a nationalist movement.

1987b, 1992). By contrast, critics of the rationalist perspective argue that nationalist politics cannot be understood in the light of individual self-interest and selective incentives. In their view, collective action derives from strong irrational and emotional drives (Smith 1986; Connor 1994).

The ecological perspective favored here allows us to steer a middle course between these extremes. I assume that there is some small proportion of both idealistically motivated and cunning entrepreneurs whose motivations differ completely from the more risk-averse masses.[11] Members of the former group, here collectively referred to as dissidents, are willing to act regardless of the power balance between the periphery and the center: "Bravery to the point of apparent foolishness is essential to many social movements, especially the most radical" (Calhoun 1991, 51). In keeping with the hypotheses of rational choice, by contrast, the bulk of the regional population predicate their actions upon power realities.[12] Finally, the imperial government intervenes from time to time, attempting to repress nationalist movements. Like the opportunism of the masses, the assertion of the center's rule depends upon the power balance; the likelihood of repression drops as the targeted movement grows stronger. It is assumed that each attempt to repress succeeds in eliminating the campaign completely as long as it does not possess resources comparable to those of the center.

To summarize, there are three simple rules: Rule 1 governs the behavior of the ideologically driven dissidents and does not depend on the prospects of success. Rule 2 stipulates that, unlike the dissidents, most of the regional actors are indeed sensitive to the power balance. Rule 3 controls the center's decisions to crack down on opposition movements.

TECHNICAL SPECIFICATION

This section provides a detailed, technical specification of the model. Readers who are more interested in the overall picture may want to turn directly to the next section.

The current framework shares many properties with the Emergent Po-

---

[11] This solution to collective action has been explored extensively in the sociological literature (for a review, see Udéhn 1993, 244–48). Students of social movements have noticed that collective action depends on a small number of resourceful persons, usually belonging to the middle class. Starting with agitation from the elites, revolutions spread as "snowballs" within social networks. This hypothesis has recently received formal confirmation in the computer simulations of Macy (1990, 1991).

[12] Here I assume rationality to be interpreted in a strictly material and survival-oriented sense.

larity Model. In fact, the Coordination Model can be seen as an extension of the two-level version of the model. In addition to using the collective-action mechanism, the current extension enables regions to coordinate their opposition to the center by forging cultural alliances. In order to manage the overwhelming complexity of this elaboration, however, we introduced a few abstractions compared to the Emergent Polarity Model. As we will see, the Coordination Model operates with simplified combat rules and without a harvest mechanism.

Structure

As we have seen, an actor's identity is implemented as a two-dimensional vector holding dichotomous traits. Transcommunal identities can also allow for wild cards.[13] The primitive community's decisions to adopt a transcommunal identity depend on the fit between their communal identity and the transcommunal one. The fit is defined as the difference between the number of corresponding traits minus the number of clashing ones, not counting the indifferent traits of the transcommunal identity (i.e., those with wild cards). This simple rule generates a fit index for each pair of individual and transcommunal identities (see table 8.1).

The decision to join a national movement presupposes that the fit is positive. In other words, the 00 regions cannot adhere to the ?1 and 01 transcommunal identities since they both violate the second trait. By the same token, the 01 actors reject the 00 and ?0 identities. How these collectivities array themselves determines the geopolitical setting. Figure 8.2 illustrates the balance between any coalition of regions against the resources of the center. Whereas the x-axis shows the center's resource level R, the y-axis indicates the resource status of the opposition. Given a

TABLE 8.1
The Fit of Transcommunal Identities

Communal Identity	Transcommunal Identity				
	00	?0	0?	?1	01
00	2	1	1	-1	0
01	0	-1	1	1	2

[13] This representation resembles John Holland's (1992a) schemas. See also Robert Axelrod's (1987) operationalization of strategy as a string of instructions and James March's (1991) implementation of organizational culture as bit-vectors. See also the earlier discussion of modeling identity with CAS techniques.

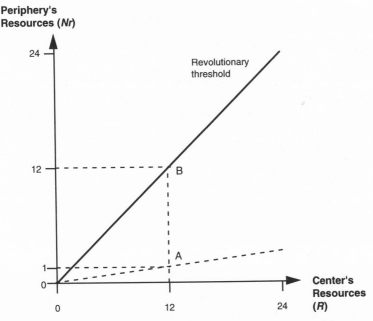

Figure 8.2. The power balance between the center and the periphery

nationalist movement with N members, the periphery is able to mobilize Nr resources where each region controls $r = 1$ resource unit. To simplify the analysis, it is assumed that the nationalist opposition needs to attain the same resource level as the center if it wants to challenge the center's hegemony.[14] The solid line from the origin represents this threshold. All points below this line correspond to situations in which the periphery is unable to attack the central government. If the center controls $R = 12$ resources, for example, it is vastly superior to any single regional challenger ($r = 1$) despite possessing only half of the opposition's total power (i.e., $Nr = 24$, see point A). This is why revolutionary leaders must forge a coalition of at least twelve regions in order to curb the center's dominance (see point B). In essence, a single dissident region must persuade enough potential allies to move from A to B. Obviously, revolutionary activity becomes increasingly harder the stronger the center (i.e., the further we move to the right along the x-axis). If the center's resource level is twenty-four units, only a grand coalition of all twenty-four regions could topple the balance.

---

[14] This is an arbitrary assumption that can easily be changed depending on which side is presumed to possess an offensive advantage.

Dynamic Properties

Within this geopolitical structure, peripheries struggle for dominance. In each time period, each communal actor decides on its transcommunal identity. If it does not already belong to a movement, it may decide to create a new one (Rule 1) or to join an existing one (Rule 2). At the same time, the center scans through all its provinces checking whether any of its subjects is disloyal. Should this be the case, it randomly singles out one such region, and decides if enforcement should be enacted (Rule 3). These three rules fully define the dynamics of the system.

RULE 1. THE CREATION OF MOVEMENTS

The rule governing the provinces' propensity to rebel is extremely simple. The probability that such an actor creates a nationalist movement is set to a low, fixed probability, in our case 0.01 per period and unit. Figure 8.3 depicts this eventuality as a flat line. The choice of a new nationalist platform involves selecting randomly from the transcommunal identities that do not violate the dissident's communal identity (cf. table 8.1). The dissidents attach an equal probability to each of the three possible transcommunal identities. For example, should the pioneering actor be of 00

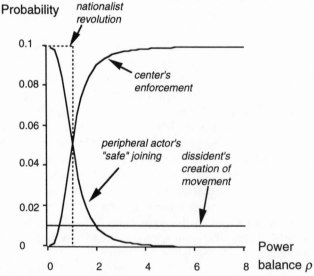

Figure 8.3. The probabilistic rules of center-periphery interaction

type, the proposed identity will be either 00, 0?, or ?0, each with a likelihood of one third.[15]

Suppose that the frequency of 01 types in the regional population is p. Then the probability of the type-specific transcommunal identities must be $\Pr(01) = \Pr(?1) = p/3$ and $\Pr(00) = \Pr(?0) = (1-p)/3$ and of the shared transcommunal identity $\Pr(0?) = p/3 + (1-p)/3 = \frac{1}{3}$. For a symmetrically split population (i.e., $p = \frac{1}{2}$), we have $\Pr(01) = \Pr(?1) = \Pr(00) = \Pr(?0) = 1/6$ and $\Pr(0?) = \frac{1}{3}$. This means that the type-independent, overarching transcommunal identity 0? is twice as likely as any of the other identities.

RULE 2. THE JOINING OF MOVEMENTS

The second rule defines the average communal actor's behavior once a dissident has already created a movement. In contrast to the unconditional rule 1, the present mechanism depends heavily on the center-periphery power balance.[16] The regional actor scans through all available movement and judges whether it would be safe to join. Its decision depends on a simple power calculation. The "safe-to-join" curve in figure 8.3 illustrates how the probability of safety falls with the resource superiority of the center ρ.[17]

Formally, if the oppositional identity already enjoys the support of N regional actors, the resource balance is defined as:

$$\rho = \frac{R}{(N+1)r}.$$

This value is used to compute the probability of joining:

[15] The process of cultural innovation may actually produce a transcommunal identity that already exists. In this case, the effect is the same as joining the already existing movement, although the motive must be idealistic rather than opportunistic (cf. rule 2).

[16] See Elster (1989) for an analysis of conditional norms of cooperation.

[17] While it does not feature nationalist collective action, the two-level extension of the Emergent Polarity Model uses a similar rule (see esp. fig. 5.9) . The S-shaped curve can be seen as an example of a "lumpy good" (Hardin 1982, 55–61; Levi 1988, 57–58). The peripheral unit bases its power comparison on the hypothetical case, presuming that it has already joined the movement (i.e., the denominator contains the factor $N + 1$ and not just N). This is not a mere technicality because it generates the type of "bandwagoning" self-feeding process that has often been observed in collective action. Along these lines, Therborn (1991) contends that "Under given conditions of alien cultural exposure, the more relatively powerful/prosperous the members of a given culture, the more stable it should be and the more attractive to members of other cultures. Isolation and relative power should be seen as multiplicative variables" (187). For another example of a positive feedback, see the discussion of "hegemonic takeoffs" in chapter 4.

$$\Pr(\text{Join}|\rho) = \frac{q}{1 + (\rho/\rho_0)^c},$$

where ρ_0 stands for the resource balance that makes the fall in probability the steepest. I set the value to one for all the simulation runs below. The parameter c controls the overall slope of the curve. High values generate a sharper edge for the threshold value ρ_0. The numerical value $c = 3.17$ was calibrated to make the probability of joining 0.01 for a resource balance of two. Finally, the probability q scales the entire function to desired proportions. The value used in the simulations was 0.1. This means that the probability of considering a movement safe never exceeds this value.

Figure 8.3 reveals that the likelihood of "safe joining" falls sharply with the power balance. If the center is stronger than the periphery ($\rho >$ 1), the likelihood of adhering to a movement drops below 0.05. In cases where the center is twice as strong ($\rho = 2$), the likelihood is only 0.01 — that is the same as the probability of dissident activity. Should the center be eight times stronger than each individual community ($\rho = 8$), the probability of safe joining is almost negligible (0.000137). Despite these low probabilities, a movement once started benefits from a bandwagoning effect: as increasing numbers join the campaign, subsequent adherence becomes more likely. This is so because each new member shifts the power balance in the movement's favor, thus facilitating further adherence. The positive-feedback process corresponds to the threshold phenomena observed in real social and political movements (e.g., Granovetter 1978; Kuran 1989, 1991; Goertz 1994).

Should there be more than one "safe" movement, the peripheral actors pick the one with the highest identity fit. For the parameter values chosen here, however, the bias in favor of better fit plays a subordinate role since the likelihood of finding any safe movement is quite low.

RULE 3. THE COLLAPSE OF MOVEMENTS

Together rules 1 and 2 produce an ecology that crystallizes into a fixed political landscape quite quickly because there is no provision for how nationalist movements could ever disappear. A fully evolutionary system needs to ensure that both variation and selection be maintained continuously. This is where the government-orchestrated elimination of oppositional organizations fits in. As in the previous rule, power plays an important role. Here the center bases its decision upon its power position compared to the periphery (cf. the enforcement curve in fig. 8.3). The probability function is the mirror image of the periphery's logistic function (i.e., the ratio ρ/ρ_0 is reversed by the negative exponent $-c$):

$$\text{Pr(Enforce}|\rho) = \frac{q}{1 + (\rho/\rho_0)^{-c}}$$

where $\rho = R/(Nr)$, that is the power ratio in the center's favor. As in the periphery's function, we use the same parameter values: $q = 1$, $\rho_0 = 1$, and $c = 3.17$.

In each time period, the center checks whether any of the provinces belongs to a nationalist organization. Should this be the case, it applies the probabilistic criterion to decide whether repression is necessary. Since the rule depends on the power balance, large nationalities will be persecuted less often than small and defenseless dissident cells. Thus there is a built-in selective logic in the enforcement mechanism.[18]

In the event of repression, all members of the same nationality as the region under attack respond to the center's challenge. As long as the center is more powerful than the group in question, the outcome is a quick victory for the government. Police repression always results in the collapse of the oppositional movement as long as the latter is in an inferior position. If the periphery manages to gather superior resources, however, a nationalist revolution takes place that ends the simulation run. The strongest movement is recorded as the "winner" and the simulation ends.

Together, the three rules define a simple ecological system. Rules 1 and 3 are responsible for the necessary variation. While rule 1 ensures that new identities are constantly created, the center's elimination of unsuccessful organizations (cf. rule 3) guarantees that the variance does not fall prematurely. At the same time, this rule contributes to selection, since the remaining movements are likely to be stronger. Rule 2 amplifies the selective logic of rule 3 by favoring stronger movements.

SIMULATION RESULTS

The three behavioral rules generate diferent outcomes depending on the overall power balance. This section illustrates the model's emergent dynamics by displaying sample runs and more systematic results. Figure 8.4 presents the history of a system with an 8:1 power balance in the center's favor. The figure plots the strength of each movement measured as the number of members over time. The maximum adherence is the entire regional population ($N = 24$), but a nationalist movement only needs eight provinces, or a third of the regional population, to stage a success-

---

[18] This is obviously not the only possible assumption. If the center decided to concentrate on larger movements first because they are more threatening, the curve would have the opposite slope. Yet to the extent that the actual success of oppression is taken into account, the current assumption seems more realistic.

Strength of movement

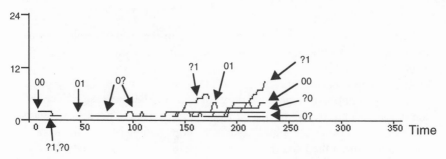

Figure 8.4. The history of a system with power balance 8 in the center's favor

ful revolution. As the simulation starts, there is no nationalist activity. Very soon, however, dissident activity emerges. At about time 5, two peripheral actors independently decide to launch a campaign of type 00 (cf. rule 1). A bit later, one of the 00 movements crumbles and is replaced by two other dissident movements, namely ?1 and ?0, both very short-lived. After another couple of attempts (type 01 and 0?), the first serious uprising occurs. At time 125, a movement of type ?1 manages to launch a more impressive though ultimately unsuccessful attempt to seize power. At about time 175, after having gathered six members (cf. rule 2), this movement perishes as a consequence of government-led repression (cf. rule 3). It is followed by another, more modest campaign that reaches the level of four members before vanishing. Around time 200, nationalist mobilization picks up again. This time there are a number of contending platforms. The one that finally gains the upper hand is ?1, the first movement to win support from the necessary eight regions, allowing it to crush the center.

To illustrate the importance of the resource balance, I ran a similar simulation in which the center's strength was twelve times that of the individual provinces (see fig. 8.5). In this harsher climate, the center's increased willingness to engage in repression makes it harder for smaller movements to survive. After starting off with exactly the same conditions as in the previous run, the new simulation starts to differ after time 150. Because of the changed power environment it is the 0? identity that dominates. With the exception for one attempt by 00, all serious challenges to the center are made in the name of 0?. In fact, the 00 movement comes quite close to toppling the center, since it manages to gather eleven members. Nevertheless, the wider popular support of the less specific 0? identity makes it more successful in the long run. On its fifth attempt, it

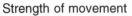

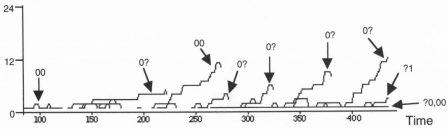

Figure 8.5. The history of a system with power balance 12 in the center's favor

succeeds in forging a sufficiently strong coalition, comprising twelve members.

These examples suggest that competitive environments tend to favor collective action drawing on inclusive identities rather than more narrow ones. To find out whether this is a general result, it is necessary to turn to counterfactual analysis based on systematic reruns of history. Much has already been said about the use of simulation to evaluate counterfactual propositions, so there is no need to reiterate the details of this methodology. Chapters 4 and 5 present similar analyses of emergent polarity in geopolitical systems. Again I ran twenty replications, each representing a separate stream of contingencies, while holding constant the independent variable (i.e., the power balance). Each replication started with a different random seed generating a distinct series of probabilistic decisions. The structural conditions remained the same for each set of twenty replications.

Figure 8.6 shows the result of this exercise. As in the previous chapters, I stacked the outcomes on top of each other. Instead of using polarity categories, the current presentation displays five classes of outcomes depending on the identity of the prevailing nationalist movement. Each run replication proceeded until a revolution took place, but was aborted after 10,000 time periods if one did not. The bottom field corresponds to the runs that ended with movements of type 0?. On top of these observations, the fields of types ?0, ?1, 00 and 01 are shown.

For very low values of the resource balance, the outcomes depend heavily on the dissidents' random selection of national identities (cf. rule 1). If the center only controls the same amount of resources as each peripheral actor ($r = R = 1$ and thus $\rho = 1$), a revolution takes place as soon as a new movement crops up. The probabilistic calculations reported in the previous section (cf. rule 1) suggest that the distribution among nationalist types should be one-third for the wide identity 0? and

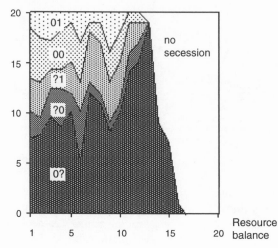

Figure 8.6. Emergent national identities with equally split population

one-sixth for the remaining identities. This seems to be the case to judge from the diagram (see the y-axis for $\rho = 1$).

The conditions differ as the power balance shifts in the center's favor. As the center grows stronger, the more general identity 0? becomes increasingly more successful at the expense of the more parochial movements. This trend culminates at power balance 12, beyond which it becomes impossible for the other movements to reach the revolutionary threshold. After this point, movements of type 0? dominate completely, but their effectiveness falls sharply as the power of the center increases further. If the center acquires sixteen times as many resources as the individual communities, collective action becomes practically impossible, at least within the time limit.

With a relatively weak center, a variety of identities can succeed. With a stronger center, only a wider oppositional identity is viable. As the center becomes even more powerful, this single oppositional identity remains the only possibility but becomes a decreasingly likely actual prospect. Asymmetry in power apparently breeds homogeneity in political culture.

The current simulation featured a perfectly split peripheral population. What happens if there are twice as many 00 types as there are 01 actors in the population? Figure 8.7 tells a dramatically different story than the previous diagram. When culture is distributed asymmetrically, there is no longer any strong tendency for the wider identity 0? to dominate as the

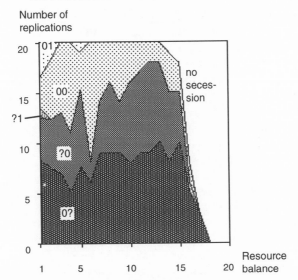

Figure 8.7. Emergent national identities with twice as many 00 types as 01 types

balance shifts in favor of the center. Since two-thirds of the population, or sixteen regions, are of type 00, any of the three identities 0?, ?0, and 00 provide enough support to topple the imperial government. On the other hand, the 01 and ?1 type movements disappear almost entirely since their more limited popular support does not suffice as a basis for collective action.

In sum, the periphery's revolutionary activity depends on both the cultural conditions and the regional power distribution. If one group dominates, overarching identities become less central to the periphery's struggle against the center. A more fragmented culture map, however, requires more coordination on the part of the regions. In these latter cases, the center-periphery power balance is likely to influence the inclusiveness of the revolutionary movement.

NATIONALIST COORDINATION AND THE FORMATION OF YUGOSLAVIA

Few historical examples illustrate the dynamics of identity politics better than the formation of Yugoslavia. A virtual laboratory of competing national ideologies, Southern Slav politics at the beginning of the twentieth century constitute a fascinating though foreboding example of variation and selection in the real world. By studying the events in the light of the ecological model, I hope to gain insights about an extremely complex political situation, shedding light not only on the formation of Yugoslavia but also on more recent events. Indeed, the roots of the contemporary tragedy can be sought in the dramatic developments preceding the creation of the Kingdom of Serbs, Croats, and Slovenes in 1918.[19]

As the peripheral actors in the formal framework, the Southern Slav peoples lived under foreign rule throughout most of the nineteenth century. After the retreat of the Ottoman Empire, the Habsburg Monarchy quickly filled the ensuing power vacuum. The Habsburgs controlled all areas inhabited by Croats and Slovenes as well as some of the Serb-populated regions, including Vojvodina. Following the Congress of Berlin in 1878, Serbia gained independence from the Ottoman Empire, but for most practical purposes the new state remained both economically and politically dependent on the dual monarchy until World War I.[20] Thus, the imperial context resembles the ecological setting in that two main nationalities, the Croats and Serbs, gradually crystallized, both dominated by an external power, Austria-Hungary.[21]

Serbs and Croats have many things in common, especially a shared language. Serbo-Croatian was the product of a series of successful reforms initiated in the early nineteenth century by the famous Serbian linguist Vuk Stefanovic Karadzic followed by the work of the Croat language reformer Gaj in the mid-nineteenth century (cf. Banac 1984, 76–80). Despite the convergence of dialects, cross-national communication suffered from the failure to standardize written communication due to the almost complete lack of literacy in the peasant population.[22] While the

[19] For the historical documentation, I have relied on Ivo Banac (1994), who presents the most complete account of nation formation up until the beginning of the twentieth century. Because of its slight Croatian bias, I also consulted Dragnich (1992) who takes a less refined, explicitly pro-Serbian stance. As historical background sources, Jelavich (1983) and Stavrianos (1959) proved useful.

[20] In a treaty, signed by Austria-Hungary and Serbia in 1891, the Serbs pledged to weed out subversive forces in its territory. Moreover, they promised not to sign any external treaties or admit any foreign forces to its territory without the prior approval of the Habsburgs. While these terms caused an uproar in Belgrade that eventually led to the treaty's rejection, the Serbian king Milan secretly assured the Austrians of Serbia's compliance. Although Serbia became more independent after the overthrow of the Obrenovich dynasty in 1903, the country remained in the Austria-Hungarian sphere of influence (Jelavich and Jelavich 1977, 185–87). Its treatment at the outset of World War I reflects its subordinate situation (cf. Lebow 1981), and following military defeat by the reinforced Habsburg army in 1915, the country was effectively occupied. For an alternative, pro-Serbian interpretation, see Dragnich (1992).

[21] In addition to the Habsburg dominance, the Balkans was continuously affected by other great powers, including the Ottoman Empire, Italy, Germany, Russia, France, and Great Britain.

[22] On the importance of written communication for nationalism, see Gellner (1983), who highlights education, and Anderson (1991), who focuses on the influence of "print-capitalism."

Croats rely on the Latin alphabet, most Serbs use the Cyrillic script.[23] This crucial difference coincides with the religious fault line between the two nationalities. Stemming from the division of the Roman Empire in 395, the Serbs belong to the Orthodox community, first within Byzantium and later within the Ottoman *millet* system. Croatia (and Slovenia), by contrast, remained loyal to the western part of the Roman Empire and the Catholic church.

At the risk of resorting to simplistic classification, we identify two conflict dimensions:

> **1.** the main ethnic/linguistic cleavage between Slavs and non-Slavs, coded as "0" and "1" respectively, the latter category being Germans and Magyars who ruled the dual monarchy together after the *Ausgleich* of 1867;[24]
>
> **2.** the intra-Slav differences, pertaining mainly to religion, with "0" denoting Orthodox, and "1" Catholic. The latter distinction in this context does not have to be interpreted in its narrow, religious sense but can also be seen as a difference between "Eastern" and "Western" culture.[25]

This crude classification endows each of the main protagonists with an identity string. We classify the "foreign" Habsburg Monarchy as type 1?, the Slav but Catholic Croats (and Slovenes) as type 01, and the Slav and Orthodox Serbs as type 00.[26] Using only this simplification of the main groups, what movements would we expect to emerge?

---

[23] In congruence with Barth's (1969) ideas about boundary formation, it was not until in this century that Serbian literary communication came to shift decisively toward Cyrillic script. Karadzic, for example, relied on the Latin alphabet. I am grateful for Stephen Tull for pointing out this to me.

[24] Following the defeat in the Austro-Prussian war, the Habsburg Monarchy finally gave in to Hungarian demands for autonomy. The agreement, often referred to as *Ausgleich* or the Dual Compromise, granted Hungary considerable autonomy in internal affairs while letting Vienna keep its dominance in foreign policy. As a result, the Habsburg Empire came to be called Austria-Hungary (see Taylor 1948, chap. 11).

[25] Adopted for technical and expositional reasons, this dichotomous representation of culture risks gives the impression that the Serbo-Croatian cleavage is unproblematic, but in fact this boundary remained blurred until the late nineteenth century. As everything else in Yugoslav history, the East-West distinction is controversial because it was introduced by the strongly pro-Croatian scholar Seton-Watson (1917; see discussion in Shoup 1968, 6–7). Many Serbs argue that their country is as Western as Croatia (e.g. Dragnich 1992). Nevertheless, it is hard to deny the Eastern, and especially Russian, influence on Serbian national identity. This trend grew stronger as the West-oriented Serbian parties declined in importance at the turn of the century (Vucinich 1963, 231).

[26] The choice of 1? rather than 11 is because the Habsburgs generally refrained from imposing Catholicism on their subject populations. Even the reforms under Joseph II at the end of the eighteenth century "implied a strong principle of noninterference by the Catholic church in the most important affairs of the state and on the other hand, a strict control of church activities by the state" (Kann 1964, 1:54–55, see also 2:xii–xiii).

The Nationalist Spectrum

The theoretical discussion above identified five possible political platforms, namely the transcommunal identity 0? and the less inclusive identities 01, ?1, 00, and ?0. In the following, I discuss what counterparts
these national ideologies had in the political process that culminated with
the formation of Yugoslavia.

YUGOSLAVISM (0?)

The movement that lobbied most strongly for Yugoslav unification in
1918 emphasized the common historical experience of all Southern
Slavs. In the later part of the Ottoman Empire's hold on the area, various
intellectuals, mostly in Croatia, saw unification of all Southern Slavs as
the only possible rescue from foreign rule. While Ivo Banac (1984) traces
the tradition back to the Dominican theologian Vinko Pribojevic in 1525,
it was not until the nineteenth century that Yugoslavism appeared as a
political force. Despite the asymmetric power relations favoring the empire, Slavic cooperation remained an exclusive, elite-based dream. Paradoxically, it was foreigners who managed to spread the pan-Slavic idea
beyond intellectual circles: as a consequence of Napoleon's victories over
the Habsburgs, in 1809 the French incorporated the Slovene and Croat
lands directly into France as the Illyrian Provinces. Although this experiment excluded the Serbs and only lasted until the Congress of Vienna in
1814, the historical precedent came to play an important role for the
subsequent attempts to unify the Southern Slavs (Jelavich 1983, 1:162–
63).

In the meantime, the Josephine reforms of the Habsburgs had stirred
Magyar nationalism. Inspired by the vernacular trend of the period and
provoked by the German pressure, the Hungarians were quick to imitate
their superiors in their own relations with the Southern Slavs. Since 1779,
most of present-day Croatia had been ruled directly by Hungary under
the scepter of Saint Stephen. From 1790 the Hungarians insisted on replacing Latin with Magyar as the official language. Predictably enough,
this move met with instant resistance among the Croat nobility. The realization that only a united front could cope with the external threat provided a new impetus to the Illyrian movement in the nineteenth century:
"The Illyrianist awakeners knew that the Hungarians would ignore a
movement of a few counties that composed Croatia-Slavonia. Their national idea therefore could not be, strictly speaking, Croatian, because
that could be misunderstood as an expression of narrow Croatian regionalism" (Banac 1984, 76).

CROATIAN NATIONALISM (01)

Although the Illyrian movement enjoyed widespread support in Croatia, an exclusively Croat form of nationalism existed simultaneously. Tracing its roots back to the late seventeenth century, the idea of Great Croatia never ceased to fascinate intellectuals and historiographers. It was not until the mid-nineteenth century, however, that Croat nationalism became a serious political force. The movement owed much to the charismatic leadership of Ante Starcevic and Eugen Kvaternik (ibid., Banac 85). Their movement, organized under the banner of the Party of Rights, asserted the historical rights of Croatia as an independent political unit.[27] By the 1890s, however, the use of the "01" label becomes fully justified, especially after the split of the party following Starcevic's death in 1896. The Party of Pure Right led by Josip Frank represents the clearest example of this identity. Rejecting any tendencies toward Yugoslavism, this Catholic-oriented party adopted an explicitly anti-Serbian ideology (cf. Stavrianos 1959, 461).

THE CATHOLIC/CLERICAL MOVEMENTS (?1)

Due to its international nature and its insistence on Latin liturgy, the Catholic church did not inspire the same degree of nationalist activity as the autocephalous Orthodox church in Serbia. Thanks to its greater religious homogeneity compared to Croatia, Slovenia fostered the strongest genuinely clerical movement (Banac 1984, 113–15). In keeping with the Holy See's aversion to revolutionary nationalism and its support of the Habsburg Monarchy, the Catholic clericalists organized in the Slovene People's Party lobbied for trial rather than full independence—that is, the creation of a Croat-Slovene entity as a complement to the dualist framework (Kann 1974, 354, 449).

SERBIAN NATIONALISM (00)

Although the peasant uprisings against Ottoman rule in the early 19th century should not be regarded as nationalist manifestations (Stokes 1976), Serbian nationalism evolved earlier than that in the other Southern Slav lands thanks to favorable geopolitical circumstances. Unlike its Croat counterpart, Serbian nationhood emerged in close association with the Orthodox church. Yet in the nineteenth century, some intellectuals

---

[27] Yet to depict their movement as an ethnonational phenomenon promoting not only Slavic values but also Catholicism is not entirely correct. The fragmented religious map of Croatia made it difficult for its politicians to stress the religious dimension (Banac 1984, 88).

inspired by Herder's nationalist writings shifted from the emphasis on religion to a predominately linguistic definition of Serbian national identity.[28] More than anyone else, it was the language reformer Karadzic who promoted this tendency. Despite the secularization of the national idea, it would be a mistake to downplay Orthodoxy as an integrated component of the Serbian nationalist program. Whether implicitly or explicitly, Serbian leaders viewed the Orthodox church as a state institution and did not refrain from promoting assimilation of non-Orthodox populations outside Serbia proper (Banac 1984, 107). Moreover, the Serbs never gave up the Cyrillic script, and continued to draw on a distinctly Serbian oral tradition based on medieval myths.

ORTHODOX CLERICALISM (?0)

Under the centuries of Turkish occupation, it was the Orthodox church that safeguarded the Serbian historical myths. The church retained its important political function as the Serbs came under Habsburg rule: "As in the Ottoman Empire, the church dignitaries became in practice the leaders of a kind of Serbian secular government, with a Serbian metropolitan, established at Sremski Karlovci, at its head" (Jelavich 1983, 1:149). Understandably enough, the church was not satisfied within the Catholic empire, but because of the Serbs' inferior power position, they preferred to cooperate with the Habsburgs. As the Serbian state crystallized in the nineteenth century, the church lost its independent political role. It would thus be a mistake to characterize the Constantinople-based Orthodox church as a promoter of Balkan nationalism. In fact, it "objected precisely to the ethnic parochialism of secular nationalism, which threatened, and eventually did destroy, the ecumenicity of transcendental values which held Balkan society together within the fold of Orthodoxy during the centuries of captivity" (Kitromilides 1989, 159).

Historical Variation and Selection

The historical survey of nationalist ideologies indicates that there are important parallels between the ecological model and the political spectrum preceding the formation of Yugoslavia. We now turn to the postulated dynamic mechanisms of variation and selection.

Southern Slav nationalism provided an ample supply of innovative intellectuals and enthusiasts ready to sacrifice their lives to overwhelming opposition. Gavrilo Princip's assassination of Archduke Ferdinand in Sar-

---

[28] German romanticism had a strong impact on the intellectual elite of other Balkan countries, especially in Greece (Kitromilides 1989, 156–57).

ajevo is but the most famous instance in a long series of conspiracies that earned the entire region a reputation in Vienna and elsewhere for intrigues. The heroic acts did not stop with single assassinations: in 1871, the Croatian nationalist Eugen Kvaternik lost his life in a desperate attempt to stage an uprising against the imperial rulers (Banac 1984, 88). Barbara Jelavich (1983) asserts that "almost all Balkan national movements had carried an element of revolutionary conspiracy. Violence and terror, justified with high romantic rhetoric, had a major role in the accomplishment of specific objectives. Secret societies, with distinctive symbols, flags, oaths, and elaborate ceremonies, were also prevalent" (2:110). Whatever motives drove these people, it was hardly material well-being or even the most rudimentary survival instinct.

Though there can be no doubt that the cultural and political conditions ensured variation, it is less obvious whether selection occurred precisely as suggested by the model. For sure, there was no lack of repression on the part of the dual monarchy. After the *Ausgleich*, the Hungarians were given direct control over Croatia. Moreover, although Vienna did not intervene directly in Serbian affairs until 1914, their annexation of Bosnia in 1909 and continued threats underline the Habsburgs' willingness to resort to force in defending their regional supremacy.

Moreover, the resource balance between the opposition and the center influenced the differential success of the transcommunal identities as expected: when the pendulum swung in favor of the center, less particularistic nationalist programs prevailed. Due to Croatia's weaker position, Yugoslavism gained more support in Croatia than in Serbia. This trend was particularly strong as both Magyar repression under Khuen-Héderváry and external pressure from Italy intensified after the turn of the century. In this threatening climate, Yugoslavism slowly gained support even among Croat nationalists (Banac 1984, 95). This tendency found intellectual backing from the Croatian bishop Josip Juraj Strossmayer and the historian Canon Franjo Racki. Despite their intellectual outlook, "these men were practical minded as well and quite aware that the Croats had little wherewithal to resist the Austro-Hungarian denationalization effort and must therefore rely on their Slavic kinsmen in the Balkans and elsewhere" (ibid., 89). These efforts led to the abandonment of Croat state rights and the papering over of Croat-Serbian differences.

Yugoslavism encountered more resistance among the Serbs, many of whom insisted on "Piedmontization" of their Balkan neighbors.[29] It was

---

[29] This term refers to unification around a core state, such as Piedmont in the Italian case or Prussia in the unification of Germany. Many Serbian politicians have traditionally viewed their role in similar terms (see Dragnich 1992, 22, 28). Cf. unification nationalism in chapter 6.

not until the Serbian leadership had been driven into exile that it at least temporarily accepted a more inclusive identity. Although the Corfu Declaration, signed in 1917, failed to resolve many contentious issues, the compromise paved the way for unification. Most historical observers link the Serbs' willingness to accept the Yugoslav program to their unfavorable situation at this historical juncture: "The Serbian leaders were in an extremely weak position. The army had been defeated; they had no assurances about the future from their allies" (Jelavich 1983, 2:143). Moreover, the Russian Revolution earlier the same year had removed Serbia's most powerful ally. The perception of weakness and fears of external intervention were not unique to the Serbs but were shared by Croats and Slovenes as well: "All of the South Slav leaders strongly feared Italian intentions; they wished to block if possible an Italian occupation of any part of their territory" (Pleterski 1990, 147; see also Taylor 1948, 249).[30]

Despite the similarity between the logic of the selectionist approach and the historical tendencies, there are important differences on a deeper level. What we observe empirically is more than simple selection through repeated elimination of movements. While the historical record contains several uprisings, the model tends to exaggerate the frequency of these attempts. In reality, the struggle did not usually assume the life-and-death character suggested by the model. In addition to the quasi-Darwinian struggle, a more subtle but no less momentous change took place: the actors learned from past experiences and were able to anticipate the course of their actions. Learning played an instrumental role in transforming the situation.

Theorists of social evolution have pointed out that Lamarckian learning is not only perfectly plausible in human affairs but more central than selection of individuals and groups. Within this context, the logical separation between variation and selection, present in biological evolution, breaks down (Harré 1979; Toulmin 1977, 23). Instead of blind variation, past experiences of selection come to guide future variation. Like other human organizations, nationalist movements have collective memories: "Cultural systems do not react to environmental imperatives like a tabula rasa. Rather they react according to built-in cognitive relevance criteria" (Eder 1985, 29, my trans.; see also Fentress and Wickham 1992). More-

---

[30] Interestingly, external power relations remained an important influence even after the unification of the Southern Slavs. As the threat from the neighboring countries increased in the late 1930s (especially Germany and Italy), the Serbs finally recognized the Croats' complaints against Serbian centralism. However, the compromise that granted the Croats wide-ranging autonomy came too late to save the Yugoslavs from foreign intervention in World War II (see Jelavich 1983, 2:202, 203).

over, individuals develop internal models of a higher complexity than those built into the modeling framework.[31] To sum up,

> we should expect people to conceive innovations, not merely by random reshuffling of their knowledge, beliefs, rules of conduct, habits, social practices and customs, but by deliberate design in the light of the conditions that the creative and rebellious amongst the people anticipate will occur. Further, in a record-keeping society experience of the fate of previous attempts at innovation can be retained and fed into the later processes by which [variation]-conditions and [selection]-conditions interact. In short, change in societies with collective memories will tend to become actually more and more Lamarckian, though we have no reason to suppose that knowledge will ever accumulate to the extent that the process will become Lamarckian in fully coupled form. (Harré 1979, 365)

An objection to this critique might draw on Milton Friedman's (1953) familiar "as-if" justification of economic equilibrium theory. In Friedman's view it matters little whether the assumption of rational agents is wrong as long as data confirm the predictions (see also Waltz 1979). To explain why actors behave as if they were rational, he referred to a selection argument. Yet, since our very purpose is to uncover the underlying mechanisms at work in nationalist mobilization, Friedman's positivist escape is of less use. Moreover the "as-if" rationale depends heavily on the turnover of organizations, and this is precisely where the analogy breaks down (Elster 1985). Genuine learning, however, can speed up evolution by several orders of magnitude (Boyd and Richerson 1980; Eder 1985, 29; Macy 1990, 1991; Udéhn 1993).

Although further elaborations of the ecological model would go beyond the scope of this chapter, some comments about possible improvements of the model are in order. First, the assumption of random cultural innovation needs to be replaced by a biased variation mechanism that features more sophisticated strategies of nationalist manipulation. In particular, the framework should allow for leaders' deliberate use of myths in the pursuit of power. Second, although real actors may show a considerable degree of loyalty to the cause of a movement, they sometimes leave it before the government cracks down. The present version of the model excludes the possibility of switching from one identity to another as soon as a communal actor commits itself to a movement. Third, in addition to these community-level decisions to join and leave organiza-

---

[31] The power-sensitive adhesion mechanism (rule 2) captures some of this dynamic, but it does not go far enough in accouting for the complex learning mechanisms that operated in the Yugoslav case.

tions, higher-level decisions also influence the way that transcommunal identities change. Voluntary mergers and splits of entire movements are an important source of redefinitions of identity even in the absence of external repression (Horowitz 1975, 1985). For example, the split of the Croat Party of Right into a pro-Yugoslav faction and Frank's anti-Serbian party strengthened the Yugoslav movement.

CONCLUSION

Notwithstanding its need for theoretical refinement, the ecological model helps us understand the dynamic and ecological aspects of nationality formation within an imperial setting. Unlike conventional rational-choice models, the framework provides an explicit representation of collective cognitive structures such as national ideologies. Yet, by including power as a conceptual category, the approach avoids the pitfalls of purely idealistic conceptions of social reality. Thus it is well suited for the study of nationalism, a phenomenon at the very nexus between culture and power.

Despite their theoretical sophistication, many sociological approaches to nationalism succumb to the temptations of functionalism. Emphasizing the modernity of the phenomenon, Ernest Gellner (1983) views nationalism as a response to the needs of industrialized society: "a modern, industrial state can only function with a mobile, literate, culturally standardized, interchangeable population" (46). Thus smaller communities became obsolete as industrialization raised the requirements for political reproduction: "Time was, when the minimal political unit was determined by the preconditions of defense or economy: it is now determined by the preconditions of education" (159).

Gellner's demand-driven explanation begs the question: "Does industrialisation really *require* nationalism? Will nothing else do as a substitute?" (Mann 1992, 139; see also Mann 1993a, 245). This is where the selectionist perspective fits in. By forcing the analyst to search for explicit microlevel mechanisms such as variation and selection, the ecological approach discourages exclusive reliance on holistic causes. In Rom Harré's (1979 353) words:

> if we consider the macroproperties of a collective of people as a selection environment, it can be taken to have differential effects on different innovatory social practices effective in a Darwinian fashion, augmenting or diminishing the population of such practices in the next time-phase of that society. In short, we can admit its existence and efficacy without having to be paralyzed by our ignorance of any but its simplest properties. (353)

Of course, there are other explanatory paradigms that attempt to uncover the microfoundations of social interaction, rational choice being the most prominent one (Elster 1983, 1985; Hechter 1987b, 24–25). Yet because of their commitment to methodological individualism based on consciously made choices, traditional rationalist explanations are ill suited to account for the formation of shared cultural identities over long time spans. These difficulties are compounded by the rational-choice theorists' tendency to reify the identity of the actors as well as their reluctance to study attitudinal changes and immaterial influences on behavior.[32]

This does not mean that economic models lack relevance for the study of nationalism. It is clear that a realistic view of the rational preselection of nationalist strategies presupposes actors equipped with more complex internal models than the simple rules of thumb in the present framework. As the best developed formal theory of human decision-making, rational choice will no doubt prove useful in the quest for more realistic ways to model nationalist decision-making. Nevertheless, the need for more sophisticated cognitive and behavioral representations does not imply the acceptance of infinite rationality; instead, the focus on large-scale historical processes such as nationalism presupposes a bounded and more context-sensitive conception of human thought and behavior (see, e.g., Simon 1981; Hayek 1973).

Whatever the future choice of methodology, it is hard to exaggerate the need for better conceptual tools in dealing with identity formation. The formation of Yugoslavia did not put an end to the quarrels over national ideology among the Southern Slavs. For many Croats the Serbian attempt to "piedmontize" their Balkan neighbors during the interwar period differed little from the German and Magyar campaigns to eliminate their national consciousness. Nor did it matter to the Serbian victims in the mass graves of World War II whether their murderers were Croat Ustashe or German SS. We now know that the papering over of simmering nationalist conflicts, though sometimes temporarily impressive as in Marshal Tito's case, have few prospects in the long run.

Moreover, it would be a mistake to regard Yugoslavia as a unique example. As soon as the former Soviet republics acquired their independence, identity conflict took center stage. For example, Ukrainian leaders currently grapple with the thorny issues of how to define their national identity (Motyl 1993). Given the religious and linguistic complexity of the demographic situation, their task hardly seems less daunting than the

---

[32] Theories based on the principles of scientific realism also explain by making explicit the underlying mechanisms (Miller 1987). As opposed to rational choice, these theories are not restricted to methodological individualism.

one facing the Southern Slavs. Indeed, Ukrainian domestic politics resembles a verbal battleground for contending national ideologies.

This pattern extends well beyond Europe. Nationalism of the Eastern European type abound in the Third World. In particular, coordination problems have continuously haunted newly independent countries in this part of the world, especially where tribal identities refuse to go away. Under certain circumstances related to the resource distribution between the center and the periphery, nationalist elites may manage to transcend such exclusive and narrow identities. Referring to Third World conditions, John Breuilly (1982) explains that this operation calls for deliberate merging of modern and traditional symbols:

> The fusion is often not very stable in terms of either organization or ideology. That is because the numerous small-scale relationships of indigenous society constantly block the extended scale of nationalist action. The problem can become particularly acute on the assumption of independence, when both a common enemy and many of the resources which maintained a central position for the colonial state become less important. (193)

To sum up, nationalist politics rests on the twin fundamentals of mobilization and coordination. While the previous chapter illustrated the importance of political consciousness for any nationalist project, the present one has highlighted the coordination aspects of revolutionary collective action. The focus on the non-trivial link between objective cultural traits and national identities contradicts reified conceptualizations of the nation as an actor. In the concluding chapter, which investigates the theoretical and policy implications of endogenizing both the state and the nation, we will have reason to return to this point.

CHAPTER 9

Conclusions for Theory and Policy

SUBSTANTIVE FINDINGS

The emergent-actor approach has important consequences for both theory and policy. Distinguishing between the state and the nation, as well as treating these actors as problematic rather than reified, puts new research questions on the agenda. This endogenization of agency also leads to surprising and unexpected results not anticipated by, and sometimes even contradicting, conventional theories that do reify states and nations. The general bewilderment following the fall of the Berlin Wall points out that our understanding of the integration and disintegration of states and nations leaves much to be desired. While my goal has not been to predict, or even to explain, the details of these momentous processes, we can reduce unpleasant surprises in the future by developing a richer conceptual framework than conventional IR theory offers. More specifically, I hope to have convinced the "mainstream" reader that emancipation from the reified-actor assumption is too important to be left to IR "dissidents." Conversely, it would be valuable if the latter have been persuaded that modeling is too useful a tool to be left to conventional IR theorists.

To summarize, we have developed the implications of two main principles. First, whenever technically feasible, the actors in world politics should be modeled as dependent rather than independent variables. The frameworks presented in this book are inherently dynamic. The modeling chapters presented path-dependent CAS models of state and nation formation in the face of historical contingencies and positive-feedback processes. Second, unlike the dominant practice in IR theory, the state and the nation are conceptualized as analytically separate categories because they are distinct organization forms and should be conceived of as such. Whereas the state constitutes a formal, hierarchical organization controlling a bounded territory, the nation is an informal community held together subjectively and emotionally by the citizen's group feeling. This terminological distinction plays an essential role in clarifying political change, especially in regions and periods characterized by noncongruence of territorial and popular sovereignty. Due to its view of the nation-state as the constitutive actor in world politics, conventional IR scholarship makes it awkward to study, and sometimes even impossible to detect, political developments violating the state-centered rules of the Westphalian system.

Highlighting emergence suggests a focus on process rather than on structure; singling out the state and the nation as the prime protagonists points to two specific processes: state formation and nationalism. More than any other historical trends, they are responsible for shaping the world as we know it. Reflecting this conceptual distinction, the modeling exercises fall into two parts. The Emergent Polarity Model traces the reciprocal link between state formation and power politics. We then introduced dynamic frameworks highlighting the micromechanisms that drive nationalist transitions. Whereas Chapter 7 analyzed how a culturally homogenous nationality within a multinational empire mobilizes against the imperial core, chapter 8 addressed a similar process involving a more heterogeneous peripheral population. In order to underline the substantive contributions of the current work, I would like to illustrate more concretely how the models presented in the previous chapters shed new light on previously neglected questions and sometimes even yield findings in contradiction to established theoretical expectations.

Neither neorealists nor neoliberals have much to say about the origin of Great Powers. While disagreeing about the prospects for cooperation among them, each focuses on behavior and therefore takes the state actors as givens. Any theory aspiring to provide general macrohistorical explanations of war and peace must also account for the formation and disintegration of the main historical actors. Like neoclassical economics, neorealism fails to do this, and should therefore be complemented by an explicit theory of structural change. Doing precisely this, the Emergent Polarity Model helped us to understand that power politics and state formation are two sides of the same coin. Tracing both the contraction and consolidation phases of power politics, we modeled state boundaries as emergent features. This is a more demanding theoretical domain than the one proposed by neorealist research. Adding the question of how states and interstate structures emerge to the scientific agenda contributes to overcoming the prevailing static nature of mainstream IR theory.

In addition to addressing neglected questions, the emergent-actor perspective generates new, counterintuitive insights about established IR theories. By going beyond the implicitly selectionist approach of neorealism, the Emergent Polarity Model demonstrated how a fully dynamic view of state formation and power politics qualifies, and under certain circumstances even contradicts, neorealist assumptions. As expected by structural realists, unit-level factors do play a subordinate role, but only under conditions of violent and persistent interstate competition. To explain why polarity reduces to a small number of Great Powers, neorealists implicitly assume a positive-feedback process that produces "hegemonic takeoffs" with unipolarity as the most likely outcome.

Responding to this eventuality, realist theory turns to balance of power theory as a solution. Contrary to what they assume will result, however, the Emergent Polarity Model showed that defensive technology and alliances may sometimes increase the chances for unipolarity rather than contribute to stability. Although these defensive mechanisms promote stability locally and in the short run, from a global perspective they widen the window of opportunity for potential hegemons by blocking competing great powers' attempts to catch up. Since defensive technology and alliances are likely to delay the campaigns of such competitors, the ascending power is free to absorb smaller states that would otherwise have been absorbed by its great-power enemies. If not stopped in time, the dominant power will gain control of the entire system, with unipolarity rather than balance of power as the final outcome.

The extensions of the Emergent Polarity Model further underlined the importance of competition. Despite its potentially dangerous consequences for state survival, the security dilemma bolstered geopolitical pluralism by forcing defensively oriented states to adopt more aggressive policies than they otherwise would have. Paradoxically enough, strategic uncertainty in the form of blurring of defensive and offensive strategies also seemed to promote the emergence of power politics. Similarly, resource absorption by the state cores proved crucial for the emergence of balance of power systems, thus suggesting that the emergence of the European state system hinged as much on internal, fiscal reforms as on external, interstate effects.

Although neorealism derives much of its inspiration from economics, it has failed to carry the analogy through. Economic theory tells us that cartels and other types of collusion distort the market equilibrium, so the realists' faith in defensive technology and alliances as stabilizing factors should have become suspect. The elegance of the neoclassical metaphor notwithstanding, Adam Smith's invisible hand is shakier in great-power politics than in the supermarket. Modeling power politics as a complex adaptive system (CAS) can alert us to potential inconsistencies in existing theories.

Whereas state formation has received limited attention in the mainstream IR literature, nation building remains an even less studied topic. To the extent that nationalism enters traditional IR theory at all, its role is usually limited to increasing the internal cohesion of existing state structures. This state-centric view obscures the independent role of nations, especially in areas characterized by noncongruence between political and cultural boundaries. The addition of nationalism widens the analytical scope to include both stateless nations and multinational states, two categories that do not fit neatly into the conventional neorealist dichotomization. Nevertheless, these cases play a central role in the post–cold war era in particular and world history in general. The conceptual blind spots explain why realists and other state-centric scholars have a tendency not only to exaggerate anarchy among states, but also to overemphasize cohesion within states. Thus, it should not come as a surprise that these observers overlooked the signs of thaw between the superpowers and of the early nationalist fissures that finally triggered the collapse of the Soviet Union.

On the neorealist view, the world of nation-states does not differ from the pre-Napoleonic era. Nevertheless, the shift to modern conditions entailed a revolution in political organization. Unlike traditional social links, nationalism constitutes a qualitatively different type of organization principle. The nation is a community based on symbolic identification with cultural or social markers rather than on a hierarchy of personal relationships. The nationalist transformation of political relations has a momentous impact on existing state structures, particularly those that do not conform with the nationalist principle of correspondence between state and nation. In these latter cases, two different effects can be expected. If the region in question is organized as a large set of small political units with a common cultural identity, unification will result. This is precisely what happened in Germany and Italy in the late nineteenth century.

In the opposite case, characterized by political unity but cultural fragmentation, nationalism is likely to cause disintegration rather than integration. As ethnic communities become politically mobilized against the imperial core, nationalist collective action threatens to explode the multinational political framework. Historical examples include the collapse of the Habsburg and Ottoman Empires, and more recent developments, such as the decolonization process in the Third World and the fall of the multiethnic communist states in the early 1990s also correspond to this pattern. In essence, the double convergence of identities illustrates the essence of nationalism, a process often overlooked in contemporary scholarship despite its historical significance.

In addition to illustrating the simultaneous trend toward integration and disintegration, this analysis suggests that nationalism is not uniquely a force of the past. It is therefore instructive to compare the workings of nationalism in different contemporary settings. The two models of nationalist mobilization and coordination address the underlying mechanisms of nationalism. The question is whether a multinational state will succeed in assimilating its nationalities or whether these will manage to secede from the imperial core's domination. To be effective, nationalist manipulation of symbols presupposes both a mobilized and culturally coordinated population. Without mobilization, the ethnic group remains unconscious of its cultural distinctiveness. In the absence of cultural coordination, even a mobilized peripheral population remains too divided to form a viable political movement.

Throughout the cold war, most IR theorists tacitly assumed that all states were nation-states. The breakup of the Soviet Union and Yugoslavia reminded them that this assumption can be grossly misleading. Rather than postulating a swift and smooth shift toward state-led assimilation, the mobilization model viewed the issue of identity formation as problematic. It did so by keeping the rate of assimilation before and after the nationalist awakening on the periphery separate. While the first rate describes direct assimilation, the second one refers to indirect assimilation. Based on this simple distinction, three sets of theoretical assumptions can be identified: assimilation theory, delayed assimilation theory, and provocation theory. Reflecting an optimistic stance toward nation-building, as exemplified by modernization theory, assimilation theory postulates a quick and frictionless drift toward the core's cultural identity. Delayed assimilation theory, however, presupposes a lower rate of indirect assimilation, but expects assimilation to prevail in the long run. Provocation theory, finally, assumes a low level of both direct and indirect assimilation. Consistent with Karl Deutsch's view of nationalist mobilization and ethnic violence, dynamic analysis shows that the conditions of provocation theory generate a short-term surge in nationalist mobilization, outpacing the state-led assimilation.

If the multinational state's attempts to instill loyalty and accelerate modernization provoke resistance in this way, a particular historical trajectory can be expected. Even if full mobilization would have occurred in the end, the provocation effect could, paradoxically, strengthen the nationalist movement, thus paving the road for secession and aborting the center's assimilation process. Assuming provocation theory to be valid, the model clarified a serious dilemmas encountered by imperial governments. Such rulers are often exposed to external military threats that force them to improve the resource extraction from their societies. But improved effectiveness, especially in the military realm, requires mobilization, a process that assumes a high degree of political participation. Trying to catch up with their more centralized competitors, large multiethnic states typically find themselves faced with internal dangers, as mobilization does not necessarily lead to assimilation. Under the assumptions of provocation theory, the imperial elite must consider both external and internal threats. This means that timing of mobilization reforms becomes critical. While too fast a transformation risks provoking secession, too conservative a policy exposes the state to great external dangers.

Thus, multinational elites face the difficult task of fine-tuning the level of mobilization that optimizes their survival chances.[1]

So far, the modeling exercise has concerned a single, culturally homogeneous periphery mobilizing against an imperial center. If this assumption is relaxed by introducing multiple cultures, the mobilization process becomes even more complicated. No one-to-one correspondence between culture and political identity can be postulated. This opens the door for political creativity. By highlighting specific ethnic or cultural markers and forgetting others, political entrepreneurs are able to manipulate the boundaries of their constituencies. Because this gerrymandering affects the power balance between the center and the periphery, culture becomes instrumental in determining the chances of successful collective action.

The prospects of nationalist collective action hinge directly upon the process of identity formation. Yet mainstream theory has little to say about the scope of national identities. To the extent that existing theories take culture into account at all, they usually treat national identities as reified entities. In contrast, we allowed them to vary in an ecological fashion, directly influenced by the imperial government's attempts to weed out opposition. As anticipated by Michael Hannan (1979), in such an environment revolutionary platforms are subject to severe selection pressures. A less favorable power balance in the periphery's favor will render the task of gathering a winning coalition more crucial than under less severe power conditions. The surprising result of this situation is that the center's attempts to stop revolutionary activity may accelerate the shift away from parochial loyalties toward more inclusive identities, a transformation that could promote collective action on the periphery in the long run. To put it briefly, the more powerful the center, the more inclusive the nationalist identities.

The model clarified how geopolitical and cultural conditions codetermine political outcomes. Theories that emphasize one at the expense of the other cannot offer a complete picture of cases in which identities are still up for grabs. I illustrated the dynamics of nationalist coordination by referring to political mobilization in the Southern Slav lands of the Habsburg Empire. The formation of Yugoslavia at the beginning of the century, however, is only one example of a general pattern. In a global perspective, the same logic explains why nationalist liberation movements, particularly in the Third World, often encounter difficulties after the initial honeymoon following independence. In the preindependence period,

---

[1] As an attempt to mitigate the pernicious effects of this dilemma, the government often grants concessions to powerful nationalities. Although such measures offer temporary relief, these compromises can endanger indirect assimilation in the long haul, thus entrenching the peripheral power brokers. Unfortunately for the center, cautious policies of this type increase the likelihood of successful challenges to the status quo.

the struggle against the imperial government necessitates coordination. Selection pressures can be expected to eliminate any movement that fails to meet this challenge. Nevertheless, these forces disappear with the crumbling of the multinational empire. Having removed the foreign rulers, the nationalist movement faces the difficult task of nation building. No longer a liberation movement, it cannot rely on the ecological mechanism provided by imperial repression. As the revolutionary glow fades, old cleavages are likely to reappear. The same factors that lead to revolutionary success cause nation-building failure.

In summary, the heuristic tools are helpful in discovering empirical patterns that would otherwise have been hard to pinpoint. The emphasis on state formation and nationalism forces the analyst to take history seriously. This is a welcome counterweight to the static tendency in contemporary IR research. Dynamic modeling in general, and CAS simulations in particular, encourage an explicitly historical outlook that directs analytical attention away from context-free regularities across time and space and toward long-term processes involving dramatic changes of the main actors' identities.

CLOSING THE METATHEORETICAL GAP

On a more general level, I am trying to accelerate the closing of the metatheoretical gap between "mainstream" IR theory and constructivist approaches. There can be no doubt that reducing this theoretical polarization is an urgent task in the face of the overwhelming complexity of the post–cold war period. We can no longer afford to regard the emergence and dissipation of states and nations as an exotic question best left for the ponderings of social theorists and historical sociologists. Nor can we defend the methodological division of labor that reserves formal modeling as the exclusive concern of conventional IR theory and deep historical investigations as the hallmark of sociologically inspired approaches.

At any rate, the model-building enterprise should be good news for both historically minded constructivists and the adherents of formal modeling. The former group has been right in calling for richer, more context-dependent theory. But in their eagerness to criticize modeling approaches for being simplistic, they have often forgotten that their advocacy of theoretical complexity actually increases the need for models, albeit of a different kind than those defended by orthodox modelers. As a complement to verbal analysis, formal frameworks serve as indispensable tools, keeping track of the internal consistency of the complicated, spatially

entangled, and history-dependent processes proposed by social constructivists and historical sociologists.

Nowhere is this more urgent than in the construction of counterfactual
scenarios. The failure to appreciate, not to mention achieve, consistency
plagues verbal theorizing in complex settings.[2] Extending neorealist analysis to the dynamic realm, and thus making it more compatible with a
less reified approach to the state, is no simple task. For example, it may
not be possible to sustain neorealist arguments about the stabilizing influence of defense dominance and defensive alliances together with the expectation of great power competition in some counterfactual scenarios. In
addition to checking internal consistency of involved theories, formal
models may help the social constructivist remember the structural underpinnings of international politics. While studying the impact of culture
and ideas on political life, it is easy to lose sight of how the underlying
power structure sets the stage for intellectual leaders' symbolic manipulation of cognitive structures.

Seen as a source of theoretical inspiration rather than a positivist, pre-
diction-generating crystal ball, the richer theoretical frameworks presented above could become useful complements to the social constructivist's verbal theorizing. Contrary to the current trend, formal modeling
does not have to reduce to ahistorical contract theory that assumes at-
omistic individuals driven by material self-interest. The fact that the proposed frameworks only manifest a fraction of the philosophical subtlety
and historical detail of constructivist accounts should not obscure their
great heuristic potential.

Formal theorists also have a lot to gain from extending their current
work to the types of models introduced here. Rational-choice theory has
proved to be a singularly abundant source of hypotheses in the social
sciences. Its simplicity and rigor have helped scholars well beyond the
confines of economics unravel complicated social dilemmas. This said, it
cannot be denied that the rational-choice theorists' reluctance to question
some of their most cherished assumptions frustrates innovation and
leaves many important questions unanswered.

Modeling long-term historical change ultimately requires the circum-
vention of two major methodological hurdles. First, postulating decreasing or constant returns to scale cannot remove the puzzle of historical
contingency. Economists have started to question the validity of this assumption in the theory of the firm (e.g., Arthur 1989, 1990), and it is now
time to confront it squarely in political science too (Krasner 1988). While
frustrating the (often vain) hope of arriving at unique equilibrium predic-

---

[2] See especially the previous discussion of counterfactual cotenability and Cederman
(1996b).

tions, a truly path-dependent perspective forces the modeler to take history seriously. Complex social institutions, most notably states and nations, are inherently emergent phenomena and should be modeled as such whenever possible. Fortunately, this does not mean giving up the focus on regularities and patterns in favor of impressionistic narration of disjointed events. Computerized counterfactual thought experiments that allow us to "rerun the tape" can filter out historical accidents and estimate the causal impact of theoretically relevant variables and parameters. In addition to their heuristic value, such experiments could also elucidate the historical robustness of deductive equilibrium theories.

Second, despite its technical usefulness, the professional norm of methodological individualism and the accompanying materialist bias obscure important aspects of international politics. Whether the assumption of self-interest refers to human individuals or entire states, the locus of identity remains reified. In the long run, however, political identities are not fixed, something that was vividly illustrated by the events that ended the cold war. These modeling techniques enable the analyst to go beyond implicit and hard-wired approaches to actor identity. Treating collective identities as emergent entities helps to demystify nationalism and opens the door for explicit theories of nation formation. In particular, the successful mobilization and persistence of decentralized, "latent" groups such as nationalist movements appears less puzzling than under the assumption of individual self-interest. Modern history abounds with successful attempts to transcend severe collective-action dilemmas by means of categorically defined group identities, phenomena for which no individualist theory of selective incentives and coercion will ever be able to fully account (cf. Taylor 1988).

By taking the rationalists' call for well-specified models seriously, CAS modeling demonstrates that it is possible to confront the challenges of historical contingency and collective identities without giving up advantages of formal representation. Rationalist scholars will have to sacrifice the dream of a context-free definition of rationality as well as the belief that social relations are always reducible to the level of the individual. But for those who are willing to pay this price, a new, exciting spectrum of formal tools is waiting to be explored.

The current study has only hinted at some promising applications. Three areas of future research illustrate further possibilities:

1. More advanced internal models. Throughout this project, the individual decision-making rules have deliberately been kept at a minimum. After all, the goal has been to get as much as possible out of a simple microlevel specification. In principle, however, there is nothing that prevents more elaborate solutions, possibly relying on full-blown strategic rationality or advanced learning theory. Yet beyond such adaptive rules of thumb, there is an infinite set of possibilities to be investigated, including more sophisticated internal models featuring entire worldviews and advanced symbol manipulation.

2. Internal-external interaction: Even though chapter 5 ended with a section discussing an example of a two-level action, no systematic tests were presented. A complete analysis of such open-ended systems, allowing for both integration and internally induced disintegration, lies beyond the scope of the current study, especially since it requires the development of more flexible statistical tools to recognize emergent polarity clusters and geopolitical regimes. Nevertheless, future work in the area promises to shed new light on the foundations of realism and IR theory in general.

3. Simultaneous emergence of states and nations: Consistent with my step-by-step approach to model development, I refrained from simultaneously endogenizing states and nations. Nevertheless, a future extension to such an emergent perspective of both actor types is likely to yield great theoretical gains. Some of the most interesting historical phenomena involve interaction between state formation and nation-building. Indeed, the dispute about peace plans in Yugoslavia in the early 1990s revolves around the clash between the norms of sovereignty and self-determination (Mayall 1990; Halperin and Scheffer 1992; Gottlieb 1993; Barkin and Cronin 1994). It would be interesting to carry the analysis in the Coordination Model beyond the artificially imposed endpoint of successful revolution. Identity issues do not cease to be relevant among national communities at the point of independence. On the contrary, the absence of a unifying threat has often spurred conflict in postcolonial situations—witness the deadly ethnic clashes between Muslims and Hindus after the British withdrawal from India.

CONSEQUENCES FOR POLICY

Punctuated equilibria, as well as the other positive-feedback processes discovered in the CAS models, illustrate how nonlinearities conspire to make prediction of particular outcomes virtually impossible. This element of unpredictability reflects the elusiveness of historical change in the real world. The abrupt end of the cold war surprised scholars and policymakers alike, on both sides of the Iron Curtain. Whether their outlook was Marxist, liberal, or realist, the events seemed equally puzzling. It was not that the swift collapse of the Soviet Union lacked precedents. After all, the twentieth century has witnessed a long series of imperial disasters, from the Habsburgs and Ottomans in World War I to the decline of the European colonial empires. Rather, the uneasiness with the post–cold war turmoil and the concomitant desire to establish "a new world order," ultimately stem from a myopic view of history rather than from the uniqueness of today's situation.

We see what we expect, and what we expect depends on our theories, whether derived from Marx, Mill, or Machiavelli. Therefore, there should not be any artificial division between theory and policy. For better or worse, Western IR scholarship in the postwar period has been more preoccupied with dissecting and justifying the prevailing order than with exploring historical contingencies, those obscure transitions from one system to another. Depending on the policy agenda, the preoccupation with stability may or may not have served us well during the cold war. Nevertheless, in the present situation it is hard to deny the need for more general heuristic tools.

Obviously, I do not want to suggest that the methods advocated here offer a panacea that will magically disentangle the puzzles of the post–cold war period. Only methodological pluralism promises to lead to theoretical progress. Interpreted in this more modest way, however, richer models do serve a useful purpose in discouraging rash policy recommendations based on "deductive" reasoning. I will highlight three ways in which the adherence to the two principles of emergent agency and the state-nation distinction could prevent mistakes and misconceptions that have been particularly common in Western policy debates.

First, I have consistently emphasized the need to distinguish the state from the nation. Although it is instructive to transplant the realist logic of the security dilemma to postimperial situations of "nascent anarchy", as in former Yugoslavia (Posen 1993; Fearon 1994), indiscriminate application of neorealist principles to nationalities and ethnic groups risks obscuring the fundamental difference between decentralized and centralized power. In Craig Calhoun's (1993) apt words: "The state-centered approach, in sum, clarifies one dimension of nationalism but obscures others. In particular, it (i) makes it hard to understand why national identity can stir the passions it does, and (ii) encourages analysts either to ignore ethnic and other identities that do not coincide with states or treat them as somehow naturally given" (219).

Despite the convergence of these two organization forms in the nation-state, national communities are different from states, something that becomes particularly obvious in regions that have lived under "imperial overlay" for long periods (Buzan 1991). Since it is precisely these areas that experience, or can be expected to experience, security problems, the analytical distinction takes on an immediate policy relevance. Examples include the Balkans and Eastern Europe, as well as large portions of the Third World. In these cases, the realist focus on nation-states as the only actors of world politics not only overestimates the degree of anarchy among states but also exaggerates the level of cohesion within them.

It is understandable that this outlook has gained popularity in the West, where the nation-state has dominated as the principal form of political organization since the nineteenth century. Yet, as Gidon Gottlieb (1993) points out, the dramatic changes prompted by the collapse of the Soviet empire require conceptual retooling: "The fact that scores of nations are struggling for self-determination calls for fresh thinking about the relationship between states and nations. This question, which raised the larger question of nationalism, has been sadly neglected since the Versailles peace settlement" (24).

There is all the more reason, then, to encourage the development of theories that help to visualize the dramatically different geopolitical and cultural conditions that dominate in areas less familiar to the Western analyst. Failure to recognize the fundamental difference between states and nations can lead to dangerous policy consequences. For example, the preoccupation with territorial as opposed to popular sovereignty delayed the response to the Yugoslav civil war (Halperin and Scheffer 1992, 32–38, 45–46), and when the West finally did react, the policy was geared mainly toward securing Slovenia and Croatia's state rights regardless of minority rights. Germany's diplomatic campaign promoting early recognition of Croatia without safeguards for the Serbian minority reflected the lack of concern with national as opposed to state boundaries.[3]

Reflecting liberal ideas, the "peaceful democracy" literature also exhibits a similar conceptual blurring between state and nation. Basing their policy recommendations on the established fact that democracies do not engage in war among themselves, scholars prescribe swift democratization as a solution to the security problems in Eastern Europe and elsewhere. Because of the static and correlational nature of these studies, the difference between stable democracy and the often risky process of democratization is usually overlooked. Almost as an afterthought to his book-length survey of the issue, Bruce Russett (1993) devotes two paragraphs to the "special complication" of nationalism. Adhering to what Ronald Suny refers to as the Sleeping Beauty theory of nationalism, Russett states: "Hatreds, long suppressed, emerge to bedevil any effort to build stable, legitimate government. They bring border conflicts to liberate or incorporate 'oppressed' minorities, and civil wars" (133–34). Apart from exemplifying an inadequate, reified attitude toward nationalism, Russett's "tagged on" comments about nationalism reveal the unresolved dilemma haunting the Wilsonian approach to world peace.

The standard reaction of liberals to the boundary-drawing problems of

---

[3] Despite the domestic preoccupation with national unification, the German *Ostpolitik* in the late 1980s and early 1990s mainly emphasized state rights and territorial sovereignty: "The principle of self-determination was indeed dear to the Germans in the light of their own reunification, but in their efforts to bolster Gorbachev they had turned a blind eye to the cause of the Baltic republics" (Zametica 1992, 64).

nationalism is to let the "people" decide. Reflecting on this problem in the decolonization debate in the late 1950s, Sir Ivor Jennings put the finger on the weak spot: "On the surface it seemed reasonable: let the People decide. It was in fact ridiculous because the people cannot decide until someone decides who are the people" (cited in Mayall 1990, 41). In the words of James Mayall: "Once it is acknowledged that no external objective criteria exist for distinguishing between legitimate and illegitimate collectives, or between real and false nations, then at first sight plebiscite . . . appears to have much to recommend to it. This was, indeed, the technique initially favored by Wilsonian liberals at the time of the Versailles Conference" (ibid., 52). Nevertheless, this voluntaristic and contractarian approach of liberal democracy rests on two implicit assumptions often taken for granted by Western scholars and policymakers: "First, it assumes that a collective identity already exists—otherwise, who or what would decide which people to poll; Second, because of the fact that whoever controls the questions on which a particular population is to be asked to vote, is in a very strong position also to control the outcome" (ibid.). Thus, due to their Western bias, liberals tend to underestimate the dilemma of identity formation. Indeed, it is often forgotten that the creation of national identities in most historical cases, including the formation of the old Western nations, has been anything but a democratic process.

Although the emergent-actor perspective does not offer any direct solutions to this thorny dilemma, explicitly modeling the interaction of political and cultural boundaries helps to clarify the issue and point to policies that deviate from the state-centered recommendations of conventional IR theorists. It is unlikely that the "special complication" of nationalism will go away as a result of Western educational campaigns designed to teach the Eastern peoples "historical truth" (e.g., Van Evera 1994). Instead of solely promoting democracy, scholars and policymakers would be well served to pay more attention to the problems of minorities. Obviously this does not prevent democracy from remaining a desirable goal; a truly lasting peace can hardly be achieved in its absence. Yet, it is unlikely that institutional fixes will solve the fundamental ethnopolitical dilemmas of the post–cold war period. Calling for nonconventional arrangements, Gidon Gottlieb (1994) outlines a promising direction:

> What is required is nothing less than a rethinking of self-determination; a revision of the Westphalian system, limited to states, from which other national communities are excluded; a readiness to update the peace settlements of 1919–23 with a scheme that reconciles the claims of national communities dispersed in the former empires of the east with the territorial integrity of existing states; a willingness to entertain national demands in terms

broader than the protection of persons belonging to minorities and individual human rights; the adoption of diverse types of intermediate status between autonomy and territorial sovereignty; the elaboration of new kinds of regional standing for national communities that have no state of their own. (112)

The formalized distinction between states and nations made here is one contribution to a better understanding of ethnopolitical dilemmas.

Second, modeling national identities as inherently emergent steers clear of the Scylla of reification and the Charybdis of relativism. The ecological framework allows us to analyze the competition among national programs without resorting to reified classifications of "bad" and "benign" nationalisms. Anglo-Saxon scholarship continues to be plagued by a tacit ethnocentric bias glorifying "Western" nationalism and correspondingly vilifying its "Eastern" counterpart, without paying attention to how different structural conditions influence the the development of nationalism. This tendency can be traced to the strongly the pro-Western position of early scholars such as Seton-Watson (1917), Hans Kohn (1944), and Elie Kedourie (1960), but is clearly visible in contemporary Western scholarship and policy. In a somewhat sweeping contribution that has attracted much attention, Liah Greenfeld (1992) even denies the French the honor of practicing Western nationalism (188) and puts German socialists in the "Eastern" camp of Nazi fanatics (although the many of them ended up in a completely different type of camp): "Whether Marxists, the preachers of communist internationalism, or anti-Semites, the prophets of National Socialism, they came from the same stock, burned with the same desire, and fought the same enemy. Their mind was still that of Pietists and Romantics; they were driven by *ressentiment* and hatred of the West" (395). Unfortunately, polemic statements of this type obscure the issues more than they clarify. Greenfeld's elite-centered analysis rarely ventures beyond normative assessments of intellectuals and historical actors.[4]

---

[4] To be fair, Greenfeld traces the historical development of French and German nationalisms, so her account is not reified in the sense of being ahistorical. Rather, reification enters the picture because of her comparative focus. Despite her commitment to "methodological individualism" (19), Greenfeld does not refrain from moral judgments of entire nations, a tendency that is further exacerbated by the organization of her book into largely unconnected country studies. This makes her study vulnerable to accusations of insufficient causal depth, a common weakness in historical debates about blame (cf. Miller 1987, 98–104). A geopolitical approach would turn attention to the fact that political-boundary problems had already been solved in the English and American cases because of the ruthless and effective crushing of the indigenous "fringe" populations (Celts and Indians respectively). These historical campaigns created clearly bounded, insular political units that never were, and hopefully never will be, present in Central and Eastern Europe. Lacking clear geographical

In policy, the labeling of the history of entire countries as "Western" or "Eastern" introduces a bias that has particularly serious consequences. To return to the Yugoslav case, the German eagerness to "help" their (allegedly) Western brethren by pushing for prompt and unconditional recognition of Franjo Tudjman's Croatia illustrates the perils of reifying cultural cleavages. Academic comparisons of "national characters," "civilizations," and "roads to modernity" often produce superficial and misleading attributions of blame that conceal the underlying causes of divergent developmental patterns.[5]

Cultural instrumentalists fall into the opposite trap of adopting a purely relativistic view of national allegiances (e.g., Hechter 1987a, 1987b, 1992; Meadwell 1989, 1993). In their opinion, identities are extremely flexible. Driven by self-interest, people shift their loyalties from one organization to the other. Convinced that European integration produces enormous economic gains and that everybody would recognize this, functionalists are surprised every time the citizens of Western European states refuse to jump on the integrationist bandwagon (e.g., Haas 1976).

Scholars with a keener appreciation for the historical inertia of collective identities have generally been better prepared to explain constraints on identity formation. While acknowledging the flexibility of political identities, they emphasize the staying power of modern nations (e.g., Gellner 1983; Smith 1986). This deep-seated resistance to change can, under

---

boundaries, political entrepreneurs in these latter areas typically appealed to ethnic markers to define their nations. Of course, this fact does not make Nazism or other nationalist excesses excusable, but does provide a better understanding of these phenomena than offered by pro-Western dichotomizations. For a qualitative study of French and German nationalism that pays more attention to the boundary problem, see Brubaker (1992).

[5] For those who still doubt that this type of reification can be exploited politically, the following statement by Croatian President Franjo Tudjman made in a press conference March 7, 1994, should be instructive:

> The world welcomes the [Croatian-Muslim] Agreement as a way out of the war crisis which posed not only the threat of expansion but also the threat of a confrontation of civilizations. Hence its importance not only for us, who are directly involved, but also for the world. After all, the involvement of the major European and global powers, the United States on the one hand and the Russian Federation on the other, shows that this is not merely a delimitation between Croatia and Serbia, Serbia and the Muslims, that this is, in a way, a delimitation between worlds and civilizations which has existed in this part of the world since the split of the Roman Empire, Christianity and the better known Yalta agreement, that this is, therefore, a determined and crucial solution which will have a crucial bearing on the future development of relations in Southeastern Europe, and accordingly in the world. (Croatian Foreign Press Bureau)

Unsurprisingly, Samuel Huntington's (1993) article on civilizations was embraced warmly by the Zagreb press and turned instantly into intellectual ammunition against the Serbs. I am grateful to Stephen Tull for pointing out this example to me.

certain circumstances, produce a reversed trend toward disintegration. Thus, state-led, instrumentalist attempts to accelerate modernization and nation-building in multiethnic states often backfire. As a formal illustration, the Mobilization Model captures the policy dilemmas of imperial elites trying to modernize their states.

Hopefully, models of this type will sensitize policymakers to the risks of accelerating the political and economic reforms in Eastern Europe and the former Soviet Union. Eager to see former communist countries adopt democracy and capitalism, these leaders forget that it took their own nation-states centuries to develop viable democratic institutions and smoothly operating markets. While economic and political reforms are clearly needed, prescriptions for shock therapy often lead to consequences not anticipated or taken seriously until it is too late. In the cautioning words of an expert conscious of these political risks:

> The new states are supposed to complete transitions to market economies and democracy as quickly as possible, under conditions—the penury and confusion bequeathed to them by the collapse of empire and totalitarianism—that are least conducive to such a transformation. And the new states are never to waver in their commitment to democratic procedures and human rights while depriving their own *demos* of their livelihood. I do not see how Ukraine, Russia, or even Poland can pull it off. If aggressively pursued, politics that promote rapid and radical economic, political, and social change are a surefire way of creating massive political instability, social chaos, and ethnic conflict. The only alternative is an evolutionary set of politics that involve the sequencing of political, social, and economic reform within countries and among countries. (Motyl 1993, viii)

Whether the advocates of the drastic reforms have to take the responsibility for their actions (as Gorbachev did) or not (as do the Western economists who can take the next plane home), they all tend to underestimate the difficulties of democratization and conversion to market economy. The same applies to integration enthusiasts lobbying for instant deepening of the European Union. Preoccupied with institutional details, these scholars and policymakers do not realize the full scope of the differences between establishing a common market and building a new pan-European nation. Faced with new challenges, including internal ones such as the establishment of a European currency and external ones such as the civil war in Yugoslavia, the European Union need a higher degree of political cohesion and sense of common purpose to be fully effective. Yet these will not come about easily: "There is little evidence that a quick, technorationalistic fix is available to solve the continental problem of cultural identity. Nor, indeed, should we expect too much of the identity-conferring potential of audiovisual media in a transnational context" (Schlesinger 1994, 46).

Third, and finally, creating alternatives to the traditional, ultraparsimonious models has another beneficial practical implication: it offers a way to investigate the robustness of "deductively" derived policy recommendations. The more open-ended results of CAS models could remind those who take advice from social scientists about the conditional nature of these seemingly unambiguous recommendations. In particular, the counterfactual perspective built into the CAS frameworks highlights the contingent nature of political change. While these models show that historical contingency does not preclude the possibility of discovering nonrandom patterns and regularity in history, they also remind us that such structural convergence often hinges upon a complex set of conditions.

The prestige of deductive theory often encourages overconfidence in rather arbitrary, and in some cases even politically biased, policy prescriptions. By contrast, explicit treatments of contingency inspire a healthy dose of skepticism to formally elegant yet context-free theories. Contemporary IR theorizing could use a higher degree of awareness of such limitations. Not only are scholars too ready to draw sweeping conclusions about the general applicability of certain abstract principles, but they frequently transform these a priori inferences directly into policy advice. Referring to the deductive power of neorealism, John Mearsheimer (1990) concludes that nuclear weapons and bipolarity guaranteed stability during the cold war. Thus, he infers, an American military withdrawal from Europe threatens to leave the continent dangerously disarmed and multipolar. To preserve stability, Mearsheimer recommends a policy of "controlled proliferation"—more specifically that Germany acquire nuclear weapons, a piece of advice he has recently extended to Ukraine (Mearsheimer 1993).

The value of these recommendations depends on whether generalization is justified from the relatively stable cold-war superpower dyad to potentially fragile relations between countries that may even lack a secure second strike. Even if we believe this to be the case—a by no means self-evident assumption—the question remains whether nuclear weapons really did guarantee the "long peace" (Gaddis 1986) between the superpowers themselves. Mearsheimer's confidence in the stabilizing effect of nuclear arms rests crucially on the cold war case, but it is not really appropriate to infer anything about the causal impact of any factor based on "running the tape once." Such a post hoc determinism succumbs to the temptation of "present-ism." How can we be sure that reliance on nuclear arms to guarantee the peace was not a recklessly risky gamble? In the Cuban missile crisis, for example, the world was not far from being blown to pieces. No technical safeguards could ever fully prevent serious incidents. Those who argue that nuclear weapons should be relied upon in the future because everything went fine during the cold war use the same logic as drunken drivers who refer to their clear record as a justification for not giving up the bottle while driving.[6]

Counterfactual scenarios of this type play an important role in policy debates. Another controversial example concerns Reagan's arms buildup in the early 1980s. Conservative scholars and politicians, including President Bush, have suggested that without this policy the cold war would never have ended. In their view, it was the Strategic Defense Initiative (SDI) that forced Soviet leaders to launch far-reaching reforms (see Kegley 1994 for a review). Arguing that the cold war ended despite, and not because of, Reagan's arms policy, Lebow and Stein (1994) use documents from the Politburo to show that the Reagan buildup helped the hard-liners. In the light of the attempted coup in 1991, we cannot be sure that rerunning the historical tape again with the SDI, but with another stream of events, would not have produced a more Pyrrhic version of the conservatives' self-proclaimed victory.[7]

To pick a third example, conservatives from the neorealist camp often argue that balance of power will take care of itself. Instead of relying on security regimes and other cooperative arrangements, these scholars use the market metaphor to bolster their laissez faire recommendations. Again, Mearsheimer's suggestion that Germany and Ukraine initiate massive armament programs come to mind. While our counterfactual analysis did not explicitly address these particular cases, it demonstrates the fundamental inadequacy of selling loose economic analogies as social science. Free competition in security affairs sometimes gets a little hotter than these theorists expect. Indeed, nicely balanced power politics of the cold-war type is far from the only plausible outcome; if not ruled out by assumption, unipolarity emerges as a serious threat to the realists' scenarios.

By refraining from expressing their causal claims in counterfactual terms, IR analysts often try to make their theories look far more persuasive than they really are. Nevertheless, there is no escape from counter-

---

[6] Of course, unlike the case of drunken driving, we may never be in a position to establish whether the cause has the hypothesized effect. We cannot be sure that inferences based on CAS models prove realistic enough to serve as a policy guide. Nevertheless, this type of model inspires a more cautious attitude to scientific prediction and prescription than characterizes contemporary IR scholarship.

[7] Although the hard-liners were finally ousted, their bid for power in 1991 showed that the conservative forces in the Soviet Union were neither unwilling nor unable to resort to force. Under slightly different circumstances, their putsch might have had an entirely different outcome.

factual reasoning (Fearon 1991; Tetlock and Belkin 1996b, Cederman 1996b). Modeling such scenarios explicitly as CAS not only provides a way to check the consistency of long causal chains but can also help us to assess the robustness of macrolevel processes in the face of historical accidents. Used in this way, "the computer plays a role similar to the role the microscope plays for biology" (Holland and Miller 1991, 367). In this book, I have studied two such processes: one pertaining to state formation and the other to identity formation in multinational states. Despite the presence of historical contingency and positive feedback, the simulations lent qualified support for general macrolevel results, including certain neorealist propositions about power politics and hypotheses about identity formation drawn from organizational ecology and social anthropology.

It is time to complement traditional modeling approaches with methods that go beyond the prevailing orthodox parsimony. Failure to do so will continue to delay a deeper understanding of complex social systems. While conventional equilibrium models provide useful information about stable periods, their weaknesses become obvious under turbulent conditions. Relying exclusively upon such deductive theories is like learning how to fly by using a flight simulator that does not allow the fictitious plane to crash. Nevertheless, grasping the full potential of CAS amounts to no less than a methodological revolution. The bad news is that social scientists will have to give up the dream of positivist predictability. The good news is that they will know more precisely the limits of their knowledge. While the tracing of robust processes may appear less glorious than the scientific norms of social physics, perhaps it will make political surprises somewhat less surprising and social science more useful as a guide to policy-making in a complex world.

Bibliography

Abrams, Philip. 1982. *Historical Sociology*. Ithaca, N.Y.: Cornell University Press.

Achen, Christopher H. 1986. *Statistical Analysis of Quasi-Experiments*. Berkeley and Los Angeles: University of California Press.

Achen, Christopher H., and Duncan Snidal. 1989. "Rational Deterrence Theory and Comparative Case Studies." *World Politics* 41:143–69.

Alexander, Jeffrey C. 1988. *Action and Its Environments: Toward a New Synthesis*. New York: Columbia University Press.

Alker, Hayward R. 1981. "From Political Cybernetics to Global Modeling." In *From National Development to Global Community*, ed. K. L. Merritt and Bruce M. Russett. London: George, Allen, and Unwin.

Almond, Gabriel, and Stephen J. Genco. 1977. "Clouds, Clocks, and the Study of Politics." *World Politics* 20:489–522.

Alt, James E., and Kenneth A. Shepsle, eds. 1990. *Perspectives on Positive Political Economy*. Cambridge: Cambridge University Press.

Alter, Peter. 1989. *Nationalism*. London: Edward Arnold.

Anderson, Benedict. 1991. *Imagined Communities: Reflections on the Origin and Spread of Nationalism*. 2d ed. London: Verso.

Ardant, Gabriel. 1975. "Financial Policy and Economic Infrastructure of Modern States and Nations." In Tilly 1975.

Aron, Raymond. 1966. *Peace and War*. Garden City, N.Y.: Doubleday.

Arthur, W. Brian. 1989. "Self-Reinforcing Mechanisms in Economics." In *The Economy as an Evolving Complex System*, ed. P. W. Anderson, K. J. Arrow, and D. Pines. Redwood City, Calif.: Addison-Wesley.

———. 1990. "Positive Feedbacks in the Economy." *Scientific American* 265:92–99.

———. 1991. "Learning and Adaptive Economic Behavior." *AEA Papers and Proceedings* 81:353–59.

Ashley, Richard. 1986. "The Poverty of Neorealism." In *Neorealism and Its Critics*, ed. Robert O. Keohane. New York: Columbia University Press.

———. 1988. "Untying the Sovereign State: A Double Reading of the Anarchy Problematique." *Millennium* 17:227–62.

Åslund, Anders. 1989. *Gorbachev's Struggle for Economic Reform: The Soviet Reform Process 1985–1988*. Ithaca, N.Y.: Cornell University Press.

Aumann, Robert. 1976. "Agreeing to Disagree." *Annals of Statistics* 4:1236–39.

Axelrod, Robert. 1984. *The Evolution of Cooperation*. New York: Basic Books.

———. 1986. "An Evolutionary Approach to Norms." *American Political Science Review* 80:1095–1112.

———. 1987. "The Evolution of Strategies in Iterated Prisoner's Dilemma." In *Genetic Algorithms and Simulated Annealing*, ed. L. Davis. Los Altos, Calif.: Kaufmann.

————. 1993. "A Model of the Emergence of New Political Actors." Santa Fe Institute Working Paper 93–11–068.

————. 1995. "The Convergence and Stability of Cultures: Local Convergence and Global Polarization." Discussion Paper No. 375, Institute of Public Policy Studies, the University of Michigan.

Axelrod, Robert, and Scott D. Bennett. 1993. "A Landscape Theory of Aggregation." *British Journal of Political Science* 23:211–33.

Axelrod, Robert, and Douglas Dion. 1988. "The Further Evolution of Cooperation." *Science* 242:1385–90.

Axelrod, Robert, and Robert O. Keohane. 1985. "Achieving Cooperation Under Anarchy: Strategies and Institutions." *World Politics* 35:226–54.

Baldwin, David. 1985. *Economic Statecraft*. Princeton: Princeton University Press.

————, ed. 1993. *Neorealism and Neoliberalism*. New York: Columbia University Press.

Banac, Ivo. 1984. *The National Question in Yugoslavia: Origins, History, Politics*. Ithaca, N.Y.: Cornell University Press.

Barkin, J. Samuel, and Bruce Cronin. 1994. "The State and the Nation: Changing Norms and the Rules of Sovereignty in International Relations." *International Organization* 48:107–30.

Barry, Brian. 1978. *Sociologists, Economists and Democracy*. Chicago: University of Chicago Press.

Barth, Fredrik. 1969. "Introduction." In *Ethnic Groups and Boundaries: the Social Organization of Culture Difference*, ed. Fredrik Barth. Boston: Little, Brown.

Bean, Richard. 1973. "War and the Birth of the Nation State." *Journal of Economic History* 33:203–21.

Becker, Gary. 1986. "The Economic Approach to Human Behavior." In *Rational Choice*, ed. Jon Elster. New York: New York University Press.

Beissinger, Mark, and Lubomyr Hajda. 1990. "Nationalism and Reform in Soviet Politics." In *The Nationalities Factor in Soviet Politics and Society*, ed. Lubomyr Hajda and Mark Beissinger. Boulder, Colo.: Westview.

Benner, Erica. 1995. *Really Existing Nationalisms: A Post-Communist View from Marx and Engels*. Oxford: Oxford University Press.

Berger, Peter L., and Thomas Luckmann. 1966. *The Social Construction of Reality: A Treatise in the Sociology of Knowledge*. Hammondsworth, England: Penguin Books.

Berlin, Isaiah. 1972. "The Bent Twig: A Note of Nationalism." *Foreign Affairs* 51:11–30.

Betts, Richard K. 1992. "Systems for Peace or Causes of War? Collective Security, Arms Control, and the New Europe." In *America's Strategy in a Changing World*, ed. Sean M. Lynn-Jones and Steven E. Miller. Cambridge, Mass.: MIT Press.

Biersteker, Thomas J., and Weber, Cynthia, eds. 1996. *State Sovereignty as Social Construct*. Cambridge: Cambridge University Press.

Binmore, Ken. 1990. *Essays on the Foundations of Game Theory*. Cambridge, Mass.: Basil Blackwell.

Birch, Anthony H. 1989. *Nationalism and National Integration.* Winchester, Mass.: Unwin Hyman.

Bohman, James. 1991. *New Philosophy of Social Science: Problems of Indeterminacy.* Cambridge, Mass.: MIT Press.

Boyd, Robert, and Peter J. Richerson. 1980. "Sociobiology, Culture, and Economic Theory." *Journal of Economic Behavior and Organization* 1:97–121.

Brass, Paul R. 1974. *Language, Religion, and Politics in North India.* Cambridge: Cambridge University Press.

———. 1976. "Ethnicity and Nationality Formation." *Ethnicity* 3:225–41.

———. 1980. "Ethnic Groups and Nationalities: The Formation, Persistence, and Transformation of Ethnic Identities." In *Ethnic Diversity and Conflict in Eastern Europe,* ed. Peter F. Sugar. Santa Barbara, Calif.: ABC-Clio.

———. 1991. *Ethnicity and Nationalism: Theory and Comparison.* Newbury Park, Calif.: Sage.

———. 1992. "Language and National Identity in the Soviet Union and India." In Motyl 1992.

Bremer, Stuart A., and Michael Mihalka. 1977. "Machiavelli in Machina: Or Politics Among Hexagons." In *Problems of World Modeling,* ed. Karl W. Deutsch. Boston: Ballinger.

Breuilly, John. 1982. *Nationalism and the State.* Chicago: University of Chicago Press.

Brubaker, Rogers. 1992. *Citizenship and Nationhood in France and Germany.* Cambridge, Mass.: Harvard University Press.

———. 1995. "National Minorities, Nationalizing States, and External National Homelands in the New Europe." *Dædalus* 124:107–32.

Bueno de Mesquita, Bruce, David Newman, and Alvin Rabushka. 1985. *Forecasting Political Events: The Future of Hong Kong.* New Haven: Yale University Press.

Bull, Hedley. 1977. *The Anarchical Society.* London: Macmillan.

Burks, Arthur W., ed. 1970. *Essays in Cellular Automata.* Champaign-Urbana, Ill.: University of Illinois Press.

Buss, Leo W. 1987. *The Evolution of Individuality.* Princeton: Princeton University Press.

Buzan, Barry. 1991. *People, States and Fear: An Agenda for International Security Studies in the Post-Cold War Era.* New York: Harvester Wheatsheaf.

———. 1993. "From International System to International Society: Structural Realism and Regime Theory Meet the English School." *International Organization* 47:327–52.

Calhoun, Craig. 1991. "The Problem of Identity in Collective Action." In *Macro-Micro Linkages in Sociology,* ed. Joan Huber. Newbury Park Calif.: Sage.

———. 1992. "Why Nationalism: Sovereignty, Self-Determination and Identity in a World-System of States." Unpubl. ms. University of North Carolina, Chapel Hill.

———. 1993. "Nationalism and Ethnicity." *Annual Review of Sociology* 19: 211–39.

Campbell, Donald T. 1969. "Variation and Selective Retention in Socio-Cultural Evolution." *General Systems* 15:69–85.

Campbell, Donald T., and Julian C. Stanley. 1966. *Experimental and Quasi-Experimental Design for Research*. Chicago: Rand McNally.

Carneiro, Robert L. 1970. "A Theory of the Origin of the State." *Science* 169:733–38.

Carr, Edward Hallett. 1963. *What Is History?* New York: Knopf.

Carrère d'Encausse, Hélène. 1980. *Decline of an Empire: The Soviet Socialist Republics in Revolt*. New York: Newsweek Books.

———. 1991. *The End of the Soviet Empire: The Triumph of the Nations*. New York: Newsweek Books.

Cederman, Lars-Erik. 1996a. "Expansion or Unity? Placing the European Union in Historical Perspective." In *Towards a New Europe: Stops and Starts in Regional Integration*, ed. Gerald Schneider, Patricia Weitsman, and Thomas Bernauer. Westport, Conn.: Praeger/Greenwood.

———. 1996b. "Rerunning History: Counterfactual Simulation in World Politics." In Tetlock and Belkin 1996a.

———. 1996c. "From Primordialism to Constructivism: The Quest for Flexible Models of Ethnic Conflict." Paper presented at the annual meeting of the American Political Science Association, San Francisco, August 29–September 1.

Chakrabarti Pasic, Sujata. 1996. "Culturing International Relations Theory: A Call for Extension." In Lapid and Kratochwil 1996a.

Christensen, Thomas, and Jack Snyder. 1990. "Chain Gangs and Passed Bucks: Predicting Alliance Patterns." *International Organization* 44:137–68.

Claude, Inis L., Jr. 1964. *Power and International Relations*. New York: Random House.

———. 1986. "Myths About the State." *Review of International Studies* 12:1–77.

———. 1989. "The Balance of Power Revisited." *Review of International Studies* 15:77–85.

Climo, T. A., and P.G.A. Howells. 1976. "Possible Worlds in Historical Explanation." *History and Theory* 15:1–20.

Cohen, Michael D., James March, and Johan P. Olsen. 1972. "A Garbage Can Model of Organizational Choice." *Administrative Science Quarterly* 17:1–25.

Cohen, Raymond. 1979. *Threat Perception in International Crisis*. Madison, Wisc.: University of Wisconsin Press.

Coleman, James S. 1990. *Foundations of Social Theory*. Cambridge, Mass.: Harvard University Press.

Collins, Randall. 1978. "Long-Term Social Change and the Territorial Power of States." *Research in Social Movements, Conflict, and Change* 1:1–34.

———. 1995. "Prediction in Macrosociology: The Case of the Soviet Collapse." *American Journal of Sociology* 100:1552–93.

Connor, Walker. 1972. "Nation-Building or Nation-Destroying." *World Politics* 24:319–55. Rep. 1994.

———. 1978. "A Nation is a Nation, is a State, is an Ethnic Group is a . . . " *Ethnic and Racial Studies* 1:377–400.

———. 1984. *The National Question in Marxist-Leninist Theory and Strategy*. Princeton: Princeton University Press.

———. 1992. "Soviet Policies Toward the Non-Russian Peoples in Theoretic and Historic Perspective: What Gorbachev Inherited." In *The Post-Soviet Na-*

tions: Perspectives on the Demise of the USSR, ed. Alexander J. Motyl. New York: Columbia University Press.

———. 1994. *Ethnonationalism: The Quest for Understanding.* Princeton: Princeton University Press.

Coser, Lewis A. 1956. *The Functions of Social Conflict.* New York: Free Press.

Cox, Robert. 1986. "Social Forces, States and World Orders: Beyond International Relations Theory." In *Neorealism and Its Critics*, ed. Robert O. Keohane. New York: Columbia University Press.

Cusack, Thomas R., and Richard Stoll. 1990. *Exploring Realpolitik: Probing International Relations Theory with Computer Simulation.* Boulder, Colo.: Lynnie Rienner.

Daase, Christopher. 1993a. "Sicherheitspolitik und Vergesellschaftung: Ideen zur theoretischen Orientierung der sicherheitspolitischen Forschung." In Daase et al. 1993.

———. 1993b. "Regionalisierung der Sicherheitspolitik—Eine Einfürung." In Daase et al. 1993.

———. 1996. "Theorie und Praxis des Kleinen Krieges: Ein Beitrag zum Verständnis des Wandels der internationalen Beziehungen." Diss., Freie Universität Berlin.

Daase, Christopher, Susanne Feske, Bernhard Moltmann, and Claudia Schmmid, eds. 1993. *Regionalisierung der Sicherheitspolitik: Tendenzen in den internationalen Beziehungen nach dem Ost-West-Konflikt.* Baden-Baden: Nomos Verlagsgesellschaft.

Dacey, Michael F. 1974. "A Model of Political Integration and Its Use in Reconstruction of a Historical Situation." In *Locational Approaches to Power and Conflict*, ed. Kelvin R. Cox, David R. Reynolds, and Stein Wiley. New York: John Wiley and Sons.

Dawisha, Karen, and Bruce Parrott. 1994. *Russia and the New States of Eurasia.* Cambridge: Cambridge University Press.

Dawkins, Richard. 1989. *The Selfish Gene.* Oxford: Oxford University Press.

Dehio, Ludwig. 1962. *The Precarious Balance.* New York: Knopf.

Delanty, Gerard. 1995. *Inventing Europe: Idea, Identity, Reality.* London: Macmillan.

Dessler, David. 1989. "What's at Stake in the Agent-Structure Debate?" *International Organization* 43:441–73.

Deutsch, Karl W. 1953. *Nationalism and Social Communication: An Inquiry Into the Foundations of Nationality.* Cambridge, Mass.: MIT Press.

———. 1961. "Social Mobilization and Political Development." *American Political Science Review* 60:493–514.

———. 1969. *Nationalism and Its Alternatives.* New York: Knopf.

Deutsch, Karl W., and J. David Singer. 1964. "Multipolar Power Systems and International Stability." *World Politics* 16:390–406.

Deutsch, Karl W. et al. 1957. *Political Community and the North Atlantic Area.* Princeton: Princeton University Press.

Diehl, Paul F., and Gary Goertz. 1992. *Territorial Changes and International Conflict.* London: Routledge.

Douglas, Mary. 1986. *How Institutions Think.* Syracuse, N.Y.: Syracuse University Press.

Downing, Brian M. 1992. *The Military Revolution and Political Change: Origins of Democracy and Autocracy in Early Modern Europe*. Princeton: Princeton University Press.

Doyle, Michael W. 1986. *Empires*. Ithaca, N.Y.: Cornell University Press.

Dragnich, Alex N. 1992. *Serbs and Croats: The Struggle in Yugoslavia*. San Diego: Harcourt Brace.

Duffy, Gavan. 1992. "Concurrent Interstate Conflict Simulations: Testing the Effects of the Serial Assumption." *Mathematical and Computer Modelling* 16:241–70.

———. 1993. "Historical Reflection and the Outcomes of War: A Massively Parallel Computer Simulation." Paper presented at the annual meeting of the International Studies Association, Acapulco, Mexico.

Durkheim, Émile. 1938. *The Rules of Sociological Method*. New York: Free Press.

Eder, Klaus. 1985. *Geschichte als Lernprozess: Zur Pathogenese politischer Modernität in Deutschland*. Frankfurt: Suhrkamp.

Eldredge, Niles, and Stephen Jay Gould. 1977. "Punctuated Equilibria: The Tempo and Mode of Evolution Reconsidered." *Paleobiology* 3:115–51.

Elias, Norbert. [1939] 1982. *The Civilizing Process: State Formation and Civilization*. Oxford: Basil Blackwell.

———. [1970] 1978. *What is Sociology?* London: Hutchinson.

Elster, Jon. 1978. *Logic and Society: Contradiction and Possible Worlds*. Chichester: John Wiley.

———. 1983. *Sour Grapes: Studies in the Subversion of Rationality*. Cambridge: Cambridge University Press.

———. 1985. *Making Sense of Marx*. Cambridge: Cambridge University Press.

———. 1989. *The Cement of Society: A Study of Social Order*. Cambridge: Cambridge University Press.

Emerson, Rupert. 1960. *From Empire to Nation: The Rise to Self-Assertion of Asian and African Peoples*. Boston: Beacon Press.

Eriksen, Thomas Hylland. 1992. *Us and Them in Modern Societies: Ethnicity and Nationalism in Mauritius, Trinidad and Beyond*. Oslo: Scandinavian University Press.

———. 1993. *Ethnicity and Nationalism: Anthropological Perspectives*. London: Pluto Press.

Evans, Peter, Dietrich Rueschemeyer, and Theda Skocpol, eds. 1985. *Bringing the State Back In*. Cambridge: Cambridge University Press.

Evans, Peter, Harold K. Jacobson, and Robert D. Putnam. 1992. *Double-Edged Diplomacy: International Bargaining and Domestic Politics*. Berkeley and Los Angeles: University of California Press.

Fearon, James D. 1991. "Counterfactual and Hypothesis Testing in Political Science." *World Politics* 43:169–95.

———. 1994. "Ethnic War as a Commitment Problem." Paper presented at the annual meeting of the American Political Science Association, New York.

Fentress, James, and Chris Wickham. 1992. *Social Memory: New Perspectives on the Past*. Oxford: Basil Blackwell.

Ferguson, Yale H., and Richard W. Mansbach. 1988. *The Elusive Quest: Theory and International Politics*. Columbia, S.C.: University of South Carolina Press.

Fischer, Markus. 1992. "Feudal Europe: Discourse and Practices." *International Organization* 46:427–66.

Fogel, Robert William. 1964. *Railroads and American Economic Growth*. Baltimore: Johns Hopkins University Press.

Fontana, Walter. 1991. "Algorithmic Chemistry." In *Artificial Life II*, ed. Christopher G. Langton, Charles Taylor, J. Doyne Farmer, and Steen Rasmussen. Redwood City, Calif.: Addison-Wesley.

Fontana, Walter, and Leo Buss. 1994. "What Would Be Conserved If 'the Tape Were Played Twice?'." *Proceedings of the National Academy of Sciences* 91:751–61.

Friedman, Milton. 1953. *Essays in Positive Economics*. Chicago: Chicago University Press.

Fukuyama, Francis. 1992. *The End of History and the Last Man*. New York: Free Press.

Gaddis, John Lewis. 1986. "The Long Peace: Elements of Stability in the Postwar International System." *International Security* 10:99–142.

———. 1992. "The Cold War, the Long Peace, and the Future." In *The End of the Cold War: Its Meaning and Implications*, ed. Michael J. Hogan. Cambridge: Cambridge University Press.

———. 1992/93. "International Relations Theory and the End of the Cold War." *International Security* 17:5–58.

Gardner, Martin. 1970. "The Fantastic Combinations of John Conway's New Solitaire Game 'Life'." *Scientific American* 223:120–23.

Geddes, Barbara. 1991. "Paradigms and Sand Castles in Comparative Politics of Developing Areas." In *Political Science: Looking to the Future*, ed. William Crotty. Chicago: Northwestern University Press.

Geertz, Clifford. 1973. *The Interpretation of Cultures*. New York: Basic Books.

Gellner, Ernest. 1964. *Thought and Change*. London: Weidenfeld and Nicolson.

———. 1983. *Nations and Nationalism*. Ithaca, N.Y.: Cornell University Press.

———. 1992. "Nationalism in the Vacuum." In Motyl 1992.

George, Alexander L. 1979. "Case Studies and Theory Development: The Method of Structured, Focused, Comparison." In *Diplomacy*, ed. Paul G. Lauren. New York: Free Press.

———. 1980. *Presidential Decisionmaking in Foreign Policy: The Effective Use of Information and Advice*. Boulder, Colo.: Westview.

George, Alexander L., and Timothy J. McKeown. 1985. "Case Studies and Theories of Organizational Decision Making." *Advances in Information Processes in Organizations* 2:21–58.

Giddens, Anthony. 1979. *Critical Problems in Social Theory*. Berkeley and Los Angeles: University of California Press.

———. 1984. *The Constitution of Society*. Berkeley and Los Angeles: University of California Press.

Gilbert, Felix. 1965. *Machiavelli and Guicciardini: Politics and History in Sixteenth-Century Florence*. Princeton: Princeton University Press.

Gilbert, Margaret. 1989. *On Social Facts*. Princeton: Princeton University Press.

Gilpin, Robert. 1981. *War and Change in World Politics*. Cambridge: Cambridge University Press.

Gitelman, Zvi. 1992. "Development and Ethnicity in the Soviet Union." In *The Post-Soviet Nations: Perspectives on the Demise of the USSR*, ed. Alexander J. Motyl. New York: Columbia University Press.

Glaser, Charles L. 1990. *Analyzing Strategic Nuclear Policy*. Princeton: Princeton University Press.

Gleick, James. 1987. *Chaos: Making a New Science*. New York: Viking.

Goertz, Gary. 1994. *Context in International Politics*. Cambridge: Cambridge University Press.

Goldstone, Jack A. 1991. *Revolution and Rebellion in the Early Modern World*. Berkeley and Los Angeles: University of California Press.

Goodman, Nelson. 1983. *Fact, Fiction and Forecast*. Cambridge, Mass.: Harvard University Press.

Gottlieb, Gidon. 1993. *Nation against State: A New Approach to Ethnic Conflicts and the Decline of Sovereignty*. New York: Council of Foreign Relations Press.

——. 1994. "Nations Without States." *Foreign Affairs* 73:100–112.

Gould, Stephen Jay. 1989. *Wonderful Life: The Burgess Shale and the Nature of History*. New York: W. W. Norton.

——. 1990. *The Individual in Darwin's World*. Edinburgh: Ritchie.

Granovetter, Mark. 1978. "Threshold Models of Collective Behavior." *American Journal of Sociology* 83:1420–43.

Grant, Charles. 1994. *Delors: Inside the House that Jacques Built*. London: Nicholas Brealey.

Green, Donald P., and Ian Shapiro. 1994. *Pathologies of Rational Choice Theory: A Critique of Applications in Political Science*. New Haven: Yale University Press.

Greenfeld, Liah. 1992. *Nationalism: Five Roads to Modernity*. Cambridge, Mass.: Harvard University Press.

Guicciardini, Francesco. 1969. *The History of Italy*. Princeton: Princeton University Press.

Gulick, Edward V. 1955. *Europe's Classical Balance of Power: A Case History of the Theory and Practice of Great Concepts of European Statecraft*. New York: W. W. Norton.

Haas, Ernst B. 1953. "The Balance of Power: Prescription, Concept, or Propaganda." *World Politics* 5:442–77.

——. 1958. *Beyond the Nation-State*. Stanford: Stanford University Press.

——. 1976. "Turbulent Fields and the Theory of Regional Integration." *International Organization* 30:173–212.

Haferkamp, Hans, and Neil J. Smelser. 1992. "Introduction." In *Social Change and Modernity*, ed. Hans Haferkamp and Neil J. Smelser. Berkeley and Los Angeles: University of California Press.

Hall, John A. 1993. "Ideas and the Social Sciences." In *Ideas and Foreign Policy: Beliefs, Institutions and Political Change*, ed. Judith Goldstein and Robert O. Keohane. Ithaca, N.Y.: Cornell University Press.

Hall, John A., and G. John Ikenberry. 1989. *The State*. Minneapolis: University of Minnesota Press.

Hall, Rodney Bruce, and Friedrich V. Kratochwil. 1993. "Mediaeval Tales: Neorealist 'Science' and the Abuse of History." *International Organization* 47:479–505.

Hallpike, C. R. 1986. *The Principles of Social Evolution.* Oxford: Clarendon Press.

Halperin, Morton H., and David J. Scheffer. 1992. *Self-Determination in the New World Order.* Washington, D.C.: Carnegie Endowment for International Peace.

Hannan, Michael T. 1979. "The Dynamics of Ethnic Boundaries in Modern States." In *National Development and the World System,* ed. John W. Meyer and Michael T. Hannan. Chicago: University of Chicago Press.

Hannan, Michael T., and John Freeman. 1989. *Organizational Ecology.* Cambridge, Mass: Harvard University Press.

Hardin, Russell. 1982. *Collective Action.* Baltimore: Johns Hopkins University Press.

———. 1995. *One for All: The Logic of Group Conflict.* Princeton: Princeton University Press.

Harré, Rom. 1979. *Social Being: A Theory for Social Psychology.* Oxford: Basil Blackwell.

Hawthorn, Geoffrey. 1991. *Plausible Worlds: Possibility and Understanding in History and the Social Sciences.* Cambridge: Cambridge University Press.

Hayek, Friedrich A. 1952. *The Counter-Revolution of Science: Studies on the Abuse of Reason.* Glencoe, Ill.: Free Press.

———. 1967. *Studies in Philosophy, Politics and Economics.* Chicago: University of Chicago Press.

———. 1973. *Law, Legislation and Liberty: Rules and Order.* Chicago: Chicago University Press.

Hechter, Michael. 1987a. "Nationalism as Group Solidarity." *Ethnic and Racial Studies* 10:415–26.

———. 1987b. *Principles of Group Solidarity.* Berkeley and Los Angeles: University of California Press.

———. 1992. "The Dynamics of Secession." *Acta Sociologica* 35:267–83.

Hempel, Carl. 1965. *Aspects of Scientific Explanation and Other Essays in the Philosophy of Science.* New York: Free Press.

Herz, John H. 1951. *Political Realism and Political Idealism.* Chicago: Chicago University Press.

Hinsley, F. H. 1986. *Sovereignty.* Cambridge: Cambridge University Press.

Hintze, Otto. 1975. "The Formation of States and Constitutional Development: A Study in History and Politics." In *The Historical Essays of Otto Hintze,* ed. Felix Gilbert. New York: Oxford University Press.

Hirschman, Albert O. 1984. "Against Parsimony." *AEA Papers and Proceedings* 74:89–96.

Hoffmann, Stanley. 1977. "An American Social Science: International Relations." *Daedalus* 106:41–60.

Holland, John H. 1992a. *Adaptation in Natural and Artificial Systems: An Introductory Analysis with Applications to Biology, Control, and Artificial Intelligence.* Cambridge, Mass.: MIT Press.

———. 1992b. "A New Era in Computation." *Daedalus* 121:17–30.

———. 1995. *Hidden Order: How Adaptation Builds Complexity.* Reading, Mass.: Addison-Wesley.

Holland, John H., and John H. Miller. 1991. "Artificial Adaptive Agents in Economic Theory." *AEA Papers and Proceedings* 81:365–70.

Holland, John H., et al. 1987. *Induction: Processes of Inference, Learning, and Discovery*. Cambridge, Mass.: MIT Press.

Holsti, Ole R., P. Terrence Hopfmann, and John D. Sullivan. 1973. *Unity and Disintegration in International Alliances: Comparative Studies*. New York: John Wiley and Sons.

Hopf, Ted. 1991. "Polarity, the Offense-Defense Balance, and War." *American Political Science Review* 85:475–93.

Horgan, John. 1995. "From Complexity to Perplexity." *Scientific American* 272:104–9.

Horowitz, Donald L. 1975. "Ethnic Identity." In *Ethnicity: Theory and Experience*, ed. N. Glazer and D. P. Moynihan. Cambridge, Mass.: Harvard University Press.

———. 1985. *Ethnic Groups in Conflict*. Berkeley and Los Angeles: University of California Press.

Howard, Michael. 1994. "The World According to Henry: From Metternich to Me." *Foreign Affairs* 73:132–40.

Hroch, Miroslav. 1985. *Social Preconditions of National Revival in Europe: A Comparative Analysis of the Social Composition of Patriotic Groups among the Smaller European Nations*. Cambridge: Cambridge University Press.

Huberman, Bernardo A., and Tad Hogg. 1987. "Phase Transition in Artificial Intelligence Systems." *Artificial Intelligence* 33:155–71.

———. 1988. "The Behavior of Computational Ecologies." In *The Ecology of Computation*, ed. Bernardo Huberman. Elsevier Science Publishers.

Hume, David. [1748] 1988. *An Enquiry concerning Human Understanding*. La Salle, Ill.: Open Court.

Humphreys, Paul. 1989. *The Chances of Explanation: Causal Explanation in the Social, Medical, and Physical Sciences*. Princeton: Princeton University Press.

Huntington, Samuel P. 1968. *Political Order in Changing Society*. New Haven: Yale University Press.

———. 1993. "The Clash of Civilizations?" *Foreign Affairs* 72:22–49.

Iida, Keisuke. 1991. "When and How Do Domestic Constraints Matter? Two-Level Games with Uncertainty." *Jounral of Conflict Resolution* 37:403–26.

Ikenberry, John, and Charles Kupchan. 1990. "Socialization and Hegemonic Power." *International Organization* 44:283–315.

Jackson, Robert H. 1990. *Quasi-States: Sovereignty, International Relations, and the Third World*. Cambridge: Cambridge University Press.

Jacobson, Harold K., William Reisinger, and Todd Mathers. 1986. "National Entanglements in International Governmental Organizations." *American Political Science Review* 80:141–59.

Jelavich, Barbara. 1983. *History of the Balkans*. 2 vols. Cambridge: Cambridge University Press.

Jelavich, Charles, and Barbara Jelavich. 1977. *The Establishment of the Balkan National States, 1904–1920*. Seattle: University of Washington Press.

Jervis, Robert. 1978. "Cooperation Under the Security Dilemma." *World Politics* 30:167–214.

———. 1983. "Security Regimes." In *International Regimes*, ed. Stephen D. Krasner. Ithaca, N.Y.: Cornell University Press.

———. 1993. *Structurationism and the Cold War: A Plausibility Probe*. New York: Department of Political Science, Columbia University.

Kann, Robert A. 1964. *The Multinational Empire: Nationalism and National Reform in the Habsburg Monarchy, 1948–1918*. 2 vols. New York: Octagon Books.

———. 1974. *A History of the Habsburg Empire 1526–1918*. Berkeley and Los Angeles: University of California Press.

Kaplan, Morton A. 1957. *System and Process in International Politics*. New York: John Wiley and Sons.

Kaufman, Stuart A., and Sonke Johnsen. 1991. "Coevolution to the Edge of Chaos: Coupled Fitness Landscapes, Poised States, and Coevolutionary Avalanches." *Journal of Theoretical Biology* 149:467–505.

Kedourie, Elie. 1960. *Nationalism*. London: Hutchinson.

Kegley, Charles W., Jr. 1994. "How Did the Cold War Die: Principles for an Autopsy." *Mershon International Studies Review, Supplement to the International Studies Quarterly* 38:11–42.

Kellert, Stephen H. 1993. *In the Wake of Chaos: Unpredictable Order in Dynamical Systems*. Chicago: Chicago University Press.

Kennedy, Paul. 1989. *The Rise and Fall of the Great Powers*. New York: Vintage.

Keohane, Robert O. 1983. "Theory of World Politics: Structural Realism and Beyond." In *Political Science: The State of the Discipline*, ed. Ada W. Finifter. Washington, D.C.: American Political Science Association.

———. 1988. "International Institutions: Two Approaches." *International Studies Quarterly* 32:379–96.

King, Gary, Robert O. Keohane, and Sidney Verba. 1994. *Designing Social Inquiry*. Princeton: Princeton University Press.

Kissinger, Henry A. 1957. *A World Restored: Metternich, Castlereagh and the Problems of Peace 1812–1822*. Boston: Houghton Mifflin.

Kitromilides, Paschalis M. 1989. "'Imagined Communities' and the Origins of the National Question in the Balkans." *European History Quarterly* 19:149–94.

Kohn, Hans. 1944. *The Idea of Nationalism: A Study in its Origins and Background*. New York: Macmillan.

Kollman, Ken, John H. Miller, and Scott E. Page. 1992. "Adaptive Parties in Spatial Elections." *American Political Science Review* 86:929–37.

Koslowski, Rey, and Friedrich V. Kratochwil. 1994. "Understanding Change in International Politics: The Soviet Empire's Demise and the International System." *International Organization* 48:215–47.

Krasner, Stephen D. 1988. "Sovereignty: An Institutional Perspective." *Comparative Political Studies* 21:66–94.

Kratochwil, Friedrich. 1986. "Of Systems, Boundaries and Territoriality." *World Politics* 34:27–52.

———. 1993. "The Embarrassment of Change: Neorealism as the Science of Realpolitik without Politics." *Review of International Studies* 19:63–80.

Kreps, David M. 1990a. *A Course in Microeconomic Theory*. Princeton: Princeton University Press.

———. 1990b. *Game Theory and Economic Modelling*. Oxford: Clarendon Press.

Kreps, David M., and Robert Wilson. 1982. "Sequential Equilibria." *Econometrica* 50:863–94.

Kreutzer, Wolfgang. 1986. *System Simulation: Programming Styles and Languages*. Reading, Mass.: Addison-Wesley.

Kupchan, Charles A., and Clifford A. Kupchan. 1991. "Concerts, Collective Security, and the Future of Europe." In *America's Strategy in a Changing World*, ed. Sean M. Lynn-Jones and Steven E. Miller. Cambridge, Mass.: MIT Press.

Kuran, Timur. 1989. "Sparks and Prairie Fires: A Theory of Unanticipated Political Revolution." *Public Choice* 61:41–74.

———. 1991. "Now Out of Never: The Element of Surprise in the East European Revolution of 1989." *World Politics* 44:7–48.

Laitin, David D. 1986. *Hegemony and Culture: Politics and Religious Change among the Yoruba*. Chicago: University of Chicago Press.

———. 1988. "Political Culture and Political Preferences." *American Political Science Review* 82:589–93.

———. 1991. "The National Uprisings in the Soviet Union." *World Politics* 44:139–177.

Lane, David A. 1992. "Artificial Worlds and Economics." Santa Fe Institute Working Paper 92-09-048.

Langton, Christopher G. 1988. "Artificial Life." In *Artificial Life*, ed. Christopher G. Langton. Redwood City, Calif.: Addison-Wesley.

Lapid, Yosef. 1989. "The Third Debate: On the Prospects of International Theory in a Post-Positivist Era." *International Studies Quarterly* 33:235–54.

Lapid, Yosef, and Friedrich Kratochwil, eds. 1996a. *The Return of Culture and Identity in IR Theory*. Boulder, Colo.: Lynne Rienner.

———. 1996b. "Revisiting the 'National': Toward and Identity Agenda in Neorealism?" In Lapid and Kratochwil 1996a.

Layne, Christopher. 1993. "The Unipolar Illusion: Why New Great Powers Will Rise." *International Security* 4:5–51.

Lebow, Richard Ned. 1981. *Between Peace and War*. Baltimore: Johns Hopkins University Press.

Lebow, Richard Ned, and Janice Gross Stein. 1994. *We All Lost the Cold War*. Princeton: Princeton University Press.

Levi, Margaret. 1988. *Of Rule and Revenue*. Berkeley and Los Angeles: University of California Press.

Levy, Jack S. 1981. "Alliance Formation and War Behavior." *Journal of Conflict Resolution* 25:581–613.

———. 1989a. "The Causes of War: A Review of Theories and Evidence." In *Behavior, Society, and Nuclear War*, ed. Philip E. Tetlock, Jo L. Husbands, Robert Jervis, Paul C. Stern, and Charles Tilly. Oxford: Oxford University Press.

———. 1989b. "The Diversionary Theory of War." In *Handbook of War Studies*, ed. M. I. Midlarsky. Boston: Unwin Hyman.

Lewis, David K. 1973. *Counterfactuals*. Oxford: Basil Blackwell.

Liberman, Peter. 1993. "The Spoils of Conquest." *International Security* 18:125–53.

Lindgren, Kristian. 1992. "Evolutionary Phenomena in Simple Dynamics." In *Artificial Life II*, ed. Christopher G. Langton, Charles Taylor, J. Doyne Farmer, and Steen Rasmussen. Redwood City, Calif.: Addison-Wesley.

Lohmann, Susanne. 1994. "Dynamics of Informational Cascades: The Monday Demonstrations in Leipzig, East Germany, 1989–91." *World Politics* 47:42–101.

Lorenz, E. 1963. "Deterministic Nonperiodic Flow." *Journal of the Atmospheric Sciences* 20:130–141.

Machiavelli, Niccolò. [1513] 1961. *The Prince*. London: Penguin Books.

Macy, Michael W. 1990. "Learning Theory and the Logic of Critical Mass." *American Sociological Review* 55:809–26.

———. 1991. "Chains of Cooperation: Threshold Effects in Collective Action." *American Sociological Review* 56:730–47.

Mann, Michael. 1986. *The Sources of Social Power: A History of Power From the Beginning to A.D. 1760*. Cambridge: Cambridge University Press.

———. 1992. "The Emergence of Modern European Nationalism." In *Transition to Modernity: Essays on Power, Wealth and Belief*, ed. John A. Hall and Ian Jarvie. Cambridge: Cambridge University Press.

———. 1993a. *The Sources of Social Power: The Rise of Classes and Nation-States, 1760–1914*. Cambridge: Cambridge University Press.

———. 1993b. "Nation-States in Europe and Other Continents: Diversifying, Developing, Not Dying." *Daedalus* 122:115–40.

March, James G. 1978. "Bounded Rationality, Ambiguity and the Engineering of Choice." *Bell Journal of Economics* 9:587–608.

———. 1991. "Exploration and Exploitation in Organizational Learning." *Organizational Science* 2:71–87.

March, James G. and Johan P. Olsen. 1984. "The New Institutionalism: Organizational Factors in Political Life." *American Political Science Review* 78:734–49.

Mattingly, Garrett. 1955. *Renaissance Diplomacy*. London: Jonathan Cape.

Mayall, James. 1990. *Nationalism and International Society*. Cambridge: Cambridge University Press.

McCagg, William O., Jr. 1991. "The Soviet Union and the Habsburg Empire: Problems of Comparison." In *Nationalism and Empire: The Habsburg Empire and the Soviet Union*, ed. Richard L. Rudolph and David F. Good. New York: St. Martin's.

McMullin, Ernan. 1964. "Two Ideals of Explanation in Natural Science." In *Midwest Studies in Philosophy*, ed. Peter A. French, Theodore E. Uehling, Jr., and Howard K. Wettstein. Minneapolis: University of Minnesota Press.

McNeill, William H. 1963. *The Rise of the West: A History of the Human Community*. Chicago: University of Chicago Press.

Mead, George Herbert. 1962. *Mind, Self, and Society*. Chicago: University of Chicago Press.

Meadwell, Hudson. 1989. "Ethnic Nationalism and Collective Choice Theory." *Comparative Political Studies* 22:139–54.

———. 1993. "Transitions to Independence and Ethnic Nationalist Mobilization." In *Politics and Rationality*, ed. William James Booth, Patrick James, and Hudson Meadwell. Cambridge: Cambridge University Press.

Mearsheimer, John J. 1983. *Conventional Deterrence*. Ithaca, N.Y.: Cornell University Press.

———. 1990. "Back to the Future: Instability in Europe After the Cold War." *International Security* 15:5–56.

———. 1993. "The Case for a Ukrainian Nuclear Deterrent." *Foreign Affairs* 72:50–66.

———. 1994/95. "The False Promise of International Institutions." *International Security* 19:5–49.

Mennell, Stephen. 1989. *Norbert Elias: An Introduction*. Oxford: Basil Blackwell.

Miller, Richard W. 1987. *Fact and Method: Explanation, Confirmation and Reality in the Natural and the Social Sciences*. Princeton: Princeton University Press.

Milward, Alan S. 1992. *The European Rescue of the Nation-State*. Berkeley and Los Angeles: University of California Press.

Mirowski, Philip. 1988. *Protecting Economics from Science*. Boston: Rowman and Littlefield.

Mitchell, Melanie. 1993. "Imitation of Life." *New Scientist* 137:13–14.

Mitrany, David. 1975. *The Functional Theory of Politics*. London: St. Martin's Press.

Moe, Terry M. 1979. "On the Scientific Status of Rational Models." *American Journal of Political Science* 23:215–43.

———. 1987. "Interests, Institutions, and Positive Theory: The Politics of the NLRB." In *Studies in American Political Development*, ed. Orren Karen and Stephen Skowronek. New Haven: Yale University Press.

Moravcsik, Andrew. 1991. "Negotiating the Single European Act: National Interests and Conventional Statecraft in the European Community." *International Organization* 45:651–88.

———. 1992. "Liberalism and International Relations Theory." Working Paper no. 92–6, the Center for International Affairs.

Morgenthau, Hans J. 1985. *Politics Among Nations*. New York: Knopf.

Motyl, Alexander J. 1987. *Will the Non-Russians Rebel? State, Ethnicity, and Stability in the USSR*. Ithaca, N.Y.: Cornell University Press.

———. 1990. *Sovietology, Rationality, Nationality: Coming to Grips with Nationalism in the USSR*. New York: Columbia University Press.

———. 1991. "From Imperial Decay to Imperial Collapse: The Fall of the Soviet Empire in Comparative Perspective." In *Nationalism and Empire: The Habsburg Empire and the Soviet Union*, ed. Richard L. Rudolph and David F. Good. New York: St. Martin's Press.

———. 1993. *Dilemmas of Independence: Ukraine After Totalitarianism*. New York: Council of Foreign Relations Press.

Motyl, Alexander J., ed. 1992. *Thinking Theoretically About Soviet Nationalities: History and Comparison in the Study of the USSR*. New York: Columbia University Press.

Moynihan, Daniel Patrick. 1993. *Pandaemonium: Ethnicity in International Politics*. Oxford: Oxford University Press.

Mueller, John. 1988. "The Essential Irrelevance of Nuclear Weapons: Stability in the Postwar World." *International Security* 13:55–79.

Mueller, Karl. 1993. "Patterns of Alliance: Geopolitics and Stability in Eastern Europe." University of Michigan. Unpubl. ms.

Nadel, S. F. 1957. *The Theory of Social Structure*. London: Cohen and West.

Nagel, Ernest. 1979. *The Structure of Science: Problems in the Logic of Scientific Explanations*. Indianapolis: Hackett.

Nau, Henry R. 1993. "Identity and International Politics: An Alternative to Neo-realism." Paper presented at the annual meeting of the American Political Science Association, Washington, D.C.

Nettl, J. P. 1968. "The State as a Conceptual Variable." *World Politics* 20:559–92.

Niou, Emerson M. S., and Peter C. Ordeshook. 1991. "Realism versus Neoreal-ism: A Formulation." *American Journal of Political Science* 35:481–511.

North, Douglass C. 1981. *Structure and Change in Economic History*. New York: W. W. Norton.

———. 1990. *Institutions, Institutional Change and Economic Performance*. Cambridge: Cambridge University Press.

Nye, Joseph S., Jr. 1987. "Nuclear Learning and U.S.-Soviet Security Regimes." *International Organization* 41:371–402.

Olinick, Michael. 1978. *An Introduction to Mathematical Models in the Social and Life Sciences*. Reading, Mass.: Addison-Wesley.

Olson, Mancur. 1965. *The Logic of Collective Action: Public Goods and the Theory of Groups*. Cambridge, Mass.: Harvard University Press.

Olzak, Susan. 1983. "Contemporary Ethnic Mobilization." *Annual Review of So-ciology* 9:355–74.

Organski, A.F.K. 1968. *World Politics*. New York: Knopf.

Ortega y Gasset, José. [1930] 1957. *The Revolt of the Masses*. New York: W. W. Norton.

Padgett, John F., and Christopher K. Ansell. 1993. "Robust Action and the Rise of the Medici." *American Journal of Sociology* 98:1259–1319.

Pagels, Heinz. 1988. *The Dreams of Reason: The Computer and the Sciences of Complexity*. New York: Simon and Schuster.

Phillips, D. C. 1976. *Holistic Thought in Social Science*. Stanford: Stanford University Press.

Pleterski, Janko. 1990. "The Southern Slav Question." In *The Last Years of Aus-tria-Hungary: Essays in Political and Military History 1908–1918*, ed. Mark Cornwall. Exeter: University of Exeter Press.

Poggi, Gianfranco. 1978. *The Development of the Modern State: A Sociological Introduction*. Stanford: Stanford University Press.

Popper, Karl. 1957. *The Poverty of Historicism*. London: Ark.

———. 1959. *The Logic of Scientific Discovery*. New York: Basic Books.

———. 1972. *Objective Knowledge: An Evolutionary Approach*. Oxford: Clarendon Press.

Popper, Karl, and John C. Eccles. 1977. *The Self and Its Brain*. New York: Springer International.

Posen, Barry R. 1993. "The Security Dilemma and Ethnic Conflict." In *Ethnic Conflict and International Security*, ed. Michael E. Brown. Princeton: Prince-ton University Press.

Putnam, Robert. 1988. "Diplomacy and Domestic Politics." *International Organization* 42:427–60.

Ragin, Charles C. 1987. *The Comparative Method: Moving Beyond Qualitative and Quantitative Strategies*. Berkeley and Los Angeles: University of California Press.

Rasler, Karen A., and William R. Thompson. 1989. *War and State Making: The Shaping of Global Powers*. Boston: Unwin Hyman.

Rasmusen, Eric. 1989. *Games and Information: An Introduction to Game Theory*. Oxford: Basil Blackwell.

Reisch, George A. 1991. "Chaos, History, and Narrative." *History and Theory* 30:1–20.

Richards, Diana. 1990. "Is Strategic Decision Making Chaotic?" *Behavioral Science* 35:219–32.

———. 1995. "Interests and Identities." Paper presented at the midwest meeting of the Political Science Association, Chicago.

Richardson, George P. 1991. *Feedback Thought in Social Science and Systems Theory*. Philadelphia: University of Pennsylvania Press.

Riker, William H. 1964. *Federalism: Origin, Operation, Significance*. Boston: Little, Brown.

Rosecrance, Richard. 1992. "A New Concert of Powers." *Foreign Affairs* 71:64–82.

Ross, George. 1995. *Jacques Delors and European Integration*. Cambridge: Polity Press.

Rothstein, Robert L. 1968. *Alliances and Small Powers*. New York: Columbia University Press.

Rubinstein, Ariel. 1991. "Comments on the Interpretation of Game Theory." *Econometrica* 59:909–24.

Ruggie, John Gerard. 1983. "Continuity and Transformation in World Polity: Toward a Neorealist Synthesis." *World Politics* 35:261–85.

———. 1993. "Territoriality and Beyond: Problematizing Modernity in International Relations." *International Organization* 47:139–74.

Russett, Bruce. 1993. *Grasping the Democratic Peace: Principles for a Post–Cold War World*. Princeton: Princeton University Press.

Russett, Bruce, and Harvey Starr. 1981. *World Politics: The Menu for Choice*. New York: Freeman.

Sagan, Scott D. 1986. "1914 Revisited." *International Security* 11:151–75.

Salthe, Stanley N. 1985. *Evolving Hierarchical Systems: Their Structure and Representation*. New York: Columbia University Press.

———. 1991. "Varieties of Emergence." *World Futures* 32:69–83.

———. 1993. *Development and Evolution: Complexity and Change in Biology*. Cambridge, Mass.: MIT Press.

Scharpf, Fritz W. 1988. "The Joint-Decision Trap: Lessons From German Federalism and European Integration." *Public Administration* 66:239–78.

———. 1990. "Games Real Actors Could Play: The Problem of Mutual Predictability." *Rationality and Society* 2:471–94.

———. 1991. "Games Real Actors Could Play: The Challenge of Complexity." *Journal of Theoretical Politics* 3:277–304.

Schelling, Thomas C. 1960. *The Strategy of Conflict*. Cambridge, Mass: Harvard University Press.

———. 1966. *Arms and Influence*. New Haven: Yale University Press.

———. 1978. *Micromotives and Macrobehavior*. New York: W. W. Norton.

Schieder, Theodor. 1991. *Nationalismus und Nationalstaat: Studien zum nationalen Problem im modernen Europa*. Göttingen: Vandenhoeck und Ruprecht.

Schimmelfennig, Frank. 1994. "Internationale Sozialisation neuer Staaten: Heuristische Überlegungen zu einem Forschungsdesiderat." *Zeitschrift für Internationale Beziehungen* 1:335–55.

Schlesinger, Arthur M., Jr. 1992. *The Disuniting of America: Reflections on a Multicultural Society*. New York: W. W. Norton.

Schlesinger, Philip R. 1994. "Europe's Contradictory Communicative Space." *Daedalus* 123:25–52.

Schrodt, Philip A. 1981. "Conflict as a Determinant of Territory." *Behavioral Science* 26:37–50.

———. 1993. "A Landscape Model of Rule-Based Co-Adaptation in International Behavior." Paper presented at the annual meeting of the International Studies Association, Acapulco.

Schroeder, Paul. 1994. "Historical Reality vs. Neo-realist Theory." *International Security* 19:108–48.

Schutz, Alfred. 1962. *Collected Papers*. The Hague: Martinus Nijhoff.

Schweller, Randall L. 1993. "Hitler's Tripolar Strategy for World Conquest." In Snyder and Jervis 1993.

Sen, Amartya. 1987. *On Ethics and Economics*. Oxford: Basil Blackwell.

Seton-Watson, Robert W. 1917. *The Rise of Nationality in the Balkans*. London: Constable.

Shapiro, Ian, and Alexander Wendt. 1992. "The Difference that Realism Makes: Social Science and the Politics of Consent." *Politics and Society* 20:197–223.

Shepsle, Kenneth A. 1979. "Institutional Arrangements and Equilibrium in Multidimensional Voting Models." *American Journal of Political Science* 23:27–59.

Shoup, Paul. 1968. *Communism and the Yugoslav National Question*. New York: Columbia University Press.

Simmel, Georg. [1908] 1971. "How is Society Possible." In *Georg Simmel: On Individuality and Social Forms*, ed. D. N. Levine. Chicago: University of Chicago Press.

———. 1955. *Conflict and the Web of Group-Affiliations*. Trans. Kurt H. Wolff and Reihard Bendix. New York: Free Press. [orig. publ. 1908, 1922]

Simon, Herbert A. 1955. "A Behavioral Model of Rational Choice." *Quarterly Journal of Economics* 69:99–118.

———. 1981. *The Sciences of the Artificial*. Cambridge, Mass: MIT Press.

———. 1986. "Rationality in Psychology and Economics." In *The Behavioral Foundation of Economic Theory. Journal of Business*, supplement, ed. Robin M. Hogarth and Melvin W. Reder, 209–24.

Singer, J. David. 1969. "The Level-of-Analysis Problem in International Relations." In *International Politics and Foreign Policy*, ed. James N. Rosenau. New York: Free Press.

Sked, Alan. 1989. *The Decline and Fall of the Habsburg Empire: 1815–1918*. London: Longman.

Skocpol, Theda. 1979. *States and Social Revolutions: A Comparative Analysis of France, Russia, and China*. Cambridge: Cambridge University Press.

———. 1987. "The Dead End of Metatheory." *Contemporary Sociology* 16:10–12.

Sloman, Aaron. 1978. *The Computer Revolution in Philosophy: Philosophy, Science and Models of Mind*. Hassocks, Sussex: Harvester Press.

Smith, Anthony D. 1986. *The Ethnic Origins of Nations*. Oxford: Basil Blackwell.

———. 1988. "The Myth of the 'Modern Nation' and the Myths of Nations." *Ethnic and Racial Studies* 11:1–26.

———. 1991. *National Identity*. Reno, Nev.: University of Nevada Press.

———. 1995. "Gastronomy or Geology? The Role of Nationalism in the Reconstruction of Nations." *Nations and Nationalism* 1:3–23.

Snyder, Jack. 1984. *The Ideology of the Offensive: Military Decision Making and the Disasters of 1914*. Ithaca, N.Y.: Cornell University Press.

———. 1991. *Myths of Empire: Domestic Politics and International Ambition*. Ithaca, N.Y.: Cornell University Press.

———. 1993a. "Introduction: New Thinking about the New International System." In Snyder and Jervis 1993.

———. 1993b. "Nationalism and the Crisis of the Post-Soviet State." In *Ethnic Conflict and International Security*, ed. Michael E. Brown. Princeton: Princeton University Press.

Snyder, Jack, and Robert Jervis, eds. 1993. *Coping with Complexity in the International System*. Boulder: Westview.

Sober, Elliott. 1984. *The Nature of Selection*. Cambridge, Mass.: MIT Press.

———. 1993. *Philosophy of Biology*. Boulder, Colo.: Westview.

Spruyt, Hendrik. 1994. "Institutional Selection in International Relations." *International Organization* 48:527–57.

Stavrianos, Leften S. 1959. *The Balkans Since 1453*. New York: Rinehart & Co.

Stein, Daniel L., ed. 1989. *Lectures in the Sciences of Complexity*. Redwood City, Calif.: Addison-Wesley.

Stokes, Gale. 1976. "The Absence of Nationalism in Serbian Politics Before 1840." *Canadian Review of Studies in Nationalism* 15:77–90.

Suny, Ronald Grigor. 1993. *The Revenge of the Past: Nationalism, Revolution, and the Collapse of the Soviet Union*. Stanford: Stanford University Press.

Sylvan, David, and Barry Glassner. 1985. *A Rationalist Methodology for the Social Sciences*. Oxford: Basil Blackwell.

Sylvan, David, and Stephen Majeski. 1995. "A Methodology for the Study of Historical Counterfactuals." Paper presented at the annual convention of the International Studies Association, Chicago.

Szporluk, Roman. 1990. "The Imperial Legacy and the Soviet Nationalities Problem." In *The Nationalities Factor in Soviet Politics and Society*, ed. Lubomyr Hajda and Mark Beissinger. Boulder, Colo.: Westview.

Sztompka, Piotr. 1993. *The Sociology of Social Change*. Oxford: Basil Blackwell.

Tajfel, Henri. 1981. *Human Groups and Social Categories: Studies in Social Psychology*. Cambridge: Cambridge University Press.

Tarrow, Sidney. 1995. "Bridging the Quantitative-Qualitative Divide in Political Science." *American Political Science Review* 78:471–74.

Taylor, A.J.P. 1948. *The Habsburg Monarchy: A History of the Austrian Empire and Austria-Hungary*. London: Harper and Row.

———. 1954. *The Struggle for Mastery in Europe: 1848–1918*. Oxford: Oxford University Press.

Taylor, Charles. 1985. *The Sources of the Self*. Cambridge, Mass.: Harvard University Press.

Taylor, Michael. 1988. "Rationality and Revolutionary Collective Action." In *Rationality and Revolution*, ed. Michael Taylor. Cambridge: Cambridge University Press.

Taylor, Paul. 1983. *The Limits of European Integration*. London: Croom Helm.

Tetlock, Philip E., and Aaron Belkin, eds. 1996a. *Counterfactual Thought Experiments in World Politics*. Princeton: Princeton University Press.

Tetlock, Philip E., and Aaron Belkin. 1996b. "Counterfactual Thought Experiments in World Politics: Logical, Methodological, and Psychological Perspectives." In Tetlock and Belkin 1996a.

Therborn, Göran. 1991. "Cultural Belonging, Structural Location and Human Action: Explanation in Sociology and in Social Science." *Acta Sociologica* 34:177–91.

Thorson, Stuart J., and Donald A. Sylvan. 1982. "Counterfactuals and the Cuban Missile Crisis." *International Studies Quarterly* 26:539–71.

Tilly, Charles. 1973. "Does Modernization Breed Revolution?" *Comparative Politics* 5:425–48.

———. 1978. *From Mobilization to Revolution*. New York: McGraw-Hill.

———. 1985. "War Making and State Making as Organized Crime." In Evans, Rueschemeyer, and Skocpol 1985.

———. 1990. *Coercion, Capital, and European States, AD 990–1990*. Oxford: Basil Blackwell.

Tilly, Charles, ed. 1975. *The Formation of National States in Western Europe*. Princeton: Princeton University Press.

Tolstoy, Leo. 1931. *War and Peace*. New York: Modern Library.

Toulmin, Stephen E. 1977. *Human Understanding: The Collective Use and Evolution of Concepts*. Princeton: Princeton University Press.

———. 1981. "Human Adaptation." In *The Philosophy of Evolution*, ed. U. J. Jensen and R. Harré. Brighton: Harvester Press.

Turner, John C. 1987. *Rediscovering the Social Group: A Self-Categorization Theory*. Oxford: Basil Blackwell.

Udéhn, Lars. 1993. "Twenty-five Years with *The Logic of Collective Action*." *Acta Sociologica* 36:239–61.

Ullman, Richard H. 1991. *Securing Europe*. Princeton: Princeton University Press.

Van Creveld, Martin. 1977. *Supplying War: Logistics from Wallenstein to Patton*. Cambridge: Cambridge University Press.

Van Evera, Stephen. 1984. "The Cult of the Offensive and the Origins of the First World War." *International Security* 9:58–107.

———. 1987. "Offense, Defense, and Strategy: When Is Offense Best?" Paper presented at the Jaffee Center Strategy Conference, Neve Ilan, Israel.

———. 1994. "Hypotheses on Nationalism and War." *International Security* 18:5–39.

von Neumann, John. 1966. *Theory of Self-Reproducing Automata*. Champaign-Urbana, Ill.: University of Illinois Press.

Vucinich, Wayne S. 1968. *Serbia Between East and West: The Events of 1903–1908*. New York: AMS Press.

Wæver, Ole. 1993. "Societal Security: The Concept." In Wæver, Buzan, Kelstrup, and Lemaitre 1993.

———. 1995. "Europe's Three Empires: A Watsonian Interpretation of Post-Wall European Security." Paper presented at the annual convention of the International Studies Association, Chicago.

Wæver, Ole, and Morten Kelstrup. 1993. "Europe and Its Nations: Political and Cultural Identities." In Wæver, Buzan, Kelstrup, and Lemaitre 1993.

Ole Wæver, Barry Buzan, Morten Kelstrup, and Pierre Lemaitre, eds. 1993. *Identity, Migration and the New Security Agenda in Europe*. London: Pinter.

Waldrop, M. Mitchell. 1992. *Complexity: The Emerging Science at the Edge of Order and Chaos*. New York: Simon and Schuster.

Walker, R.B.J. 1990. "Security, Sovereignty, and the Challenge of World Politics." *Alternatives* 15:3–27.

———. 1993. *Inside/Outside: International Relations as Political Theory*. Cambridge: Cambridge University Press.

Wallace, William. 1994. *Regional Integration: The West European Experience*. Washington, D.C.: Brookings Institute.

Walt, Stephen M. 1987. *The Origins of Alliances*. Ithaca, N.Y.: Cornell University Press.

———. 1991. "The Renaissance of Security Studies." *International Studies Quarterly* 35:211–50.

Waltz, Kenneth N. 1959. *Man, the State and War*. New York: Columbia University Press.

———. 1979. *Theory of International Politics*. New York: McGraw-Hill.

———. 1986. "Reflections on *Theory of International Politics*: A Response to My Critics." In *Neorealism and Its Critics*, ed. Robert O. Keohane. New York: Columbia University Press.

Watson, Adam. 1992. *The Evolution of International Society*. London: Routledge.

Weber, Eugen, 1976. *Peasants into Frenchmen: The Modernization of Rural France, 1870–1914*. Stanford: Stanford University Press.

Weber, Max. 1946. *From Max Weber: Essays in Sociology*. New York: Oxford University Press.

———. 1949. "Objective Possibility and Adequate Causation in Historical Explanation." In *The Methodology of the Social Sciences*, ed. Edward A. Shils and Henry A. Finch. New York: Free Press.

———. 1958. "The Social Psychology of the World Religions." In *From Max Weber: Essays in Sociology*, ed. H. H. Gerth and C. Wright Mills. New York: Oxford University Press.

———. 1962. *Basic Concepts in Sociology*. London: Peter Owen.

Weiner, Myron. 1971. "Political Participation: Crisis of the Political Process." In *Crises and Consequences in Political Development*, ed. Leonard Binder et al. Princeton: Princeton University Press.

Weisbuch, Gérard. 1991. *Complex Systems Dynamics*. Redwood City, Calif.: Addison-Wesley.

Wendt, Alexander E. 1987. "The Agent-Structure Problem in International Relations Theory." *International Organization* 41:335–70.

———. 1992. "Anarchy Is What States Make of It: The Social Construction of Power Politics." *International Organization* 46:391–425.

———. 1994. "Collective Identity Formation and the International State." *American Political Science Review* 88:384–96.

———. 1995. "Constructing International Politics." *International Security* 20:71–81.

White, Harrison C. 1992. *Identity and Control*. Princeton: Princeton University Press.

Wolfers, Arnold. 1962. *Discord and Collaboration: Essays on International Politics*. Baltimore: John Hopkins University Press.

Wolfram, Stephen. 1986. *Theory and Applications of Cellular Automata*. Singapore: Worlds Scientific.

Wolton, Dominique. 1993. *La dernière utopie: Naissance de l'Europe démocratique*. Paris: Flammarion.

Wright, Quincy. 1965. *A Study of War*. Chicago: University of Chicago Press.

Young, Crawford. 1993. "The Dialectics of Cultural Pluralism." In *The Rising Tide of Cultural Pluralism: The Nation-State at Bay?*, ed. Crawford Young. Madison, Wisc.: University of Wisconsin Press.

Zametica, John. 1992. "The Yugoslav Conflict." *Adelphi Paper* 270.

Index

Achen, Christopher H., 10, 54
adaptation, 50, 52. *See also* strategic adaptation
agency, 4–7, 14–15, 19–22, 25, 32–33, 48, 213, 223
alliances, 7, 73; implemented, 89–91, 109–12; in Renaissance Italy, 100–2; simulation results of, 98–100, 111–12, 215
anarchy, 5, 76, 107, 138–40, 223
Anderson, Benedict, 11, 61, 167, 202
Arthur, W. Brian, 43, 55, 61, 106, 220
assimilation, 145, 152–63, 216–17; defined, 154; direct and indirect, 155
assimilation theories, 157–59, 217
Axelrod, Robert, 27, 32, 49, 60–61, 66, 68, 85–86, 113

balance of power, 7, 8, 72, 76–77, 95–96, 215; automatic and manual, 77–78, 91, 105–6; regional vs. global, 102–4
Banac, Ivo, 202–7
Barth, Fredrik, 26, 153, 162, 185–86, 203
bit-string. *See* identity
Brass, Paul R., 26, 147, 155, 162, 186
Bremer, Stuart A., 82–85, 88, 90, 96, 122
Breuilly, John, 148–49, 165, 177, 212
Brubaker, Rogers, 19, 144–45, 147, 153–56, 165
bounded rationality, 34, 62, 86–87, 103, 211

Calhoun, Craig, 21, 45–46, 136, 149, 158, 167, 184, 186, 191, 223
Carr, E. H., 39, 43–44
Carrère d'Encausse, Hélène, 14, 173
CAS. *See* complex adaptive systems
causal mechanisms: in CAS, 66–68, 209–11; in counterfactuals, 38–42; in neorealism, 76
causation, 9–10, 38–42, 55, 57, 67. *See also* counterfactuals
cellular automata, 53, 82
chaos theory, 40, 52, 68
classifier systems, 60
collective action, 12–13; CAS models of, 120, 163–70, 185–91; dilemmas of, 45, 221; and nationalism, 149, 216

combat rules, 87–88, 123–24, 128
common knowledge, 33–34, 52, 63
complex adaptive systems (CAS), 7, 49–69; defined, 50–54
complexity, defined 50; in philosophy, 37–38, 42; of the post-cold war period, 3–7; and social constructivism, 30–31; and rational-choice theory, 32–34. *See also* complex adaptive systems
computer simulation, 7, 49–50; advantages of, 54–62; limitations of, 62–66. *See also* complex adaptive systems
Connor, Walker, 17–18, 144, 158, 160–61, 164, 191
conquest, 7, 22, 74, 142; implemented, 78–79, 88–91, 124–25; and positive feedback, 98–98; historical examples of, 100–2
constructivism. *See* social constructivism
coordination. *See* nationalist coordination
cotenability. *See* counterfactuals
counterfactuals, 6, 9–12; and CAS simulation, 57–60; cotenability of, 41–42, 57–58, 117, 220; and policy, 229–31; simple and complex, 55–57
critical theory, 6, 27–29. *See also* social constructivism
Cuban missile crisis, 41, 228–29
Cusack, Thomas R., 75, 82–91, 94, 98, 100, 122, 123, 128, 135
culture, 21, 25–26; and boundaries, 184–87; CAS models of, 60–61, 134, 187–88; and mainstream theory, 45–46, 136–39; and nationalism, 139–51; and political mobilization, 152–55; and power, 210. *See also* identity; nationalism

Daase, Christopher, 27, 102, 107
decision rules, 85–87, 123; stochastic, 126–28; tit-for-tat, 68, 85, 123
decolonization, 8, 22, 145, 216. *See also* nationalism
defense-offense balance, 7, 73; effects of, 92–96, 215–20; implemented, 85; in neorealist theory, 76–78. *See also* superiority ratio